Lutheran Quarterly Books will advance the same aims as *Lutheran Quarterly* itself, aims repeated by Theodore G. Tappert when he was editor fifty years ago and renewed by Oliver K. Olson when he revived the publication in 1987. The original four aims continue to grace the front matter and to guide the contents of every issue, and can now also indicate the goals of *Lutheran Quarterly Books*: "to provide a forum (1) for the discussion of Christian faith and life on the basis of the Lutheran confession; (2) for the application of the principles of the Lutheran church to the changing problems of religion and society; (3) for the fostering of world Lutheranism; and (4) for the promotion of understanding between Lutherans and other Christians."

For further information, see www.lutheranquarterly.org.

The symbol and motto of *Lutheran Quarterly*, VDMA for *Verbum Domini Manet in Aeternum* (1 Peter 1:25), was adopted as a motto by Luther's sovereign, Frederick the Wise, and his successors. The original "Protestant" princes walking out of the imperial Diet of Speyer in 1529, unruly peasants following Thomas Müntzer, and from 1531 to 1547 the coins, medals, flags, and guns of the Smalcaldic League all bore the most famous Reformation slogan, the first Evangelical confession: The Word of the Lord remains forever.

For the complete list of *Lutheran Quarterly Books*, please see the final pages of this work.

Praise for *United with Christ*

Volker Leppin, the leading expert on Martin Luther and medieval mysticism, at last has a book dedicated to the subject in English. This collection of essays establishes itself as the definitive English reference for understanding the mystical aspects of Luther's theology. By reading this book, it becomes increasingly difficult to maintain a strict dichotomy between Protestantism and mysticism, as well as the notion of a sudden breakthrough in Luther's understanding of justification by faith. Instead, Leppin reveals how Luther's early theological development revolved around a mystical transformation of his understanding of penance, shifting from a sacrament mediated by the church hierarchy to a direct and internal encounter with God. Beyond dispelling long-standing stereotypes about Luther, this book has the potential to reshape our contemporary understanding of theology, inviting us to embrace theology not solely as an academic discipline but as an existential orientation.

—Samuel J. Dubbelman, assistant professor of church history, Lutheran Theological Seminary, Hong Kong

Volker Leppin's studies of Martin Luther's "mystical roots" and "transformations" of medieval mystical traditions have challenged our historical understanding of the reformer and have major implications for the further development of the Lutheran tradition. This volume makes a judicious selection of Leppin's essays available in English and will be welcome and thought-provoking reading for anyone interested in Luther's theology.

—Vincent Evener, assistant professor in the history of Christianity, Missouri State University

Martin Luther transformed medieval Christianity into something else. Some forms were left behind, but their substance endured in difficult-to-see ways. In this deeply learned book, Volker Leppin, one of our finest interpreters of medieval and Reformation Christianity, shares his vision of this transformation. The vision is remarkable both in its microscopic attention to text and context, and also in its breadth of survey of centuries of history. Read this convincing, engaging, and delightful book.

—Derek R. Nelson, professor of religion, Wabash College, and coauthor of *Resilient Reformer: The Life and Thought of Martin Luther*

Martin Luther stands at the crossroads of medieval mysticism and early modern university theology. German, American, and Scandinavian scholars interpret Luther's vision in diverse ways. Volker Leppin masters this complex field and provides an academic synthesis that leads the reader to the heart of the Reformation.

—Risto Saarinen, professor, University of Helsinki

United with Christ

United with Christ

Martin Luther and Christian Mysticism

VOLKER LEPPIN

FORTRESS PRESS
MINNEAPOLIS

UNITED WITH CHRIST
Martin Luther and Christian Mysticism

30 29 28 27 26 25 2 3 4 5 6 7 8 9

Library of Congress Cataloging-in-Publication Data

Names: Leppin, Volker, author.
Title: United with Christ : Martin Luther and Christian mysticism / Volker Leppin.
Description: Minneapolis, MN : Fortress Press, [2025] | Includes bibliographical references and index.
Identifiers: LCCN 2024025688 (print) | LCCN 2024025689 (ebook) | ISBN 9798889833505 (print) | ISBN 9798889833512 (ebook)
Subjects: LCSH: Mysticism--Germany--History. | Luther, Martin, 1483-1546.
Classification: LCC BV5077.G3 L36 2025 (print) | LCC BV5077.G3 (ebook) | DDC 230/.41--dc23/eng/20240807
LC record available at https://lccn.loc.gov/2024025688
LC ebook record available at https://lccn.loc.gov/2024025689

Cover design and illustration: Josh Eller

Print ISBN: 979-8-8898-3350-5
eBook ISBN: 979-8-8898-3351-2

Contents

Introduction

> Decades of careful research have made it possible finally to leave behind the outmoded assumption that mysticism and Protestantism have always stood in contradiction to one another.[1]

This conclusion drawn by Ronald Rittgers and Vincent Evener demonstrates that today's research is departing from the old Protestant prejudice toward mysticism. Albrecht Ritschl once declared that mysticism was "only the pronounced stage of Catholic piety" and, of course, intended this negatively.[2] The whole spectrum of Protestant thinkers followed him as seen in Adolf von Harnack (1851–1930), who proposed that whoever claimed mysticism for Protestantism "emptied [Catholicism] of its character, and evangelical faith becomes deteriorated,"[3] and with Karl Barth (1886–1968), who considered mysticism to be the sister of atheism.[4]

There were and are good reasons for this negative opinion, most importantly the Protestant doctrine of justification. Is it really possible for human beings, subject to original sin, to find their way to direct contact with God? To immerse themselves into him? The answer tends to be no. Well-profiled *forensic* justification (Christ's attribution of justification to the believer) made this problem unavoidable. Forensic justification views mystical spirituality as giving more agency to the human person than is appropriate in the tradition of Paul, Augustine, and Luther. It *is* undeniable

1. Ronald K. Rittgers and Vincent Evener, eds. "Introduction," in *Protestants and Mysticism in Reformation Europe* (Leiden: Brill, 2019), 1–16, 14.
2. Albrecht Ritschl, *Geschichte des Pietismus. Erster Band: Der Pietismus in der reformierten Kirche* (Berlin: De Gruyter, 1966), 28.
3. Adolf von Harnack, *Lehrbuch der Dogmengeschichte. Bd. 3: Die Entwicklung des kirchlichen Dogmas*, 4th ed. (Tübingen: Mohr, 1909), 435. Trans. after: Adolph Harnack, *History of Dogma*, vol. 6. Trans. Neil Buchanan (Boston: Little, Brown, 1907), 98.
4. Karl Barth, *Kirchliche Dogmatik. Bd. I/2*, 8th ed. (Zürich: Theologischer Verlag, 1990), 344.

that mystical theology can lead to works-righteousness, an inappropriate mixture of the divine and human, and—in cases where mysticism has been abused—*has* certainly led to catastrophic consequences. We must, therefore, remain discerning and self-discerning regarding mysticism.

National Socialism provides but one example of this danger. Theologians such as Erich Seeberg[5] and Erich Vogelsang,[6] both adherents of the German Christians, attempted to appropriate Luther into the National-Socialist ideology using the language of mysticism. Their misappropriation can be seen in *The Myth of the 20th Century*, the main work of the Nazis' chief ideologue Alfred Rosenberg. Rosenberg held Meister Eckhart (c. 1260–c. 1328) to be a thinker of the soul's nobility and divinity. For Rosenberg, this concept meant that the soul comes to a status where it no longer needs grace.[7] He considered the theology of grace to be Pauline and not Christian,[8] and, to him, this meant that it was Jewish.[9] Rosenberg identified a "völkisches Bekenntnis" or "folkian creed" in Eckhart[10] and saw in him the founder of a new religion.[11] Eckhart would supposedly free Christianity from the Protestant "error" of keeping the Old Testament in its canon.[12]

All of this sounds absurd. It is. Historical research has shown that Rosenberg's Eckhart has little or nothing to do with the historical one,[13] and that Rosenberg's image of Eckhart was based on a poor translation of Eckhart made by Hermann Büttner in the nineteenth century.[14] But identifying the basic errors in Rosenberg's ideology does not change the fact that it had an immense effect on Protestant theologians, or that the Lutherans were the most affected. Seeberg and Vogelsang used the concept of Luther as a mystic to terrible effect to make him acceptable for

5. Thomas Kaufmann, "*Anpassung als historiographisches Konzept und als theologiepolitisches Programm. Der Kirchenhistoriker Erich Seeberg in der Zeit der Weimarer Republik und des 'Dritten Reiches'*," in *Evangelische Kirchenhistoriker im "Dritten Reich,"* ed. Thomas Kaufmann and Harry Oelke (Gütersloh: Gütersloher Verlagshaus, 2002), 122–272.
6. Volker Leppin, "Luther and Mysticism: The Case of the Seebergs and Vogelsang," in *Luther, Barth, and Movements of Theological renewal (1918–1933)*, ed. Heinrich Assel and Bruce McCormack (Berlin: De Gruyter, 2020), 109–124.
7. Alfred Rosenberg, *Der Mythus des 20. Jahrhunderts. Eine Wertung der seelisch-geistigen Gestaltenkämpfe unserer Zeit*, 91st–94th ed. (Munich: Hohenzeichen-Verlag, 1936), 237.
8. Rosenberg, *Mythus*, 235.
9. Rosenberg, *Mythus*, 235.
10. Rosenberg, *Mythus*, 235.
11. Rosenberg, *Mythus*, 239.
12. Rosenberg, *Mythus*, 218.
13. Ingeborg Degenhardt, *Studien zum Wandel des Eckhartbildes*, Studien zur Problemgeschichte der antiken und mittelalterlichen Philosophie 3 (Leiden: Brepols, 1967), 261–274.
14. Degenhardt, *Studien*, 275.

the Third Reich. Today's research must be aware that this has happened and could happen again, hence why German-speaking researchers have long been very cautious about addressing Luther's mystical roots. Those roots, however, have always been lurking on the edge of the scholarly discussion, as seen with Wilhelm Maurer, a church historian in the era of the Third Reich who was close to the Confessing Church.[15] Maurer published a paper in 1949 analyzing *The Freedom of a Christian*, in which he distinguished Luther from medieval mysticism while also identifying a line of continuity between them, which in turn was rooted in the early church's "Theology of Mysteries."[16] Maurer provided us with a relatively non-ideological approach to this topic which remains helpful for today's work. It would take decades, however, for this impulse to gain traction, especially in Germany.

At the 1966 Luther Congress, Heiko Augustinus Oberman (a Dutch Reformed Luther scholar), Erwin Iserloh (a German Catholic), and Bengt Hägglund (a Swedish Lutheran) held presentations on Luther and mysticism. But not a single Lutheran Luther researcher from Germany did. One of the most important books in this area, a work that has significantly shaped today's research, was written by the Dutchman Theo Bell,[17] who identified the enormous significance of Bernard of Clairvaux (1090–1153) for Martin Luther. Nowadays, Finnish scholars such as Tuomo Mannermaa have engaged with Russian-Orthodox theologians and have discovered the idea of *theosis* (becoming divine) as a moment in Luther's doctrine of justification. They have done so while confronted with sharp criticism from German-language researchers.[18] Their work has made it possible for us to rediscover a mystical structure within Lutheran theology.

15. Gerhard Müller, "In memoriam Wilhelm Maurer," in *LutherJahrbuch*, vol. 50 (Göttingen: Vandenhoeck & Ruprecht, 1983), 16.
16. Wilhelm Maurer, *Von der Freiheit eines Christenmenschen. Zwei Untersuchungen zu Luthers Reformationsschriften 1520/21* (Göttingen: Vandenhoeck, 1949), 51.
17. Theo Bell, *Divus Bernhardus. Bernhard von Clairvaux und Martin Luthers Schriften* (Mainz: Zabern, 1993).
18. Examples can be found in: *Luther und Theosis. Vergöttlichung als Thema der abendländischen Theologie*, ed. Simo Peura and Antti Raunio (Helsinki: Martin-Luther-Verlag, 1990); Simo Peura, *Mehr als ein Mensch? Die Vergöttlichung als Thema der Theologie Martin Luthers von 1513 bis 1519* (Mainz: Zabern, 1994); for more on the Finnish critique of modern Luther scholarship, see: Risto Saarinen, *Gottes Wirken auf uns. Die transzendentale Deutung des Gegenwart-Christi-Motivs in der Lutherforschung* (Stuttgart: Steiner, 1989). A summary listing of the Finnish works produced by Tuomo Mannermaa has been provided by: Juhani Forsberg, "Die finnische Lutherforschung seit 1979," in *LutherJahrbuch*, vol. 72 (Göttingen: Vandenhoeck & Ruprecht, 2005), 147–182.

More recently, international researchers such as Ronald Rittgers, Vincent Evener,[19] and Erik Hermann[20] have provided major contributions to our image of mysticism and Luther. This image is one of continuity and fruitful developments of medieval heritage during and beyond the Reformation. Within Lutheranism, justice and justification grow out of and blend with a rich medieval palette. Johann Arndt's early seventeenth-century reform orthodoxy would not have been utterly implausible without impulses from mysticism. Philipp Jacob Spener (1635–1705), arguably *the* father of Lutheran Pietism in early modernity, recommended reading mystical literature and provided his own theories about Luther's development out of mysticism:

> It might also be useful to make more effort to put into the hands of students and recommend to them the use of such simple little books as the Theologia Germanica and the writings of Tauler, which, next to the Scriptures, probably made our dear Luther what he was. Such was the advice of Luther himself, who in a letter to Spalatin wrote thus of a man of God (as he called Tauler elsewhere): "If you desire to read the old, pure theology in German, you can obtain the sermons of the Dominican friar, John Tauler. Neither in the Latin nor in the German language have I found a purer, more wholesome theology or one that agrees more with the Gospel."[21]

Readers of the following chapters will notice that they have a lot in common with Spener. Their purpose, however, is not to identify Lutheran mysticism with Pietism. Friedrich Daniel Ernst Schleiermacher (1768–1834), one of the great fathers of nineteenth century liberal theology, also mentioned the "mystical disposition which is so essential to me" from his youth,[22] and his *On Religion* is indeed deeply shaped by mystical thought. In light of the experiences of the twentieth century, it has become clear to us that we need to conduct clean, philological work with the texts themselves in order to truly understand how mysticism has influenced

19. Vincent Evener, *Enemies of the Cross: Suffering, Truth, and Mysticism in the Early Reformation* (Oxford: Oxford University Press, 2021).

20. Erik Herrmann, "Luther's Divine Aeneid: Continuity and Creativity in Reforming the Use of the Bible," in *LutherJahrbuch*, vol. 85 (Göttingen: Vandenhoeck & Ruprecht, 2018), 85–109.

21. Philipp Jakob Spener, *Pia desideria: Die Werke Philipp Jakob Speners*, Studienausgabe, ed. Kurt Aland. vol. I/1 (Gießen: Brunnen, 1996), 236, 6–10. Trans. after: Philipp Jakob Spener, *Pia Desideria*, Seminar Editions, trans. and ed. Theodore G. Tappert (Philadelphia: Fortress Press, 1964), 110–111.

22. Schleiermacher and Georg Reimer, April 30, 1802 (Friedrich Daniel Ernst Schleiermacher, *Briefwechsel 1801–1802*, ed. Andreas Arndt and Wolfgang Virmond [Berlin: De Gruyter], 1999 [Friedrich Daniel Ernst Schleiermacher, kritische Gesamtausgabe vol. 5], 393 [No. 1220, 17–18, 20–21]). My translation.

Protestant theology. This volume seeks to do precisely that. It is the fruit of a long and wandering journey through medieval studies which started with my rather uncommon detour from Scholastic studies into mysticism. For a Protestant church historian though, especially for someone interested in Luther and the Reformation, this made a bit more sense. I believe this approach has borne fruit, as seen in the now substantial body of evidence that collectively indicates that much of Martin Luther's Reformational theology can be explained by his reception of mysticism.[23] That means, however, that late-medieval mysticism (and I am thinking especially of *German-speaking*, Dominican mysticism of the Upper Rhine region in the fourteenth century—still occasionally referred to today as "Deutsche Mystik" or "German Mysticism") provides theological elements and basic structures which the theology of the Reformation could employ—and it did so very productively.

Thus, I am committed to a Reformation-historical heuristic, not in the sense of, say, Ullmann's inadequate "Reformers before the Reformation,"[24] but rather in the sense of questions which a previous generation of researchers such as Heiko Augustinus Oberman (1930–2001) brought to Scholastic texts.[25] I am mostly interested in reconstructing those aspects of mystical theology according to their original logic and contexts, aspects which could and later would be received productively by the Reformation. For Protestants, this method does sometimes mean reminding ourselves over and over again that we dare not overestimate Luther's innovations, and we need the help of mystical theology to accurately qualify them. We have to look carefully at the original sources. Consequently, the following studies will present the reader with a collection of pertinent Middle High German and Latin texts in accessible translation. The goal is to remain as close as possible to the original thought of Luther.

These studies are mostly occupied with tracing how Luther received earlier thought. As Bell has demonstrated, Martin Luther read Bernard of Clairvaux very intensively. This book will place this engagement with Bernard within the context of Luther's simultaneous occupation with *Theologia Deutsch* and John Tauler (1300–1361), the fourteenth-century student of Meister Eckhart. While Tauler did further develop Eckhart's thought, his real accomplishment was to simplify and clarify it, making

23. See Volker Leppin, "'Omnem vitam fidelium penitentiam esse voluit.' Zur Aufnahme mystischer Traditionen in Luthers erster Ablaßthese," *Archiv für Reformationsgeschichte* 93 (2002), 7–25.
24. See Carl Ullmann, *Reformatoren vor der Reformation: Vornehmlich in Deutschland und den Niederlanden*, vol. 1 (Hamburg: FA Perthes, 1866).
25. Heiko Augustinus Oberman, *The Harvest of Medieval Theology; Gabriel Biel and Late Medieval Nominalism* (Grand Rapids, MI: Eerdmans, 1967).

it much easier for future generations to understand and receive. While Eckhart's sermons were passed on to further generations in clandestine ways, the Tauler sermons succeeded in the world of manuscript copying and printing. Many of Eckhart's sermons were copied anonymously or under pseudonyms—in many cases under the name of Tauler. Thus, the Reformation did not have a clear idea of how extensive Eckhart's oeuvre really was. But Tauler *was* a major topic of the time. People had begun collecting Tauler's sermons and organizing the manuscripts according to the liturgical year before he died. By the mid-fifteenth century, we can find a fairly stable, standard collection of sermons considered to be Tauler's. This collection served as the source for early editions such as the one from 1498 in Leipzig and the one from 1508 in Augsburg. But we should not forget that the Tauler corpus was still in evolution at the beginning of the sixteenth century. In 1521 a new edition was published in Basel, and here a noteworthy amount of obviously Pseudo-Tauleriana was integrated into the corpus. The editor of this edition even marked these passages as dubious. We see two really interesting things here: first, that people were aware of the problem of originality of texts, and second that they did not really care about it.[26]

For the young monk named Martin Luther, mysticism was not just a genre of literature—it was also lived experience. Luther research has given very little attention to Luther's mystical experiences despite him having mentioned them explicitly. Georg Rörer, who transcribed many of Luther's sermons, reports the statement from 1523:

> I saw many monks and clerics who are unsure and I was transported once into the third heaven.[27]

Contrary to the usual Protestant perception, Luther did not just follow Paul in the sense of a quick conversion. He *did* explain himself in this manner, but so did his fellow Augustinian brother Natin.[28] A Pauline conversion experience was part of the repertoire of late-medieval, monastic piety.

26. These Tauler passages are based on Volker Leppin, "The Mystics the Protestants Read," in *Protestants and Mysticism in Reformation Europe*, ed. Ronald K. Rittgers and Vincent Evener (Leiden: Brill, 2019), 25–26.

27. Martin Luther, *D. Martin Luthers Werke: kritische Gesamtausgabe* (WA: Weimarer Ausgabe), vol. 11 (Weimar: H. Böhlaus Nachfolger, 1900), 117, lines 35–36. "*Multos vidi monachos et clericos, qui incerti sunt, et ego semel raptus fui in 3um celum.*" My translation. Hereafter, all citations from the *Weimarer Ausgabe* will be abbreviated as WA, followed by the volume number, page number, and line number.

28. Otto Scheel, ed., *Dokumente zu Luthers Entwicklung (bis 1519)*, 2nd ed. (Tübingen: Mohr, 1929), 53 No. 136.

It was accompanied, however, by the experience of "Pauline rapture," mentioned briefly in 2 Corinthians 12:2, in which Paul reports having been transported to the third heaven.[29] This too belonged to medieval spirituality. If we believe in the historicity of Luther's later recollections, then this experience was by no means restricted to biblical ideas but was also explained in the sense of the *Corpus Dionysiacum*, a pseudonymous collection of mystical texts from the fifth or sixth century. In a very late recollection during his Lectures on Isaiah in 1543/44, Luther explains:

> Therefore I was also in that school where I meant to be among the choirs of angels while I was among the devils.[30]

When we consider that Luther was already acquainted with Pseudo-Dionysius very early on (during the period of his *Commentary on the Sentences*),[31] then the choirs of angels might be understood as pointing to the Dionysian heavenly hierarchies. Both texts are recollections (and, as source material, not always to be taken at face value) of the young monk Luther. They do, however, agree that young Luther had mystical or visionary experiences that found a medium in the Dionysian corpus.

Luther explored mysticism in his monastic context. He would focus his mystical reflection with the help of John Staupitz (1460–1524), who would serve as a polestar of Luther's thought until he took his job as a theology professor in Wittenberg.[32] There is a clear consensus in Luther research that Staupitz as a father-confessor was very important for Luther. That importance can be seen in a very famous scene, which Wilhelm-Ernst Winterhager has dated to 1516:[33] Luther was seized with terror upon seeing the Most Holy during a Corpus Christi procession in his hometown

29. For more, see: Volker Leppin, *Geglaubte Wahrheit. Das Theologieverständnis Wilhelms von Ockham* (Göttingen: Vandenhoeck & Ruprecht, 1995), 125–126.

30. WA 40/3, 657,35–36. "*Nam fui et ego in ista schola, ubi putavi me esse inter choros Angelorum, cumtamen inter Diabolos potius sim versatus.*" My translation.

31. WA 9, 63,67–68; Josef Wieneke, *Luther und Petrus Lombardus. Martin Luthers Notizen anläßlich seiner Vorlesung über die Sentenzen des Petrus Lombardus Erfurt 1509/11* (St. Ottilien: EOS 1995), 84–88; for more on Luther's relation to Dionysius, see Erich Vogelsang, "Luther und die Mystik," *LutherJahrbuch 19* (1937), 32–54, here: 33–37. It must be said, however, that Vogelsang's paper requires a clear contextualiztion within its period (see Leppin, *Luther and Mysticism* [footnote 6]).

32. Ulrich Köpf, "Martin Luthers theologischer Lehrstuhl," in *Frömmigkeitsgeschichte und Theologiegeschichte. Gesammelte Aufsätze* (Tübingen: Mohr, 2022), 540–555, has clearly demonstrated that we cannot speak of a specific professorship for biblical studies.

33. Wilhelm Ernst Winterhager, "Martin Luther und das Amt des Provinzialvikars in der Reformkongregation der deutschen Augustiner-Eremiten," in *Vita Religiosa Im Mittelalter*, ed. Franz J. Felten and Nikolas Jaspert (Berlin: Duncker u. Humblot, 1999), 707–738.

of Eisleben.[34] When he approached Staupitz with this matter, he received comfort: "It is not Christ who is terrifying you, for Christ does not terrify but consoles."[35] Throughout his life, Luther consistently emphasized that Staupitz taught him about a Christ who was different from the terrifying judge he had learned in his childhood home. According to a late recollection, his novitiate master Johann Grevenstein[36] (whom Luther later held to be a true Christian among the "damned habit"[37]) responded to his despair by pointing out that God instructed his Christians to hope.[38] The monastery was by no means determined by the singular idea of Christ the Judge, despite Luther's frequent generalizations.[39] Luther could certainly experience[40] "proximate grace"[41] in the monastery, starting with his novitiate master and then later with his superior Staupitz.

As we can see as early as Eisleben, Staupitz is the one who lends Luther's mystical experiences a strongly Christ-centered focus. It is expressed in the gentlest of tones, and with a mystical influence. The key image for this mystical experience is that of the relation between Christ and the

34. Martin Luther, *D. Martin Luthers Werke: kritische Gesamtausgabe* (WA.Tr: Weimarer Ausgabe Tischreden), vol. 1 (Weimar: H. Böhlaus Nachfolger, 1912), 59, lines 8–12 (No. 137): "What happened in my case? I was once terrified by the sacrament which Dr. Staupitz carried in a procession in Eisleben on the feast of Corpus Christi. I went along in the procession and wore the dress of a priest. Afterward I made a confession to Dr. Staupitz and he said to me, 'Your thought is not of Christ.'" Trans. after: Martin Luther, "Table Talk Recorded by Viet Dietrich, 1531–1533," in *Luther's Works*, vol. 54, *Table Talk*, trans. Theodore G. Tappert, ed. Helmut T. Lehmann and Theodore G. Tappert, 3–115 (Philadelphia, PA: Fortress Press, 1967 [5th ed. 1983]). Hereafter, all citations from the *Weimarer Ausgabe Tischreden* will be abbreviated as WA.Tr.

35. WA.TR 2, 417,14f (No. 2318a): "*Non est Christus, quod te terruit, quia Christus non terret, sed consolatur.*" My translation.

36. For more on him, see Adalbero Kunzelmann, *Geschichte der deutschen Augustiner-Eremiten. Fünfter Teil: Die sächsisch-thüringische Provinz und die sächsische Reformkongregation bis zum Untergang der beid* (Würzburg: Augustinus, 1974), 461.

37. WA 30/3, 530,25–26; cf. also Martin Luther, *D. Martin Luthers Werke: kritische Gesamtausgabe* (WA.B: Briefwechsel), vol. 9 (Weimar: H. Böhlaus Nachfolger, 1930), 133,40–41: "*Mein Praeceptor Im Closter, ein feiner alter Man.*" (Hereafter, all citations from *Briefwechsel* will be abbreviated as WA.Br, followed by volume number and page number.)

38. WA 40/2, 411,14–412,1; cf. WA.TR 5, 439,35 (No. 6017), which is clearly refering to the same event.

39. WA 10/3, 357,25–26; cf. WA 41, 197,5–201,19; WA 47, 99,34–39; 109,42–110,2; 590,1–6.

40. For more on the formative influence of Luther's time in the cloister, see Ulrich Köpf, "Martin Luther als Mönch," *Luther* 55 (1984), 66–84; Ulrich Köpf,"Monastische Traditionen bei Martin Luther," in *Luther—zwischen den Zeiten. Eine Jenaer Ringvorlesung*, ed. Christoph Markschies and Michael Trowitzsch (Tübingen: Mohr, 1999), 17–35.

41. Berndt Hamm, "Die 'Nahe Gnade'—innovative Züge der spätmittelalterlichen Theologie und Frömmigkeit," in *Herbst des Mittelalters? Fragen zur Bewertung des 14. und 15. Jahrhunderts*, ed. Jan A. Aertsen and Martin Pickavé (Berlin: De Gruyter, 2004), 541–557.

believer taking the form of a groom and a bride. Luther would return to this image in *The Freedom of a Christian*, but he likely discovered it with Staupitz's help, who had used it in his *Libellus de exsecutione aeternae praedestinationis* just before Luther started publishing:

> The connection between Christ and the Church is perfectly described as such: "I take you to be mine, I take you to me, I take you into me." Conversely, the Church or the soul says to Christ: "I make you to my own, I take you to me, I take you into me." Thus, Christ says: "The Christian is mine, the Christian is taken to me, I am the Christian" and the bride says: "Christ is mine, Christ is taken to me, I am Christ."[42]

This should ring a bell for anyone who has read Bernard of Clairvaux, the father of medieval bridal mysticism in the Western Christian tradition. But the trails leading to Staupitz do not all originate with Bernard. There is another mystical author who was read very intensely in Staupitz's circles and Staupitz may have even introduced him to Wittenberg: John Tauler.[43] Luther's recollections appear to indicate that his reading of Tauler confirmed Staupitz's Christ-centered conception of the gracious God. As we will explore in chapter 3, Luther's introduction to the *Resolutiones* provides us with central insights into this significance, especially when paired with his "Grand Self-Testimony," a late recollection that purports a "Reformational Discovery." Luther recalls how Staupitz had directed him to God's gracious inclination while wrestling with questions of penance:

> Reverend Father: I remember that during your most delightful and helpful talks, through which the Lord Jesus wonderfully consoled me, you sometimes mentioned the term "poenitentia." I was then distressed by my conscience and by the tortures of those who through endless and insupportable precepts teach the so called method of confession. Therefore I accepted you as a messenger from heaven when you said that poenitentia is genuine only if it begins with love for justice and for God and that what they consider to be the final stage and completion is in reality rather the very beginning of poenitentia.[44]

42. Johann von Staupitz, *Sämtliche Schriften*, vol. 2, *Lateinische Schriften: Libellus de exsecutione aeternae praedestinationis*, ed. Lothar Graf zu Dohna and Richard Wetzel (Berlin: De Gruyter, 1979), 145–147. My translation.

43. See Henrik Otto, *Vor- und frühreformatorische Tauler-Rezeption. Annotationen in Drucken des späten 15. und 16. Jahrhunderts* (Gütersloh: Gütersloher Verlagshaus, 2003).

44. WA 1, 525,4–14. Translation after Martin Luther, *Luther's Works*, vol. 48, *Letters I*, trans. Gottfried G. Krodel, ed. Helmut T. Lehman and Gottfried G. Krodel (Philadelphia, PA: Fortress Press, 1963 [3rd ed. 1981]), 65. (Hereafter, all citations from *Luther's Works* will be abbreviated as LW, followed by volume number and page number.)

Staupitz guided Luther, both as a pastor and by providing him with a reading list. That list included the Bible as well as the mystic Tauler. While working on the *Lectures on the Romans*, Luther read Tauler with great intensity from the edition that had been published in 1508. In doing so he became acquainted with a form of thought that conceived of the human as being entirely founded through God, something we will explore in chapter 1. These ideas pertaining to some existential foundation of the person have frequently been claimed to be original innovations of Luther. It is, however, more accurate to say that the young monk was greatly shaped by the ideas derived from Tauler, and their influence would remain perceptible in the more mature Reformer. Seeing Tauler's profound influence on Luther means that we cannot be righteously skeptical about the compatibility between mystical thought and the doctrine of justification. Mystical thought cannot be reduced to the idea that there is something in the human person that is sensitive to God and the divine, but rather it means that the human being is reliant, to a great extent, on external entities and means for their constitution. Ultimately, the human soul is reliant on God. That is music to Lutheran ears! But it is also a kernel of church criticism, for where God encounters the human being immediately, the church is not needed to mediate salvation and consequently, neither is the church's Sacrament of Consecration for the priests (see chapter 2). A cornucopia of conflicts emerged from this tension, and the general picture they yield indicates that mysticism *could* remain institutionally conforming (e.g., Bernard of Clairvaux) but did take on an attitude within medieval Catholicism which was distinct from the church's hierarchy and its prevailing culture.

This is right where the Reformation picks up, and this is what makes a new evaluation of the sacraments plausible in the first place. Luther was fascinated by Tauler's conception of penance which was far more than just the Sacrament of Penance. Western medieval Christianity understood the Sacrament of Penance to consist of three steps: remorse, oral confession, and atonement, which in turn became tightly linked to indulgence as its expression. Luther followed the mystics and then took a further step when he argued that true penance does not necessarily require the church's administered Sacrament. This is the core of his *95 Theses* on indulgence (see chapter 3). This appears to be and indeed is innovation, but it is still medieval innovation. This point does not contest the fact that Luther was an Augustinian who was thinking more and more along the lines of Pauline-Augustinian justification theology. Many texts from the late Middle Ages, however, also indicate that this strain of theology had long been integrated into mystical thought (see chapter 4). The old skepticism about mystical thought and justification living peaceably together must be put to rest. The evidence says that these are not the polar opposites that earlier research considered them to be. Luther seems to have lived with a close connection to mystical thought and emerged out of it. The same can be said about the emphasis on the passivity of human beings in the process of justification. When we consider how believers self-identified in late-medieval mysticism, then we see that an important idea had been fully formed by the beginning of the sixteenth century: the sinner has nothing to give God (see chapter 5). This idea would become central to Lutheran spirituality and piety, as can be seen in its chorales and oratories.

So, what does this all have to do with Luther's basic theology? Chapter 6 tries to weave all these threads into a meaningful tapestry. Three basic moments of Luther's (and Lutheran) theology demonstrate how this tradition received mysticism and was shaped by it. Law and Gospel, justification, and the priesthood of all believers all demonstrate the influence of mystical thought. Of course, this study would not dream of claiming that these moments can be completely described by medieval mystical theology, nor am I claiming that the entire Reformational theological tradition can be brought into harmony with mysticism or Tauler.[45] But I do see mysticism as having contributed to Luther's theology in a significant way and I believe there are good reasons for this conviction. This is also true for a positive understanding of sacraments in Lutheranism, for Luther not only remained critical of medieval sacraments (and indulgence), but also developed a new understanding of the Lord's Supper by using mystical material (see chapter 7), which maintained the presence of Christ in, with, and under the elements in such a fashion that the faithful are bound with Christ into one "bread." These ideas about the Lord's Supper underwent thrilling developments in Luther's middle and late period; however, an examination of Luther's mystical thought is also helpful for better understanding young Luther. In the disputations of the 1530s, Luther gives us a "new language" within the framework of Scholastic methodology, and it is a language that draws heavily on mystical ideas (see chapter 8).

In sum, I hope that the reader of this book comes away with the impression that we cannot understand Luther without mysticism. I intend this primarily in a historical sense, which should surprise nobody since Luther was deeply rooted in his late-medieval context, which was developing according to its own logic, a logic which included mysticism. But it goes without saying that Luther's theological developments are interesting

45. See the erroneous interpretation of my theses by Ulrich Köpf in "Martin Luther und Tauler," in *Frömmigkeitsgeschichte und Theologiegeschichte. Gesammelte Aufsätze* (Tübingen: Mohr, 2022), 515–539.

beyond him as a historical person: mysticism taught theologians how to think and speak with humility. It led to a new understanding of theology, with a living relationship between God and the faithful replacing a collection of doctrinal statements. This living process binds Christians of various confessional identities together, as seen in the common mystical sources for both Luther and Catholics. Mysticism belongs to all of us Christians; directly encountering God serves as the basis for all Christian confession. We better understand Luther as a historical person when we appreciate his mystical sources—and those insights make him an inspiration for today's ecumenical dialogue and a living Christian faith.

1.

John Tauler's External Constitution of the Person

In his groundbreaking study on modern Luther research, Risto Saarinen has shown how post-Kantian concepts shaped the image of Luther in modern German research and how this led those researchers to ignore moments of mystical presence in the believer.[1] Post-Enlightenment anthropology played a major role in fostering what was seen as Luther's exceptional role in the history of mind. Scholars such as Wilfried Joest have emphasized anthropology,[2] particularly the eccentric grounding of the person. In so doing, they have focused on one of the elements of Luther's theology which really does make him unique. They exhibited impressive diligence when reading Luther's texts and we can still learn from their deep insights as to how Luther formed his arguments. Today, we have to ask them if they were always right in stressing Luther's differences from mysticism to the extent that they did. The following study will try to reassess this assumption. It does so by looking at the mystic whose work was most familiar to Martin Luther. Thus, I will take the aforementioned concepts in Luther research as reason enough to concentrate on anthropology in the work of John Tauler.[3] As I trace his external constitution of the person, I will start by handling the decisive concept of the birth of God in the soul in his theological framework before turning my attention to the

1. Risto Saarinen, *Gottes Wirken auf uns. Die transzendentale Deutung des Gegenwart-Christi-Motivs in der Lutherforschung* (Stuttgart: Steiner, 1989).
2. Wilfried Joest, *Ontologie der Person bei Luther* (Göttingen: Vandenhoeck u. Ruprecht, 1967).
3. For more on Tauler's biography and work, see Volker Leppin, "Tauler, Johannes (ca. 1300–1361)," in *Theologische Realenzyklopädie Online* (Berlin: De Gruyter, 2010), 745–748.

anthropological meaning of this birth of God. Then I will conclude by posing a few theses about self-consciousness and personhood.

THE BIRTH OF GOD: THE IDEA OF AN EXEMPLARY SERMON

The theme of the birth of God occupies a prominent place in Tauler's rather small body of work. The first of the collected sermons (perhaps dating back to Tauler's days) devotes extensive attention to this concept.[4] The collection is ordered according to the church year, which begins with Advent and Christmas. But the collection actually skips Advent, placing Christmas—and thus the birth of God—right at the beginning. That sermon may well be Pseudo-Taulerian, but that does not really matter for the point made here: skipping Advent indicates that the compiler did not heedlessly follow chronology, instead placing the texts according to their content. The birth of God runs through all of the sermons and, as a sort of introductory thesis, can be regarded as the sum of their parts.

Sermon 1 is also one of the most theologically dense sermons in the entire oeuvre ascribed to Tauler. It is introduced with a motive taken from Isaiah 9: "For a child has been born for us, a son given to us." Tauler explains this verse with a three-fold hermeneutic. The biblical text initially speaks of the intra-Trinitarian birth of the Son through the Father, secondly of the historical birth of Jesus in time (Tauler likely sees this one as the historical sense of Isaiah's prophecy), and thirdly of the birth of God in the soul of a faithful person. This allegorical reading not only interlocks various levels of meaning but also draws on two levels of metaphor. The text is not only to be read allegorically; the various Christmas masses are presented in an allegorical light and thus related to the various ways of the birth of God in the Soul.[5]

4. For a representative look at the (occasionally too aggressive) critique of this research direction, cf. Risto Saarinen, *Gottes wirken auf uns: die transzendentale Deutung des Gegenwart-Christi-Motivs in der Lutherforschung*, vol. 137, *Veröffentlichungen des Instituts für Europäische Geschichte Mainz. Abteilung Religionsgeschichte* (Stuttgart: Steiner Verlag Wiesbaden, 1989).
5. For more on the involvement of allegorical textual interpretation into an allegorical understanding of the liturgy, see Volker Leppin. "'Als wir diese spise essent, so werden wir gessen': Reale und metaphorische Nähe Christi bei Johannes Tauler," in *Metaphorik und Christologie* (Berlin: De Gruyter, 2003), 167–177; Kirstin Faupel-Drevs, "Vom rechten Gebrauch der Bilder im liturgischen Raum. Mittelalterliche Funktionsbestimmungen bildender Kunst," in *Rationale divinorum officiorum des Durandus von Mende (1230/1–1296).* Studies in the History of Christian Thought 89 (Leiden: Brill, 2000).

Interestingly, the historical birth of Jesus is a non-starter in this interpretation. Tauler does mention it as the second birth event in his list, but he only gets around to Jesus's historical birth as a tertiary consideration and then almost as an afterthought, using it as a springboard for another metaphorical jump to Mary, who in turn is interpreted as an allegory for the faithful soul. It is a whirlwind journey to Tauler's ultimate destination: the birth of God in the soul.

Thus, when interpreting this sermon, we can concentrate on the intra-Trinitarian and soul-internal births. They are definitely related to each other, which makes things more interesting. With reference to Boethius and Augustine, the intra-Trinitarian birth of God is interpreted as "*uzgiesse(n)*" ("pouring out") in neo-Platonic terminology.[6] Thus, divine self-generation is defined as being divine in itself. It is, however, even more significant that in basically the same statement Tauler shares that "the Father has thus poured Himself out into the other two Divine persons; after that He communicated Himself to creatures."[7] The intra-Trinitarian act of self-generation is barely distinguished from that of worldly creation (a frequent point of contention with neo-Platonic thought). This is the same process with only gradations in the intensity of the handling. It is interesting to note that this idea stands in rather stark contrast with other cosmological statements in which Tauler clearly articulates the concept of *creatio ex nihilo*: "He made everything from nothing."[8]

This thought space does not force us to relate the various allegorical levels of interpretation to the biblical accounts of the birth of God, the immanent Trinity, and internal events of the soul. It is however possible to speculate that the Trinitarian self-distinction, by which the Father divides himself and yet remains identical with himself,[9] is now an image for what happens in the human person, who is said to "enter wholly into himself, and again go out of himself."[10] Tauler is borrowing ideas from Augustine here, who famously interpreted the faculties of the soul (*memoria*, *intellectus*, and *voluntas*) as "vestiges of the Trinity." According to Tauler, these

6. *Die Predigten Taulers aus der Engelberger und der Freiburger Hs. sowie aus Schmidts Abschriften der ehemaligen Straßburger Hss*, Deutsche Texte des Mittelalters 11, ed. Ferdinand Vetter (Berlin 1910 = Dublin 1968), 8, 23.

7. Vetter, *Die Predigten Taulers*, 8, 23–24. Cited after: John Tauler, *The Sermons and Conferences of John Tauler*, trans. and ed. Walter Elliott (Washington, DC: Apostolic Mission House, 1910), 67.

8. Vetter, *Die Predigten Taulers*, 205,5. "*Er machte alle ding von nute.*" My translation.

9. Vetter, *Die Predigten Taulers*, 8,32–34.

10. Vetter, *Die Predigten Taulers*, 9,8–9. "*in sich gon und denne usser sich gon.*" Trans. after: Tauler, *The Sermons and Conferences of John Tauler*, 68.

three faculties are directed toward earthly things.[11] They require some form of "struggle" ("*widerlouf*").[12] This takes place with the soul of the person becoming entirely "empty, passive, and free."[13] It is true of God, though, that "without doubt, God must fill it wholly, or sooner the heavens would burst and fill the void. Still less does God leave anything empty, so contrary is this to His nature and to His ordinance."[14] Tauler describes a sort of *horror vaccui* for God: God cannot tolerate the emptiness within the human and fills it himself. This is the moment of the birth of God, or to put it differently, of a person's "go[ing] out of himself." Tauler is clearly working with a two-sided dynamic in which God is drawn into the person and the person into God. The main requirement for the person is that they relinquish any control and become purely passive: "When all our powers of sense and motion are thus by an inward movement assembled together in the highest power, which is the force and foundation of them all, then happens an outward, yea, an overflowing movement, beyond and above self, by which we renounce all ownership of will, of appetite, and of activity."[15] This is Augustinian hamartiology taken to its ultimate conclusion, in which desire (*concupiscientia*), experienced in the "waves and desires," as well as pure self-centeredness become the main features of sinful humanity. Only when the person is free of all desires does God work in them. And he works in the entire person as the Trinitarian God, taking the person into the Trinitarian action by enacting the birth of God in the person.

THE "NOBLE PERSON" AND THEIR CONSTITUTION THROUGH THE BIRTH OF GOD

For us, it might be somewhat incredible to believe that a soteriological framework defines an anthropological condition in the true, real sense. It gets even wilder when Tauler reaches the statement that the birth of God

11. Vetter, *Die Predigten Taulers*, 9,9–18.
12. Vetter, *Die Predigten Taulers*, 9,19: Cf. Tauler, *The Sermons and Conferences of John Tauler*, 68.
13. Vetter, *Die Predigten Taulers*, 10,3. "*itel, lidig und wan.*" Trans. after: Johannes Tauler, *Johannes Tauler: Sermons*, trans. Maria Shrady, Classics of Western Spirituality (Mahwah, NJ: Paulist Press, 1985), 38.
14. Vetter, *Die Predigten Taulers*, 10,9–11. "*Gott müsse do alzuomole erfüllen, der himel risse e und erfulte daz itel, und Got lot nu vil minre die ding itel, es wer wider alle sin nature und wider sin gerehtikeit.*"
15. Vetter, *Die Predigten Taulers*, 9,28–30. "*Denne sol do geschehen ein uzgang, jo ein ubergang usser ime selber und uber in, do sullent wir verlougenen allen eigenschaft wellens und begerens und wurckens.*" Trans. after: Tauler, *Johannes Tauler: Sermons*, 38.

is ultimately the birth of a human person. "And as the Son is begotten of the Father and returns again into the Father, so shall the soul of this man be born of the Father in the Son, return into the Father with the Son, and be made one with Him."[16] In a certain sense, the birth of God in the soul is constitutive, or at least restitutive for a person and their existence.

Of course, it would seem that this cannot be true for a person in their created body-soul existence. And Tauler did not mean this either. He later introduces the semantically exact distinction between a "noble" person (who is, however, to be distinguished from a morally "good" one)[17] and the "natural" person. This juxtaposition neatly matches the juxtaposition of the inner person and the external/natural person.

The inner, noble person is the one who has been drawn into the events of salvation, into mystical reciprocity with God. The natural person is one who places their trust entirely in something outside of themself. That external instance could be reason, for example, if reason replaces God for the orientation of the person.[18] But it might also be one's own "good-looking" (*guotschinenden*) works.[19] These definitions make clear that tension between the noble and the natural person is internal to the human person—and by no means just another version of the classic body-soul dichotomy. We are not dealing with various domains of the human. We are instead dealing with various structures of relation. Tauler explicitly mentions the problem of a person who has been equipped with the highest faculties of the soul and is nevertheless oriented toward temporal things.[20] Resolving Tauler's anthropology as a dichotomy would be insufficient.[21] His anthropology is far more relational.[22]

16. Vetter, *Die Predigten Taulers*, 301, 27–29: "*also der sun wurt geborn zu dem vatter und widerflusset in den vatter, also wurt dis mensche in dem sune von dem vatter geborn und flusset wider in den vatter mit dem sune und wurt eine mit ime.*" Trans. after: Tauler, *The Sermons and Conferences of John Tauler*, 365.
17. Vetter, *Die Predigten Taulers*, 92,11–13.
18. Vetter, *Die Predigten Taulers*, 288,1–3.
19. Vetter, *Die Predigten Taulers*, 288,2.
20. Vetter, *Die Predigten Taulers*, 9,15–17.
21. Louise Gnädinger, *Johannes Tauler: Lebenswelt und mystische Lehre* (Munich: C. H. Beck, 1993), 130–132, tends in this direction, even though she interprets the external person according to their dependence on the world of senses—nevertheless, the main part of the relevant factors consists of certain properties of the soul.
22. Alois M. Haas, *Nim din selbes war: Studien zur Lehre v. der Selbsterkenntnis bei Meister Eckhart, Johannes Tauler u. Heinrich Seuse*. Dokimion 3 (Freiburg, Schweiz: Universitaetsverl, 1971), 133–134; Alois M. Haas, *Gottleiden—Gottlieben: Zur Volkssprachlichen Mystik Im Mittelalter*. 1. Aufl. (Frankfurt am Main: Insel-Verlag, 1989), 84.

So, the burning question is: How is the created, body-soul person (or, to draw in Plotinus, the body-spirit-soul person)[23] to be related to the person newly constituted in the birth of God?

The key is found in the Ground of the Soul.[24] The above-mentioned recourse of the person means returning to the fundamental place where we can discern the image of the Trinity.[25] That in turn means carrying this image around with us. Tauler is building his theory on the biblical anthropology of the image of God; he even gives it some treatment in the context of the birth of God while discussing the faculties of memory, understanding, and will as the vestiges of the Trinity. The image of God is anchored profoundly deeply in his thought, so much so that he can describe the path to salvation with the concept of an image. He does this by referring to Proclus and arguing that a person must reject all earthly images to become the perfect image of God. The image becomes the true relation. It is interesting, however, to note that Tauler always speaks of the grammatically singular, Trinitarian expressed God in contrast with the many images of the world. With God thought of as the origin of all things, a moment of singularity is inherent to Tauler's thought. This singularity cannot be found by knowing the many images of the world.

Tauler believes that this Ground of the Soul has been preserved in all people. He never once mentions a corruption of this ground or the image itself. We can assume, however, that, while he did not know the difference between *imago* and *similitudo* (Iraneus of Lyon's terminology), he did convey the basic concept. In any case, he assumes the idea that the image of God and human alienation from God exist simultaneously with the Ground of the Soul as the location of the image (*imago*) while the alienation corrupts its coherence (corresponding to Ireneus's *similitudo*).

23. Vetter, *Die Predigten Taulers*, 365,30–366,9; for more on this three-fold structure and its background in Plotinus, cf. Gnädinger, *Johannes Tauler*, 133; Gnädinger, *Johannes Tauler*, 496–497. The latter sees the three-fold structure to be so central as to suppress the significance of the two-fold one (as does D. M. Schlüter, "Philosophische Grundlagen der Lehren Johannes Taulers," in *Johannes Tauler. Ein deutscher Mystiker. Gedenkschrift zum 600. Todestag*, ed. Ephrem Filthaut [Essen: Driewer, 1961], 122–161, 125–126). Thomas Gandlau, *Trinität und Kreuz. Die Nachfolge Christi in der Mystagogie Johannes Taulers*. Freiburger Theologische Studien 150 (Freiburg im Breisgau: Verlag Herder, 1993), 45–54, draws out the internal interdependence of the twofold and threefold structures by distinguishing the external, internal, and most internal person.

24. Cf. Gnädinger, *Johannes Tauler*, 241; Steven E. Ozment, *Homo Spiritualis. A Comparative Study of the Anthropology of Johannes Tauler, Jean Gerson and Martin Luther (1509–16) in the Context of Their Theological Thought*, Studies in Medieval and Reformation Thought 6 (Leiden: Brill, 1969), 18; Stefan Zekorn, *Gelassenheit und Einkehr. Zu Grundlage und Gestalt geistlichen Lebens bei Johannes Tauler*, Studien zur systematischen und spirituellen Theologie 10 (Würzburg: Echter, 1993), 53.

25. Vetter, *Die Predigten Taulers*, 300,1–4.

As we have seen, Tauler considers this corruption to be humanity's orientation toward worldly things, a corruption of the Ground of the Soul. The task of Christian proclamation is to call such people to turn away from precisely that.[26] Only occasionally does Tauler discuss this with the concept of the fall into sin, his language of the "poison of the first fall" (*vergiftikeit des ersten valles*) by no means negating this traditional concept. He is, however, much less interested in the events of the first corruption of humanity, focusing instead on the given ontological conditions of the current person.

The concept of conversion or turning ("*keren*")[27] brings a semantic field into play which is accessible to thought structures beyond neo-Platonism recast into Christian terms. According to medieval theology, penance is the basic process of conversion. It has a three-fold structure of contrition of the heart (*contritio cordis*), oral confession (*confessio* oris), and satisfaction by works (*satisfactio operis*). Tauler strongly emphasizes the first step. He understands the conversion from earthly things as regret,[28] but it predominantly means turning away from all personal forms of attachment and property.[29] In the world of mysticism, such a concentration on an internal event between one's conscience before God is familiar territory. It does mean, though, that the church's hierarchy is largely bypassed,[30] even while intentionally doubling down on the church's doctrines of penance: the first step of the mystical path to salvation, the *purgatio*, is interpreted as an element of the Sacrament of Penance. Tauler does not see penance coming to its completion by means of the other classical steps of penance, but rather through the following mystical step of *illuminatio*, the illumination of the Ground of the Soul through God thus leading into the third step, the unification of the soul with the birth of God.[31]

Thus, when we speak of a conversion or a turn in Tauler's theology, we are talking about the birth of God in the context of a basic essence of the created human being. In a way, the birth of God restitutes that essence:

> The inner, noble person has been drawn out of the noble Ground of divinity and has been shaped according to the noble, pure God and is invited and

26. Vetter, *Die Predigten Taulers*, 97,23–26.
27. Vetter, *Die Predigten Taulers*, 97, 24.
28. Vetter, *Die Predigten Taulers*, 36,10–15.
29. Vetter, *Die Predigten Taulers*, 251,25–30.
30. For more on the tension between hierarchy and mysticism, cf. Volker Leppin, "Mystische Frömmigkeit und sakramentale Heilsvermittlung im späten Mittelalter", *Zeitschrift für Kirchengeschichte 112* (Stuttgart et al.: Kohlhammer, 2001), 189–204.
31. The unio conception is unfolded very clearly in: Vetter, *Die Predigten Taulers*, 363,11–15.

> called into him and is drawn into a life such that he can participate in all good things. What the noble, pleasant Ground has from its nature they can get passively by grace.[32]

The noble person is not constituted by the birth of God but is identified with the Ground of the Soul in which the image of God has been present since creation. Put precisely, the birth of God is not the constitution but rather the reconstitution of the true, noble human being. Accordingly, Tauler describes God as being born in the soul of the human (and thus made manifest) and simultaneously "lying hidden and covered" ("*verborgen und bedecket lit*")[33] in the soul's Ground. We are faced with a set of statements that cannot be brought easily into logical harmony with each other. Sometimes we hear of a dynamical relation to God, later it becomes static; sometimes the biblical kingdom of God is in us, and sometimes it must be sought out.[34] The solution to this apparent tension in the content of proclamation is the dynamic element of conversion and penance and the static dimension of the never-lost image of God and thus the presence of not only a single image but also of God Himself in the human being according to their created nature.

Both sets of statements converge, not only in the idea that the true human being comes from God (for Christians a banal statement about the creator God), but also that being is ultimately in God. Tauler demands pure passivity when establishing the necessary condition for the birth of God as letting go of all personal cares and connections to the world. That means that entering into one's own Ground is really entering into nothing itself.[35] The human being stops being and working and God alone performs God's work in the person.[36] These individuals who experience this way into themselves are "sublime above themselves" ("*erhaben uber sich selber*").[37] Tauler explicitly describes this relation to God as precluding all human works. That is how the human is reconstituted according to the nature of their creation. They can only attribute everything to the God who effects that.[38]

32. Vetter, *Die Predigten Taulers*, 25, 19–24. "*Der innewendige edel mensch der ist uz dem edelen grunde der gotheit heruzkummen und ist gebildet nach dem edeln lutern Gotte, und ist do wider ingeladen und wider ingeruoffet und wurt wider gezogen, das er alles des guotes teilhaftig mag werden das der edel wunnencliche grunt hat von naturen, das mag su erkriegen von genoden.*"
33. Vetter, *Die Predigten Taulers*, 25,25.
34. Vetter, *Die Predigten Taulers*, 144,1–7.
35. Vetter, *Die Predigten Taulers*, 90,22–25.
36. Vetter, *Die Predigten Taulers*, 23,8–15.
37. Vetter, *Die Predigten Taulers*, 24,11.
38. Vetter, *Die Predigten Taulers*, 64,9–11.

However, that only applies to the redeemed person. Tauler's anthropology is not a universal anthropology when it presents us with the external constitution of the person. It is an anthropology of the faithful, which also implies that it is only the faithful person who really exists and lives in accordance with the purpose and essence of a created human being.

TAULER'S CONCEPTS OF SELF-CONSCIOUSNESS AND THE PERSON

The previous passages may have gone well beyond the stated purpose of this text. What Tauler is presenting is a theory of destroying the self. But how does this have anything to do with self-consciousness? It has a lot to do with it, at least in Tauler's theological framework. And it does so even in a social-historical or at least social-ethical perspective.

The destruction of the self—Tauler's precondition for the birth of God—is, strictly speaking, the destruction of *self-centeredness* and, in Augustinian language, *incurvatus in se*. His whole point is to reorient the person away from the earthly and toward God/away from God.

The decisive aspect is the relation of the person to the world after their reconstitution. The statement that God is everything, and effects all things in the person, does not lead to devaluing the banal, everyday activity of human life. Instead, it leads to a very worldly theology and anthropology. As seen by Tauler, the person led by God is *not* only a monk or nun in a monastery. Interestingly, only those sermons intended for a *monastic* audience have been transmitted to us (they were usually delivered to Beghards, whose integration into the Dominican order was an ongoing project at the time). We have sadly lost Tauler's many sermons to lay audiences.[39]

The point still stands, though, that Tauler continuously talks about the sanctification of everyday life, a very unusual feature of his time. He is one of the earliest voices who explicitly describes the working life of a person as a "calling" ("*ruoff*") from God,[40] two centuries before Martin Luther would catapult the German word *Beruf* (vocation/calling) into the prominence it enjoys in today's German language. Spinning and cobbling attain the status of grace for Tauler, a space for the spirit of God to work.[41]

It made sense, therefore, that there was a clear opportunity for Tauler's ideas to become reality in late-medieval everyday life. Tauler's God sees

39. Ruh, "Meister Eckhart und die Spiritualität der Beginen," 490.

40. Vetter, *Die Predigten Taulers*, Vetter, *Die Predigten Taulers*, 243,13–22; cf. Gnädinger, *Johannes Tauler*, 311.

41. Vetter, *Die Predigten Taulers*, 177,19–22.

handwork as specifically *noble*. Because it is not the works of a person that constitute their relation to God but rather their letting go of all of their own initiatives, allowing God to simply act in them, all of a person's deeds have no material effect on their salvation. This irrelevance does not only *not* contribute to the constitution of a relation with God (a negative consequence), but it sees all acts as coming from God within that constituted relation (a positive consequence). Of course, Tauler does not even entertain the idea that God could recognize morally despicable deeds as acceptable as did, say, William of Ockham at about the same time.

Tauler is much less concerned with a speculative engagement with this topic and more interested in what it meant for the civic public of his time: an individual's everyday life could be a sanctified everyday life. That places Tauler in a spectrum of thinkers, emanating from Meister Eckhart, who explore the possibility of experienced mysticism on the part of urban workers, far from being restricted to the walls of a monastery. However, that means that his doctrine of receiving one's own being from God takes on an individual aspect—a person's being is received with uniquely differentiated gifts of the Spirit. An individual's capabilities are seen as being given by God and therefore not deficient compared to other ways of life, even monastic ones.

The destruction of the self is precisely what legitimizes action in the world as desired by God. It is also the only thing which can bring a person to themself at all. A person lacking God in their Ground is the external person who is not true to themself.[42] Only by sacrificing one's self can one do away with this deficiency and thus allow a space for the truly human relation to be constituted: the center of the human person in God. After this, a person can see themselves as a person in the sense that God does: a being through which God becomes active in the world.

42. Vetter, *Die Predigten Taulers*, 413,19–24.

2.

Mystical Piety and Sacramental Mediation of Salvation in the Late Middle Ages

Mysticism is complicated and controversial; as Protestantism has repeatedly emphasized, it *can* become an "alternative" to the Bible and many throughout history have felt the need to reject it decisively. However, mysticism *does* have some common ground with Protestantism, notably as concerns its tension with ecclesiality. Ernst Troeltsch (1865–1923) gave us a clear scholarly account with his *Social Teachings of the Christian Church*, in which he took Max Weber's types of religion (church and sect) and added a mystical category to them.[1] He characterized this type's arrival in the late Middle Ages as "a powerful competition with the previous world of thought, which had been controlled by the Church and particularly by the priests."[2]

This idea of mysticism being somehow independent of the church had been circulating for some time, but Troeltsch brought it to a point that was eagerly repeated and embraced as a model for interpreting mysticism for generations to come. At first glance, it has a lot going for it. As difficult as it is to define mysticism, one discernable characteristic is that mystical Christianity has an (at least momentary) unification of an earthly being

1. See Arie L. Molendijk, *Zwischen Theologie und Soziologie: Ernst Troeltschs Typen der christliche Gemeinschaftsbildung: Kirche, Sekte, Mystik. Troeltsch-Studien*, vol. 9. (Gütersloh: Gütersloher Verlagshaus, 1996) 43.
2. Ernst Troeltsch, *The Social Teaching of the Christian Churches*, trans. Olive Wyon, Harper Torchbooks, TB71—The Cloister Library (New York: Harper, 1960), 376; cf. Molendijk, *Zwischen Theologie und Soziologie*, 58; Alois Maria Haas. *Kunst rechter Gelassenheit: Themen und Schwerpunkte von Heinrich Seuses Mystik* (Bern: P. Lang, 1995), 67–70, has attacked Troeltsch's interpretation of mysticism and its consequences.

or will with God as central content.[3] If such an *unmediated* unification with God is possible, then the question becomes very pressing: Why *do* we need a priest who mediates sacramental wholeness at all?

The late Middle Ages knew many different forms of mystical spirituality which competed with the church. Such competition can be seen especially among the Brothers and Sisters of the Free Spirit who are mentioned repeatedly starting in the thirteenth century. Ecclesiastical authors portray them as a dangerous offshoot, almost certainly an inaccurate portrayal, but one which served their narrative of priestly mediation. In fact, the "Free Spirit" term was applied without much distinction to subsume many broadly similar phenomena during the High and late Middle Ages. The Sisters usually attract most of the attention, and in many cases the Beguines are the particular object of focus. The latter's unique social situation was associated with heresy—and sometimes the association was legitimate. The priestly mediation of grace would have been greatly challenged by statements such as those from the Beguine Marguerite Porète who wrote that the mystically joined, free soul need no longer search for God in the sacraments.[4] The same was true when the church's investigations discovered that the Lower-Rhine Beghards were teaching that the elevated eucharistic elements need not be honored.[5] All this demonstrates that there were indeed mystical currents which drew upon mystical experience to undermine sacramental mediation.

That is, however, not the whole story. Let us not forget that the mystics of the High Middle Ages—Bernard of Clairvaux or the Victorines—were

3. In the following, I understand "mysticism" to be a character of theology or spirituality centered with a worldly possibility of unification of a believer's will, or essence, with God. This unification can be the origin or goal of mystical theology. Within the spectrum of late-medieval mysticism, there are distinct types in the form of speculative and devotional mysticism.

4. *Corpus Christianorum. Continuatio mediaevalis*, vol. 69, 242,20–21: "*Ceste, qui telle est, ne quiert plus Dieu par penitance ne par sacrement nul de Saincte Eglise*" ("Whoever is so does not inquire of God by means of penitence or the sacrament or even the Holy Church.") My translation. (Hereafter, all citations from *Corpus Christianorum* will be abbreviated as CChr.CM, followed by volume number, page number, and line number.); cf. Marguerite Porète, *Der Spiegel Der Einfachen Seelen: Wege Der Frauenmystik*, ed. Louise Gnädinger (Munich: Artemis, 1987), 131; For more on the relation of Porète with the Brothers and Sisters of the Free Spirit, see Raoul Manselli, "Brüder Des Freien Geistes," *Theologische Realenzyklopädie*, vol. 7 (Berlin: De Gruyter, 2010), 218–220, here: 219. https://doi.org/10.1515/tre.07_218_18.

5. *Kompendium der Glaubensbekenntnisse und kirchlichen Lehrentscheidungen*, 4th ed, ed. Heinrich Denziger and Peter Hünerman (Freiburg im Breisgau: Verlag Herder, 2005), 898. (Hereafter, all citations from *Kompendium der Glaubensbekenntnisse* will be abbreviated as DS, followed by page number.); cf. Peter Browe, *Die verehrung der Eucharistie im Mittelalter* (Munich: M. Hueber, 1933), 50. For the relation between this verdict and that of Marguerite Porète, cf. Kurt Ruh, "Meister Eckhart und die Spiritualität der Beginen." *Perspektiven der Philosophie* vol. 8 (1982): 323–334, here 324.

deeply church-oriented in their spirituality. Meister Eckhart and his school of the fourteenth century worked very hard to conduct their lives *within* the church. Mystical groups outside of the church were the exception to the rule; mysticism within the church dwarfed it. Such details are critical for a clear picture of how ambivalent late-medieval mysticism really was. That is the purpose of this chapter, where we will examine how priests mediated salvation through the sacrament.[6]

MYSTICAL THEOLOGY SUITABLE TO THE CHURCH

The most important mystical texts of the fourteenth and fifteenth centuries were written by clerics deeply involved in the system of ecclesial mediation. They were active as confessors and priests who performed the sacrifice of the mass.[7] The sources we have do not make a big deal of this because they were focusing on the *extra*-ordinary interests of these preachers and did not want to devote time and writing materials to describing the day-to-day reality of the church. We do not have a single one of John Tauler's famous sermons to ordinary people. We only have those that he held before nuns and Beguines, who were already very religious. And yet, we continue to stumble upon little mentions of "background noise," a day-to-day ritual praxis in the church. The mystics never stop encouraging their listeners to frequently receive communion,[8] as seen in Henry Suso's *Vita*, which gives us a very vivid account of the traditional understanding of the Eucharist. Like most vitas, this stylized self-portrayal cannot be considered an autobiography in today's sense and was initiated by the Dominican nun Elsbeth Stagel before undergoing another redaction,

6. As far as I can see, this question has not been systematically approached by scholarship. There are a number of individual studies on Tauler including: Adolf Hoffmann, "Sakramentale Heilswege bei Tauler," in *Johannes Tauler: Ein deutscher Mystiker.* Gedenkschrift zum 600. Todestag, ed. Ephrem Filthaut (Essen: Driewer, 1961), 247–267 (this one *does* have a systematic tendency); Stefan Zekorn, *Gelassenheit und Einkehr: Zu Grundlage und Gestalt geistlichen Lebens bei Johannes Tauler*, Studien zur systematischen und spirituellen Theologie 10 (Würzburg: Echter, 1993), 149–160.
7. Louis Cognet, *Gottes Geburt in der Seele. Einführung in die Deutsche Mystik* (Freiburg im Breisgau: Verlag Herder, 1980), 101, also emphasizes this concrete background.
8. For example, see Johannes Tauler, *Die Predigten Taulers aus der Engelberger und der Freiburger Handschrift sowie aus Schmidts Abschriften der ehemaligen Strassburger Handschriften*, ed. Ferdinand Vetter (Berlin: Weidmannsche Buchhandlung, 1910), 283, 18–25; Johannes Tauler and Georg Hofmann, *Predigten: Vollständige Ausgabe* (Freiburg im Breisgau: Verlag Herder, 1961), 120; Heinrich Seuse, *Deutsche Schriften*, ed. Karl Bihlmeyer (Stuttgart: W. Kohlhammer, 1907 [Frankfurt, 1961]), 301, l.14—302, l.4; Heinrich Seuse and George Hofmann, *Deutsche mystische Schriften* (Düsseldorf: Patmos-Verlag, 1966), 305.

likely from Suso himself. Suso reports that as a young man, he made an agreement with a friend: whoever survived the other would read a mass for them twice per week for a year. But when Suso's friend died, he had forgotten about this pact, so his friend had to visit him from the afterlife to remind him.[9] This is a world steeped in the tradition of a satisfactory effect of the mass sacrifice and provides us with utterly no indication that mystical experience somehow competed with it.[10]

This harmony becomes an outright agenda in the *Imitation of Christ*, one of the most influential and most printed works in the area of late-medieval mysticism. Edited by Thomas á Kempis, this small text is divided into four books. The last (it was originally the second-to-last but was pushed to the end in accordance with medieval customs)[11] is titled "*De sacramento*" (on the sacrament). It was entirely clear to late-medieval readers that "the" sacrament mentioned here could only mean the Lord's Supper, the particular inclination of Christ to his church in the form of bread and wine. The entire book celebrates Christ drawing near to his church: "Marvelous and hidden grace of this Sacrament, which only the faithful of Christ know."[12] Sacramental adoration ascends into a great acclamation of praise for the priests: "Great is this mystery and great is the dignity of priests."[13] Directly after this, the church's official policy of mandatory oral confession and reception of the Eucharist are emphasized.[14] Basically, the *Imitation* is a collection of tracts, in which we see mystical theology being

9. Heinrich Seuse, *Deutsche Schriften*, ed. Karl Bihlmeyer (Frankfurt: Minerva, 1961), 144, l.3–10; cf. Heinrich Seuse and George Hofmann, *Deutsche mystische Schriften* (Düsseldorf: Patmos-Verlag, 1966), 151–152.

10. Stefan Zekorn, *Gelassenheit und Einkehr: zu grundlage und Gestalt geistlichen Lebens bei Johannes Tauler*, Studien zur systematischen und spirituellen Theologie, vol. 10 (Würzburg: Echter, 1993), 154, has demonstrated similar phrases (some even word-for-word) to Thomas Aquinas in Tauler. Also worthy of mention is the fact that Thomas á Kempis could write about Gert Groote, the founder of the Brothers of Common Life. He was granted a place in Deventer where he could perpetually see the Eucharist. For more, see Peter Browe, *Die verehrung der Eucharistie im Mittelalter* (Munich: M. Hueber, 1933), 57. Here we see purely visual spirituality in the midst of the mystical crowd!

11. Rudolf van Dijk, "Spiritualität der 'inicheit'. Mystik und Kirchenkritik in der Devotio Moderna," in *Die Kirchenkritik der Mystiker: Prophetie aus Gotteserfahrung*, vol. 2, ed. Mariano Delgado (Stuttgart: Kohlhammer, 2005), 9–38, 26

12. Thomas Von Kempen, "De imitatione Christi," in *Nachfolge Christi und vier andere Schriften. Lateinisch und deutsch*, ed. Friedrich Eichler (Munich: Kösel-Verlag, 1966), 414: "*O admirabilis et abscondita gratia sacramenti; quam novunt tantum Christi fideles*." Trans. after: Thomas á Kempis, *The Imitation of Christ* (Phoenix, AZ: Aquinas Press, 2017), 244.

13. Von Kempen, "De imitatione Christi," 434. Trans. after: Thomas á Kempis, *The Imitation of Christ* (Phoenix, AZ: Aquinas Press, 2017), 256.

14. Von Kempen, "De imitatione Christi," 426, 454; cf. similarly Tauler, *Predigten* (Vetter), 283,18–25; Tauler, *Predigten* (Hofmann), 120.

employed to stabilize the given clerical mediation and the embedding of the faithful in a structure of norms and practices. The Eucharist does not stand alone here: sacramental Penance is also glorified, and Henry Suso was regarded as one of its great practitioners. In his *Vita*, he gives the account of a woman who had told a grievous sinner about him:

> Oh my dear fellow, go and say your confession to him [Suso]! Those among us believe that whoever says their confession to him, regardless of how sinful they are, can rest assured that God will not cast them away.[15]

This is, of course, heavily stylized. But stylized accounts convey an ideal of oneself, and here we see that Suso had the ideal of being a perfect mediator of God's nearness through the Sacrament of Penance.

This ideal was presented very officially. The reason for this likely had to do with the fact that mystical theology had come under heavy pressure from the church. The Beguine Marguerite Porète had been burned and Meister Eckhart had been condemned. Any mystic who wanted to avoid conviction had to keep a clear distance from any heretical business. We see this caution very clearly in the anonymous author of the *Theologia Deutsch*, who was likely a senior ordered cleric in Frankfurt in the second half of the fourteenth century.[16] At the very beginning of his text, he distinguishes himself from the Free Spirits[17] and subsequently attacks the "spiritual arrogance" which believes:

> They do not require Scripture or doctrine or anything like it, ensuring that the authorities, ordinances and laws and commandments of the Holy Church and the Sacrament are held in no regard whatsoever.[18]

15. Seuse, *Deutsche Schriften*, 79,28–30: "*eya, lieber geselle, ga hin und biht och! Su sind da heime in guotem globen gen ime: wer im gebihtet, wie sundig er ist, daz den got niemer well gelassen.*" My translation; cf. Seuse and Hofmann, *Deutsche mystische Schriften*, 88.
16. Thus, the dating undertaken by Alois Maria Haas. *Kunst rechter Gelassenheit: Themen und Schwerpunkte von Heinrich Seuses Mystik* (Bern: P. Lang, 1995), 267; the same is true of Wolfgang von Hinten, ed., "Der Franckforter" ("*Theologia deutsch*"). In VerfLex 2 (1979) 802–808, who also refers to the linguistic reasons and the transmission in the same currents as that of Tauler and Eckhart.
17. 'Der Franckforter' ('Theologia Deutsch'), Wolfgang von Hinten, München 1982 (= Münchener Texte und Untersuchungen zur deutschen Literatur des Mittelalters 78), 67,7; cf. *'Der Franckforter', Theologia Deutsch*, translated by Alois M. Haas, (Einsiedeln: Johannes-Verlag, 1980), 37.
18. Cf. Von Hinten, *'Der Franckforter'* 105,31–33: "sie bedorff nicht schrifft noch lere und des gleich, ßo werden do alle wiße, ordenunge und gesetze unnd gebote der heiligen kirchen und die sacrament czu nichte geachtet." My translation; cf. Haas, *'Der Franckforter'*, 80.

While this exemplifies clear opportunism, practiced as extensively then as in any other time, not everything the mystics said can be explained by it. For example, Suso defended Meister Eckhart's orthodoxy without any clear advantage to himself.[19]

The church conformity of mysticism is also emphasized by the special mandate which the church gave to its own leading voices. The great theologians of late-medieval mysticism were given the task of maintaining and restoring orthodox faith in the church—Suso, Eckhart and John Tauler in Strasbourg were active in the *cura monialium*, pastoral care for nuns, especially Dominican ones whose spirituality was often very closely aligned to that of the Beguines (many female Dominican communities emerged from Beguine communities). The mystical preachers had been sent into a milieu of spirituality that had great potential for heretical mysticism. Their task was to influence these nuns through discipline and moderation—and keep them orthodox. Otto Langer has demonstrated that Meister Eckhart's numerous expressions about this can be read as an attempt to soothe the extremely excited mysticism of these women.[20] Langer has portrayed Eckhart—who can be considered the father of the following generation of mystics—as one whose main work was to bring mystical excitement into the church's own channels.

Taken together, these points support the idea of a well-defined *ecclesial mysticism*. This is certainly true for the most important mystical preachers in their own contexts. We have not yet, however, carefully examined the relation between ecclesiality and the potential critique of the church in the content of mystical teaching. To this task we now turn.

INTENSIFICATION AND INTERNALIZATION OF SACRAMENTAL SPIRITUALITY IN THE CHURCH'S MYSTICISM

If we search for the church's mediation of salvation in late-medieval mystical texts, we might not believe our eyes. The church's normal mechanisms of granting grace are not just recognized and practiced in the thick of

19. Thus, Eckhart's verdict did not stop Henry Suso from considering him to be holy and from speaking about him in a vision from heaven (see Seuse, *Deutsche Schriften*, 22,20–23,12; Seuse and Hofmann, *Deutsche mystische Schriften*, 32–33). It makes sense then that Suso was also repeatedly accused of heresy, as his *vita* indicates (Seuse, *Deutsche Schriften*, 69,17–69,3; cf. Seuse and Hofmann, *Deutsche mystische Schriften*, 77).

20. Otto Langer, *Mystische Erfahrung und spirituelle Theologie: zu Meister Eckharts Auseinandersetzung mit der Frauenfrömmigkeit seiner Zeit* (Munich: Artemis, 1987).

mystical thought, they are also deeply intertwined and actively affirmed by the mystics. Many, many passages bring to the fore that the Sacrament of the Eucharist was interpreted by the mystics as the most prominent place to encounter God.[21]

John Tauler is a textbook case of this. His sermons have been transmitted to us in a collection ordered according to the liturgical year. Among them, we find several devoted to the Corpus Christi feast, which had become a festival of *visual* spirituality (contrary to its original intentions).[22] In one of his sermons, Tauler seems to be acting against this reduction to the visual when he practically screams, "We feed upon our God,"[23] and adds just a few lines later: "No act in our material existence is so close to us, or enters so intimately into our bodily life, as eating and drinking."[24]

External consumption means that God is drawn near. In the rest of the sermon, following the above lines, Tauler takes the Real Presence to be an occasion for extensive mystical reflection. Such tight connections between the Eucharist and mystical experience are well-known facets of mystical praxis. We also see in the accounts about mystically moved nuns in Kirchberg zu Sulz. The Kirchenberg document was written by multiple hands and miraculously escaped destruction over the centuries. It provides us with a unique insight into the practical implementation of mystical spirituality, the trance-like ecstasy of the *genad contemplativa* (contemplative grace)[25] as well as the extroverted *genad jubilus* (jubilant grace).[26] We even hear of one sister who was seen floating above the ground during the singing of the choir.[27]

21. The same can be found with Eckhart; see chapter 20 of the teachings, where the Sacrament is depicted as the prominent location of encountering God: Meister Eckhart and Josef Quint, eds., *Die deutschen Werke: Die deutschen und lateinischen Werke / Meister Eckhart*, vol. 4 (Stuttgart: Kohlhammer, 1963), 262–265; For more on this: Reiner Mansetten, *Esse est Deus: Meister Eckharts christologische Versöhnung von Philosophie und Religion und ihre Ursprünge in der Tradition des Abendlandes* (Freiberg im Breisgau and Munich: K. Alber, 1993), 494.
22. Browe, *Verehrung*, 87–88, points out that Urban IV emphatically called the believers to receive the Sacrament in his inaugural bull, and that this call apparently had no effect.
23. Tauler, *Predigten* (Vetter), 293,27; cf. Tauler, *Predigten* (Hofmann), 208. Trans. after: Tauler, *The Sermons and Conferences of John Tauler*, 369.
24. Tauler, *Predigten* (Vetter), 293,31–33: "Nu ist enkein materielich ding das als nahe und inwendiklich den menschen kume als essen und trinken, das der mensch zuo dem munde in nimet." Trans. after: Tauler, *The Sermons and Conferences of John Tauler*, 369. Cf. Tauler, *Predigten* (Hofmann), 208.
25. Friedrich Wilhelm Emil Roth, "Aufzeichnungen über das mystische Leben der Nonnen von Kirchberg bei Sulz Predigerordens während des XIV. und XV. Jahrhunderts," *Alemannia* 21 (1893): 103–148.
26. Roth, "Aufzeichnungen über das mystische Leben," 105, 107.
27. Roth, "Aufzeichnungen über das mystische Leben," 106.

It is a demanding, multilayered text, but in all of its complexity, there is never even a hint of competition between mystical experience and the Sacrament. In fact, one nun falls into ecstasy when she receives the Lord in the bodily consumption of the Eucharist.[28] Receiving the mass is essentially used as a catalyst for mystical experience, and mystical experience conversely means a deep intensification in eucharistic piety. Put simply, mystical experience makes the Real Presence of the Lord in the Sacrament—thus the church's teaching—into a real experience. And this presence need not be physically consumed, as reflected in the declining rates of oral consumption of the Eucharist in the late Middle Ages. Henry Suso's self-reflection tells us of how he entered mystical experiences simply by observing the *elevation* of the host by a priest.[29]

Thus, the basis of mystical interpretation of the Eucharist is not found in the "brute fact" of Real Presence. John Tauler does not extend his emphasis of God's proximity in food by referring to the Real Presence. Much like Bernard, he ends up inverting the line of argumentation: "When we eat this food, we ourselves are eaten."[30] The focus has shifted away from a human physically eating the Sacrament to being consumed by God. Initially, Tauler uses this idea to amplify and intensify the process of the Eucharist. But his thoughts continue to drift away from the concrete actions at the altar. We are eaten by God: "He scourges us for our sins, which He reveals plainly to us. His divine presence scourges our conscience."[31] The first association to be made here relates the material consumption of the Eucharist to the conscience of a person.[32] An essential aspect of Tauler's mysticism is consuming the Eucharist as a cipher for

28. Roth, "Aufzeichnungen über das mystische Leben," 106–107, 111 et. al.
29. Seuse, *Deutsche Schriften*, 386,11ff; cf. Seuse and Hofmann, *Deutsche mystische Schriften*, 392.
30. Tauler, *Predigten* (Vetter), 294,3–4: "als wir diese spise essent, so werden wir gessen." Trans. after: Tauler, *The Sermons and Conferences of John Tauler*, 370. Cf. also Tauler, *Predigten* (Hofmann), 208. Tauler is likely thinking of the seventy-first sermon on the Song of Songs, where Bernard develops this relationship between eating and being eaten, cf. Bernard von Clairvaux, *Sämtliche Werke. Lateinisch/deutsch*, vol. 6, ed. Gerhard B. Winkler (Innsbruck: Tyrolia, 1995), 448–449.
31. Tauler, *Predigten* (Vetter), 294,24–26; Tauler, *Predigten* (Hofmann), 209.
32. By emphasizing the internal events, the Dominican Tauler reclaims a dimension of the Sacrament which had been suspended by an occupation with Augustine's symbolic interpretation of the Sacrament, such as when Bonaventure and others explained that the external sign of the Sacrament accompanied the unmediated effect of God in the soul of the person. For more on this, cf. Karl-Heinz zur Mühlen, "Zur Rezeption der Augustinischen Sakramentsformel 'Accedit verbum ad elementum, et fit sacramentum' in der Theologie Luthers," *Zeitschrift für Theologie und Kirche (ZThK)* 70 (1973): 50–76, 52–53; Karl-Heinz zur Mühlen, *Reformatorisches Profil: Studien zum Weg Martin Luthers und der Reformation* (Göttingen: Vandenhoeck & Ruprecht, 1995), 13–39, 15–16.

self-understanding and regret.[33] It makes the human person free from all selfish perception, yielding a free, empty person with space for God. It is in this sense that Tauler can interpret this central mystical process, using the forty-first Psalm, as an internal vacuum that draws God into the human being: "Deep calleth unto deep."[34]

The mystic who interprets the Sacrament in this manner can claim to understand it not only according to its external sense but also to have reached its internal sense as well. Tauler's interpretation of eucharistic spirituality does not compete with the Eucharist but leads to an internalization of the Eucharist in a full sense. And it goes even further: Tauler has almost imperceptibly opened the way to another Sacrament with his internalization of the Eucharist. Tauler's thought of the Eucharist always remains in touch with the penitential regret of the person in the presence of God. He is not alone in making this tight association between penance and Eucharist. The *Theologia deutsch* also describes the process of letting go of oneself as conversion and uses the verb "*büßen*" (confessing/repenting) in a context that is otherwise not particularly sacramental. The result is, however, surprising: when Tauler attempts to intensify the understanding of the Eucharist with a theology of penance, he ends up eroding the Sacrament of Penance itself. This brings us to the statements by this great mystic which best support the thesis of mysticism as a competitor to the church's all-encompassing provision.

THE AMBIVALENCE OF THE CHURCH'S MYSTICISM: SUBSTITUTING SACRAMENTS AND DESTABILIZING HIERARCHY

Tauler's tight relation between intensification and relativization of sacramental spirituality can be seen best in another text:

> Amid all this distress our heavenly Father has comforted us . . . God has given us His holy sacraments, beginning with the grace of the true faith in holy baptism, and then the sacrament of confirmation; holy penance, with its deep sorrow for sin, humble confession, and sincere satisfaction; our Redeemer's

33. Louise Gnädinger, *Johannes Tauler: Lebenswelt und mystische Lehre* (Munich: C. H. Beck, 1993), 121.
34. Tauler, *Predigten* (Vetter), 176,7: "abyssus abyssum invocat, das abgrunde das inleitet das abgrunde"; Tauler, *Predigten* (Hofmann), 315; cf. the equally paradoxical formulation in the *Imitatio*, 322: "Tanto etiam [homo] altius iad Deum ascendit; quanto profundius in se descendit et plus sibi ipsi vilescit."

precious body and blood in holy communion; and in our last moments the sacred anointing. All these Divine gifts has He given us, in order that when we unhappily fall from His grace we may the more readily be restored to His friendship.[35]

This is explicit praise for the sacraments, but it has great nuance. The sacraments are *only* help and support for something else.[36] We can see this merely supportive function of the sacraments in a few other texts by Tauler. In another sermon about the three-fold way to God, he describes the sacraments as useful aids in the first two steps, but in the third step all these aids actually get in the way.[37] Ultimately, the faithful person faces God directly, even without sacramental help.

No matter how well-intended his demotion of the sacraments may have been, it and his preference for innerness in his theology opened Tauler up to the accusation of competing with priestly mediation. The above-mentioned Corpus Christi sermon neatly portrays these moments together. After mentioning that a Christian should allow themself to be chewed up by God, he warns against trying to escape this "by going directly to the confessor." Instead, he insists: "no, confess to God directly."[38] We should not overlook the Middle High German term "zem ersten" (first of all). This little particle preserves Tauler's church-conformity. He never entirely negates the normal Sacrament of Penance, but he does relegate it to second place. He removes the mediation from the decisive act of the *confessio oris*.[39] It is no longer necessary to appear before a priest.[40] The

35. Tauler, *Predigten* (Vetter), 49,29–50,2: "Wider die mannigvaltige hindernisse so het uns der minnecliche Got gegeben grosse helffe und trost . . . uns er het uns die heiligen sacramente gegeben, von erst den heiligen tof und den heiligen crisemen [Salbung, Firmung], darnoch also wir usvallent, die heilige bihte und die penitencien, darzuo sinen heiligen lichamen und an dem lesten daz heilige oley. Dis sind iemer starckeund grosse sture und helffe wider in zuo gon in den ursrpung und in unsern begin." Trans. after: Tauler, *The Sermons and Conferences of John Tauler*, 210; Tauler, *Predigten* (Hofmann), 73.
36. It is interesting to note at this point that Tauler does not bind the reception of the Holy Spirit to the sacraments, but rather to the proper "bereitunge" (preparations) which can make a daily reception of the Spirit possible for a Christian (Tauler, *Predigten* [Vetter], 91,12–16).
37. Tauler, *Predigten* (Vetter), 316,2–3: "in diesem so hindert alles, daz behelffen mag" / "everything that ordinarily helps the soul is liable to become a hindrance." Trans. after: Tauler, *The Sermons and Conferences of John Tauler*, 381; cf. Tauler, *Predigten* (Hofmann), 223. However, we also see in Kempen, *Imitatio* 168, the idea of penance being outperformed by being emptied within the soul.
38. Tauler, *Predigten* (Vetter), 294,33–250,1; cf. Tauler, *Predigten* (Hofmann), 209.
39. For the centrality of oral confession in the Sacrament of Penance, cf. Martin Ohst, *Pflichtbeichte: Untersuchungen zum Busswesen im Hohen und Späten Mittelalter.* Beiträge zur historischen Theologie, vol. 89 (Tübingen: J.C.B. Mohr (P. Siebeck), 1995), 240, which refers to the *Summa Angelica* from the late fifteenth century.
40. *Imitatio*, 102.

decisive act is the individual, private confession before God Himself. And if he could replace the *confessio*, then he could also replace the *satisfactio*. Meister Eckhart takes an almost sarcastic tone when writing about the way of faith:

> Many people think they are performing great works by outward things such as fasting, going barefoot, or other such things which are called penance. But the true and best penance is that whereby one improves greatly and in the highest degree; and that is that a man should experience a complete and perfect turning away from whatever is not entirely God and divine in himself and in all creatures, and have a full, perfect, and complete turning toward his beloved God in unshakeable love, so that his devotion and yearning for Him are great.[41]

As with Eckhart, we also see Tauler emphasizing the internal part of the act of penance. His most extreme statements also tend to disregard the external aspects of the Sacrament. In both cases, the listener is left utterly unconvinced that they *must* go to a priest when they have already carried out an intensive confession of sin before God. *Contritio* becomes so important that it displaces the salvific effect of *confessio* and *satisfactio*. They become appendices; they do not hurt, but the proclamation of the mystics does not see them as necessary.

If one were to extend the logic of (over)emphasizing *contritio*, then it would implicitly erode the church's sanctioned praxis of Penance. *Some*times this is true, such as when Tauler criticized the ritualized and externalized penitential praxis in his time because it was lacking the *contritio cordis*:

> There are many who go to confession for twenty or thirty years, and never do it rightly, nor are ever rightly absorbed, and yet always afterwards receive the blessed Sacrament.[42]

The comment at the end makes clear how one should understand the fact that some individuals did not receive absolution. If they were going to the Eucharist afterward, then their penance must have taken place by officially

41. Meister, Eckhart, *Die deutschen Werke*, vol. 5, ed. Josef Quint, (Stuttgart: W. Kohlhammer Verlag, 1963), 244,5–245,2. Translation after: "Meister Eckhart, 16. Of True Penance and Holy Living." In *The Complete Mystical Works of Meister Eckhart*, trans. and ed. Maurice O'C. Walshe, Foreword by Bernard McGinn (New York: Crossroad Publishing, 2009), 503.

42. Tauler, *Predigten* (Vetter), 282,7–9: "*Man vindet vil menschen, die bichtent zwenzig oder drissig jar und engetaten nie recht bichte noch sienwurden nie absolviert und gont do mit zuo dem heiligen sacrament.*" Trans. after: Tauler, *The Sermons and Conferences of John Tauler*, 290; Tauler, *Predigten* (Hofmann), 118–119.

legitimate means. Otherwise, they would not have been permitted to approach the altar. Not receiving absolution in this case, however, likely means hearing the *words* of absolution but not really being absolved. The Sacrament therefore becomes effective only through an assumed *contritio*. Tauler's interest in stopping a mechanistic understanding of the Sacrament is obvious here. The consequence, however, is that the security of having received salvific absolution through the words of a priest acting in the place of Christ has been greatly diminished. The effectiveness of the Sacrament has become subjective and thus unsure. Tauler extends this train of thought even further when, with the assumption of a positive increase of potency, he starts to couple the effectiveness of the Sacrament with the individual virtue of the administrating priest. Tauler advises everyone to go to the celebrations of the mass all over the world because of their internal desire for God, but they should especially go "to those Holy priests . . . whose sacrifice is pleasing to God."[43] Here we see quite clearly the full commitment to the idea that the personal quality of a priest is a measure of the quality of the sacrament. The objective effect for the well-being of the recipient, however, is entirely questionable. The same danger is clear and present in the earlier mention of Suso as an excellent father confessor. If penance is particularly effective with him, then we have created a hierarchy within the ostensibly egalitarian priesthood and that is a big, ugly problem for sacramental theology. Mystical experience brings us to a conceptual world of penance in which the internal aspect of penance is so strong that the external, ecclesial aspect becomes very diffuse. At this point, who *needs* a diversified system of sacramental piety? We even see this pertaining to the Eucharist. Henry Suso has his fictional Christ saying just what we can learn from mystical authors of his time: "There are many who go to confession for twenty or thirty years, and never do it rightly, nor are every rightly absorbed, and yet always afterwards receive the blessed Sacrament."[44]And the *Imitation of Christ* ascertains: "As often as a person meditates on the mystery of Christ's incarnation and passion, so often does he communicate with him in a mystical way and so often is he refreshed by Christ and inflamed with love for him."[45] Now, it *is* true that these statements are far less common when pertaining

43. Tauler, *Predigten* (Vetter), 319,5–7: "zuo den heiligen priestern . . . von den dis opher Gotte als geneme ist." My translation; Tauler, *Predigten* (Hofmann), 248.

44. Seuse, *Deutsche Schriften*, 302,12–15; cf. Seuse and Hofmann, *Deutsche mystische Schriften*, 306; similar thoughts can be found in Tauler, *Predigten* (Vetter), 313,30–33; Tauler, *Predigten* (Hofmann), 219–220; for more on the origins on Eckhart, cf. Manstetten, *Esse est deus*, 495–496.

45. *Imitatio*, 456–457: "*Nam totiens mystice communicat et invisibiliter reficitur; quotiens incarnationis Christi mysterium passionemque devote recolit: et in amore eius accenditur.*" Trans. after: Thomas

to the internalized Lord's Supper than they are for penance. The latter's basis in *contritio* made it much more of an internal process. This process could subsume and replace everything else. When Tauler spoke of an act of *confessio*, then verbal communication was no longer necessary. The encounter with God takes place ontologically, just as we would expect from a thinker who was so inspired by Eckhart's mystical world. The sinner's act of self-discernment creates a vacuum which sucks God into them. The emptied person gets filled up by God, who transforms them with gushing divine love. This encounter between God and a person is so direct that a priest does not seem necessary anymore.[46]

This logic of cleaning the sacramental house goes even further. In another sermon, Tauler describes a woman who recognized her lowliness before God in a divine vision. In this situation, the Saints or the (personally imagined) pain and wounds of Christ could not help her but rather God alone.[47] Any mediation whatsoever over against God Himself has become entirely obsolete.

Thus, the mystical conceptions do not just seem to question the necessity of oral confession, which the Fourth Lateran Council had made mandatory.[48] They also question the distinction between layperson and priest. Tauler manages to bridge this distinction when he explains "this high priest may be taken as a figure to show forth the interior man" who carries out the priestly office by going into their innermost being.[49] Such metaphorical statements appear to suspend the strict separation between clerics and laypersons.

If we emphasize these aspects in high resolution, then it is easy to come to an interpretation of the mysticism embodied by Eckhart and his school as competition to the church. It looks as if they bring about a substitution of the sacraments, which would imply a destabilization of the church's hierarchy. And yet, the idea of mysticism as "powerful competition" scarcely rhymes with the observations at the beginning

à Kempis, *The Imitation of Christ: A Timeless Classic for Contemporary Readers*, Trans. William C. Creasy (Notre Dame, IN: Ave Maria Press, 2017), 209.

46. While discussing a mystical path, Tauler expressly speaks of being directly touched by the Holy Spirit—and without anything in the way of priestly mediation (Tauler, *Predigten* [Vetter], 38,4–11; Tauler, *Predigten* [Hofmann], 57).

47. Tauler, *Predigten* (Vetter), 45,11–46,4; Tauler, *Predigten* (Hofmann), 66–67; cf. Tauler, *Predigten* (Vetter), 117,26–28: "*Diesen ker den kundent alle engele und alle heiligen nut gegeben, noch alles daz in himmelrich und errtrich ist, nut gemachen, noch alle ding, sunder alleine daz goetteliche abgrunde in aller siner unmassen*"; Tauler, *Predigten* (Hofmann), 197.

48. For more, cf. Ohst, *Pflichtbeichte*, 32–49.

49. Tauler, *Predigten* (Vetter), 165,31–33: "*ein ieklich guot inwendig mensche*"; Tauler, *Predigten* (Hofmann), 327–328.

of this chapter. The practitioners of mysticism may have gone very far in certain formulations, but they never dared to leave the church. That really did mean not leaving the sacramental community of the church but remaining in it and helping to keep it going. They never intended to compete with the church. Any interpretation of medieval mysticism would do well to avoid one-sided conclusions based on its potentially critical elements.

CONCLUSION: MYSTICAL ECCLESIALITY

Ernst Troeltsch tried to be an honest intellectual, something evident in his engagement with ecclesial mysticism. He managed to fit it into his theory of types, but it was not a type where he personally felt comfortable, and he remarked with palpable astonishment: "This type, [i.e., the mystical], however, only attained its universal historical significance in the later Protestant Dissenters, and in their connection with Humanism."[50]

Late-medieval mysticism must therefore point to something different and bigger. As we can see, Troeltsch was not entirely free from Carl Ullmann's conception of "Reformers before the Reformation" in his classification of medieval phenomena.[51] This perspective has long provided a certain space for Protestant church-historians to find mysticism attractive.[52] Such generous application of this construct, however, which evaluates the Middle Ages according to Protestant standards, really does get in the way of a thorough understanding of medieval spirituality.

And *that* is ultimately the problem we have been working on here. A perspective, that is dumbstruck by the absence of voices critical of the institution of the church, eagerly paints a picture of mystical theologians based on fringe cases and unusually bold statements. As I have tried to demonstrate, these *would* be theological bombs if taken out of their theological and communicative contexts. To draw a bold comparison, sniffing out unusual statements as evidence in a case is what the inquisitors also did when they summoned Eckhart to Avignon or combatted the thought of Suso.

50. Ernst Troeltsch, *The Social Teaching of the Christian Churches*, trans. Olive Wyon, Harper Torchbooks, TB71—The Cloister Library (New York: Harper, 1960), 377.
51. Haas, *Kunst rechter Gelassenheit*, 69, also critically emphasizes the context of appreciating mysticism as institutional with this model.
52. Citations from Ignaz Weilner and Johannes Tauler, *Johannes Taulers Bekehrungsweg: die Erfahrungsgrundlagen seiner Mystik. Studien zur Geschichte der katholischen Moraltheologie*, vol. 10 (Regensburg: Pustet, 1961), 45–47.

On the other hand, their potential cannot be entirely defused by their situation. It is more than clear that especially Tauler, but also likely Suso, was trying to make it through times in which an ecclesial interdict prevented them from administering the sacraments. That is an important factor in understanding the ambivalence we have described here, but it is *only* one. Those statements that appear to relativize the sacraments are too deeply embedded in the theologies of their respective authors to be fully explained by pressure from the authorities. Instead, the theological context I have been describing makes clear that the medieval mystics did not intend for their punchy statements to compete with the church's traditional system. Their primary work was to intensify the given mediation of grace, not to destabilize or substitute the system of mediation! That is brilliantly demonstrated in Tauler's tight combination of intensified eucharistic spirituality with a substitution of the Sacrament of Penance. Tauler did not want to provide an alternative to the sacraments. He and other mystical authors used *contritio* as a launch point for an intensified form of the sacrament. *Because* of his deeply internalized concept of penance, Tauler apparently practiced extremely stringent forms of external penitential discipline. In any case, he had to defend himself against the accusation of being a too-strict father confessor in a sermon:

> I have been misrepresented by those who claim that I said I do not want to hear anybody's confession as long as they wouldn't vow to do whatever I want them to do. That "What I want" is a blatant falsehood. I want nothing other from anyone than what is written, and I urge no one to vow. I only cannot absolve anyone of their sins if they do not regret them.[53]

Contritio becomes Tauler's harsh criterion for proper, ecclesial confession. It is the vehicle for an internalization process capable of critiquing the church and has an intrinsic attachment to the idea of substitution. But in Tauler's eyes, it is also the only way to make the act of confession authentic and real—it is clear that he does *not* want to water down sacramental piety, but rather wants to bring its practitioners to authenticity. The idea of substitution is only plausible because the internalized sacrament is brought to its

53. Tauler, *Predigten* (Vetter), 202,30–35: "*Ich bin begriffen ze unrecht als ob ich sulle han gesprochen, ich enwelle niemans bichte hoeren, er sulle mir geloben das er tuon sulle das ich welle. Das ist gar unreht gesprochen: das ich welle; ich enwil von nieman nut denne als geschriben stat und das selbe enbit ich mir nieman geloben. Ich enmag nieman absolvieren, im ensin denne sine sunde leit.*" My translation; Tauler, *Predigten* (Hofmann), 418. Cf. also the occasional Tauler statements which allude to the idea that the Sacrament of Penance had no substitute for *deadly* sins. Cf. Thomas Gandlau, *Trinität Und Kreuz: Die Nachfolge Christi in Der Mystagogie Johannes Taulers*, Freiburger Theologische Studien 155 (Freiburg im Breisgau: Verlag Herder, 1993), 143.

true sense. The apparent church-critical posture of ecclesial mysticism is properly understood, not as the result of a critique of norms, but rather as the result of norms fulfilled beyond measure. A mystical movement that propagated such overfulfillment of norms was certainly not a "powerful competition." It was a reform movement from the very core of the church.

3.

"*Omnem vitam fidelium penitentiam esse voluit*": Luther's Adoption of Mystical Tradition in His First Thesis on Indulgence

"*Ego sane secutus theologiam Tauleri et eius libelli, quem tu nuper dedisti imprimendum Aurifabro*[1] *nostro Christianno.*"[2] (I have only followed the theology of Tauler and his little book, whom you have given to our goldsmith Christian to be printed.) So wrote Luther to his father confessor John of Staupitz on March 31, 1518. It was five months after he had written and sent off his famous theses on indulgence, and he felt it necessary to explain to his mentor how he had gotten into such trouble. He did so with an unusually clear admission of standing in the tradition of mysticism, making reference to a little book next to John Tauler.[3] It was likely the *Theologia Deutsch*[4] (see Chapter 3).

1. Despite being capitalized, "*Aurifaber*" is best understood as Christian Düring's profession since he was a goldsmith—cf. Josef Benzing, *Die Buchdrucker des 16. und 17. Jahrhunderts im deutschen Sprachgebiet.* 2nd ed. (Wiesbaden: O. Harrassowitz, 1982), 499. Düring was also the publisher of the full edition of the *Theologia Deutsch*, while the printer was Johannes Grunenberg (see WA.Br 1,161).
2. WA.Br 1, 160, 8–9: "Freilich bin ich der Theologie Taulers und jenes Büchleins gefolgt, das du neulich unserem Christian Goldschmied in den Druck gegeben hast." Alphons Victor Müller, *Luther und Tauler auf ihren theologischen Zusammenhang* (Bern: Ferd. Wyss, 1918), 23–24, makes a strong reference to this passage, but drastically overestimates the significance of Tauler for Luther.
3. The fact that Tauler does not appear in the index of Reinhard Schwarz, *Vorgeschichte der reformatorischen Bußtheologie* (Berlin: De Gruyter, 1968), demonstrates that this connection has long been neglected.
4. For more on this identification, cf. WA.Br 161; Martin Luther, *Luthers Werke in Auswahl*, 3rd ed., vol. 6, ed. by Otto Clemen (Berlin: De Gruyter, 2019), 10. (Hereafter, all citations from

His concession did not merely relate to a few statements about indulgence but rather to the basic theological convictions running throughout all his *95 Theses*. His first thesis reads: "When our Lord and Master Jesus Christ said, "Repent" [Matt 4:17], he willed the entire life of believers to be one of repentance."[5] The second thesis draws critical conclusions from it: "This word cannot be understood as referring to the sacrament of penance, that is, confession and satisfaction, as administered by the clergy."[6]

This radical, comprehensive understanding of penance can actually be brought into connection with certain elements of the mystical tradition. In this chapter, I will try to demonstrate this by first examining an early self-testimony of Luther in which he describes his discovery of a new understanding of penance. In the second section, I will explore how this is related to his reception of mysticism. The third section will be devoted to Luther's application of this understanding of penance to the topic of indulgence. Finally, the fourth section will attempt to demonstrate the consequences for our general understanding of Luther's Reformational development.

A DOUBLE BREAKTHROUGH FOR YOUNG LUTHER?

For the last few decades, research on Luther's early years has tended to focus on his so-called Reformational turn. That research has reliably sought to utilize his famous self-testimony from the foreword of the 1545 collection of his Latin writings. It provides an invaluable insight into how Luther was reflecting on the events of the early Reformation thirty years prior. The theological core of this self-depiction is his description of his transition, *away* from an understanding of God's justice as a principle of reward and punishment and *toward* an understanding that God justifies people through faith. Researchers have come to the unfortunate consensus that Luther is vague on the date of this breakthrough, a fact which has caused this document to occasion more exegetical work than scarcely any other text in church history.[7]

Luthers Werke in Auswahl will be abbreviated as BoA, followed by volume number and page number).

5. WA 1,233,10–11: "Dominus et magister noster Iesus Christus dicendo 'penitentiam agite etc.' omnem vitam fidelium penitentiam esse voluit." Trans. after LW 31:25.
6. WA 1,233,12–13: "Quod verbum de penitentia sacramentali (id est confessionis et satisfactionis, que sacerdotum ministerio celebratur) non potest intelligi." Trans. after LW 31:25.
7. Cf. the research summaries from Otto H. Pesch, "Zur Frage nach Luthers reformatorischer Wende. Ergebnisse und Probleme der Diskussion um Ernst Bizer," in *Der Durchbruch der reformatorischen Erkenntnis bei Luther*, ed. Bernhard Lohse (Darmstadt: Wissenschaftliche

The 1545 foreword owes its prominence mostly to the picture of Luther which was painted by Karl Holl and his school. The Luther Renaissance in the early twentieth century focused heavily on justification, a focus which strengthened the association between a breakthrough and the *iustitia* concept. This is a theologically justified interest, but it broadly neglected a text which Reinhold Seeberg saw as *the* key document to understand Luther's Reformational turn.[8] That document was the dedicatory text to John of Staupitz which Luther dated May 30, 1518, intended to accompany the *Resolutiones*, the more extensive explanation of his *95 Theses*. In this dedicatory text, Luther also speaks of a breakthrough moment—right in the thick of things and not after thirty years. Yet, the theological point in this text is a new understanding of penance. Luther recollects how Staupitz advised him when he was deeply distraught about his own election,[9] that love of justice and God is the *root* of all penance and not its goal.[10] If we compare this text to the famous self-testimony from 1545 we can see that there are some obvious parallels (many, however, are in very different places in the text!) which clarify one important point: Luther is describing two different processes of understanding which have different objects but a very similar procedure.[11] To make this point, I will compare them concurrently in the following.

Buchgesellschaft, 1968), 445–505; id., Neuere Beiträge zur Frage nach Luthers "Reformatorischer Wende", *Catholica*. Jahrbuch für Kontroverstheologie 37 (1983), 259–287; 38 (1984) 66–133.

8. Reinhold Seeberg, *Lehrbuch der Dogmengeschichte*, vol. 4. (Basel: Benno Schwabe, 1953–1954), 66–67. On p. 67 footnote 2, Seeberg explicitly argues against restricting our reception of the Reformational development to the development of a theology of justification. As late as 1926, Ernst Stracke, *Luthers großes Selbstzeugnis 1545 über seine Entwicklung zum Reformator historisch-kritisch untersucht. Schriften des Vereins für Reformationsgeschichte* (Leipzig: M. Heinsius nachfolger, Eger & Sievers, 1926), 119–120, felt it necessary to incorporate this text into his historiography. Since then, it has only rarely played a prominent role, such as for Heiko Augustinus Oberman, "'Iustitia Christi' und 'Iustitia Dei'. Luther und die scholastischen Lehren von der Rechtfertigung," in *Der Durchbruch der reformatorischen Erkenntnis bei Luther*, ed. Bernhard Lohse (Darmstadt: Wissenschaftliche Buch Gesellschaft, 1968) 413–444, here p. 430, or—especially interesting considering his emphatically biographical method—for Kurt Aland, "Der Weg zur Reformation: Zeitpunkt und Charakter des reformatorischen Erlebnisses Martin Luthers," in *Theologische Existenz heute*, Neue Folge, Nr. 123 (Munich: C. Kaiser, 1965), 63. An extensive treatment can be found in Richard Wetzel, "Staupitz und Luther," in, *Martin Luther: Probleme seiner Zeit*, ed. Volker Press and Dieter Stievermann (Stuttgart: Klett-Cotta, 1986), 75–87.
9. Cf. for more Wetzel, "Staupitz und Luther," 75.
10. For more on the background of Luther's worries in the confrontation of attritionism and contritionism, cf. Seeberg, *Lehrbuch*, 65; for more on the concrete roots of the advice to do penance in Staupitz's theology see Wetzel, "Staupitz und Luther," 79, which treats Staupitz's text *De exsecutione aeternae praedestinationis*.
11. Wetzel, "Staupitz und Luther," 80 makes a strong point of this.

First: In both cases, Luther speaks of a word which previously had been incomprehensible or even bitter to him, but which had now become particularly pleasant or even "sweet":

1518	1545
". . . ita, ut, cum prius non fuerit ferme in scriptura tota amarius mihi verbum quam 'poenitentia' (licet sedulo etiam coram deo simularem et fictum coactumque amorem exprimere conarer), nunc nihil dulcius aut gratius mihi sonet quam 'poenitentia'." (WA 1,525,18–21)	"Iam quanto odio vocabulum 'iustita Dei' oderam ante, tanto amore dulcissimum mihi vocabulum extollebam . . ." (WA 54,186,14f)
". . . while formerly almost no word in the whole Scripture was more bitter to me than poenitentia (although I zealously made a pretense before God and tried to express a feigned and constrained love for him), now no word sounds sweeter or more pleasant to me than poenitentia." (LW 48:66)	"And I extolled my sweetest word with a love as great as the hatred with which I had before hated the word "righteousness of God." (LW 34:338)

Second: Luther chooses a palate of figurative metaphors that convey how his discovery of the new meaning of a word has significance for heavenly matters. He understands this word to mean more than just philological comprehension:

1518	1545
". . . te velut e caelo sonantem excepimus . . ." (WA 525,10–11)	"Hic me prorsus renatum esse sensi, et apertis portis in ipsam paradisum intrasse. . . . , ita mihi iste locus Pauli fuit vere porta paradisi." (WA 54, 186,8–9, 15–16)
"Therefore I accepted you as a messenger from heaven[.]" (LW 48:65)	"Here I felt that I was altogether born again and had entered paradise itself through open gates. . . . Thus that place in Paul was for me truly the gate to paradise." (LW 34, 338)

Third: In both cases, the proof and confirmation of this discovery is found in the testimony of all of Holy Scripture:

1518	1545
". . . coepique deinceps cum scripturis poenitentiam docentibus conferre, Et ecce iucundissimum ludum, verba undique mihi colludebant planeque huic sententiae arridebant et assultabant . . ." (WA 525,15-18)	"Discurrebam deinde per scripturas, ut habebat memoria, et colligebam etiam in aliis vocabulis analogiam, ut opus Dei, id est, quod operatur in nobis Deus, virtus Dei, qua nos potentes facit, sapientia Dei, qua nos sapientes facit, fortitudo Dei, salus Dei, gloria Dei." (WA 54, 186,10-13)
"As a result, I began to compare your statements with the passages of Scripture which speak of *poenitentia*. And behold—what a most pleasant scene! Biblical words came leaping toward me from all sides, clearly smiling and nodding assent to your statement." (LW 48:66)	"Thereupon I ran through the Scriptures from memory. I also found in other terms an analogy, as, the work of God, that is, what God does in us, the power of God, with which he makes us strong, the wisdom of God, with which he makes us wise, the salvation of God, the glory of God." (LW 34:338)

No matter how distinct the theological content was, Luther describes two very similar processes in 1518 and 1545. In both cases, *one* word in the Bible had a deeply negative sense in its traditional understanding before making a radical transformation, now being understood very positively. This new definition leads to intense intellectual activity to understand its implications for other tangential topics—penance in the first case, and justification in the second.

This double account of the breakthrough experience begs the question of whether Luther had one or two breakthroughs—or perhaps none at all.[12] I think there are three valid possibilities to interpret this material. The first would be to understand both accounts as conveying accurately what really happened. That would mean that Luther had his first breakthrough

12. Authors as early as Heinrich Bornkamm argued for abandoning the concept of a "tower experience" or a psychological "breakthrough." Cf. Heinrich Bornkamm, "Probleme der Lutherbiographie," in *Lutherforschung Heute: Referate und Berichte Des 1. Internationalen Lutherforschungskongresses, Aarhus 18.-23. August 1956,* ed. Vilmos Vajta (Berlin: Luth Verlagshaus, 1958), 15–23, 17.

experience in 1518 and then a second, very similar one in the same year. We cannot entirely discredit this possibility, but it does not seem probable to me.

The second possibility would be that only one of the two accounts is correct in a historical sense: Luther had only one breakthrough experience.[13] We would give chronological priority to the account from 1518 as being a real event. According to this model, Luther had a leaky memory in 1545 when writing about his breakthrough in justification, replacing penance with justification. Perhaps he even gave an intentionally altered account. This interpretation does the best job of clearing up the difficulties in dating the self-testimony from 1545. It is well known that the verifiable details in 1545 line up best with the period of the lectures on the Psalms (1518–19)[14] or with the period of Luther's exegesis of Paul. As I will attempt to demonstrate below, the 1518 account of Luther's discovery of penance locates his breakthrough in the period of his reading Paul. The earlier date thus served as a rudimentary form for Luther's memory of the "real" psychological breakthrough. The later date would then serve as an approximate location for his new theological profile for the *iustitia*-concept but without the psychological component.

Such an interpretation runs the risk of playing the two texts against each other. It makes the most sense to me, therefore, to suspend the truly autobiographical character of *both* texts and to accept that both texts give a tendentious portrayal of events. Neither of the reported breakthroughs has any other form of evidence in the form of letters or diary entries close to the event itself. Both are accounts at a distance. In fact, we can find even more relation between the two texts, for in both cases Luther wants to present his own development to a public audience (the dedicatory writing to Staupitz was printed along with the *Resolutiones*) and to legitimize it. In 1518, Luther wanted to emphasize the orthodoxy of his understanding of the critique of indulgence; in 1545, he wanted to excuse himself from any previous statements which now sounded too papist for a 1545 audience. He did this by emphasizing that he came to his insight only later.

Bernd Ulmer has undertaken a helpful study of the sociological and communicative aspects of conversion experiences,[15] whose findings can

13. This is explained by Stracke, Luthers großes Selbstzeugnis 119–120, who attempts to use this to contest the historicity of the testimony from 1519.

14. For the matter of dating this, cf. the pieces by G. Hammer in: *Archiv zur Weimarer Ausgabe 1*, 108–113.

15. Bernd Ulmer, "Konversionserzählungen als rekonstruktive Gattung: Erzählerische Mittel und Strategien bei der Rekonstruktion eines Bekehrungserlebnisses," *Zeitschrift für Soziologie* 17, no. 1 (Stuttgart: De Gruyter, 1988), 19–33. https://doi.org/10.1515/zfsoz-1988-0102

also be seen in both of the Luther testimonies. Both are autobiographical texts which aim to legitimate reconstructions of a biography. Luther's description does not remember a real process but rather stylizes it and composes a theologically decisive development into a psychological breakthrough experience. With this self-stylization, he places himself twice into what Heiko Oberman categorizes as a pattern of sudden conversion.[16] We see the same sort of pattern with Paul and with Augustine.[17] As researchers have combed through the sources, they have never found any indication of such a punctual breakthrough, only a continuous development. That is true of Luther's discovery of justification, but also for his discovery of a new understanding of penance.

The latter case of self-interpretation as a sudden, punctual development is especially interesting because it really must have had to do with a "pre-Reformational" event. The decisive turn in Luther's understanding of penance is presented explicitly as standing in the lineage of his experiences with Staupitz. Luther blends theological continuity and self-interpretation in the sense of a biographical-psychological breakthrough. This polyvalent model is *much* more helpful for our understanding of Luther's development emerging out of the late Middle Ages. It certainly provides a better framework than, say, a sole fixation on the "Reformational turn." Luther's own statement demonstrates the misunderstanding of scholars such as Martin Brecht when he describes Luther's theology in this period as "obscure and heavy. . . not letting the bright tones of the Christian message emerge."[18] The dedicatory text to Staupitz from 1518 never mentions obscurity at all concerning Luther's spiritual advisor. In fact, the contrary is true: when speaking of his turn to a new understanding of penance, Luther speaks joyfully of a voice from heaven and from the utterly sweet savior.[19]

THE MYSTICAL CONCEPT OF PENANCE AS RECEIVED BY LUTHER

With his usage of "sweet" when talking about the savior and "bitter" for his earlier understanding of penance, Luther has entered into a semantic field which, as mentioned at the beginning of this chapter, fits very neatly

16. Oberman, "'Iustitia Christi' und 'Iustitia Dei'," 424.
17. Ulmer, *Konversionserzählungen*, 19, refers to both in his study, which is otherwise occupied with matters of the present day.
18. Martin Brecht, *Martin Luther*, vol. 1, *Sein Weg zur Reformation 1483–1521*, 3rd ed. (Stuttgart: Calwer Verlag, 1990), 133. My translation.
19. WA 1,525,22.

to Luther's own engagement with mysticism. Luther clearly sees the sweet Christ as part of the mystical experience.[20] On December 14, 1516, less than a year before the publication of the *95 Theses*, Luther recommended the sermons of John Tauler to Spalatin and wrote in rather sacramental tones that Spalatin would here taste and see how sweet the Lord is once he had seen how bitter is everything that we are.[21]

Luther's usage of this collection of concepts demonstrates Tauler's significance for him. The dedicatory text to Staupitz thus truly does testify to a gradual solidification of his new understanding of penance, which, if we follow Martin Brecht, did begin in 1515 with a conversation with Staupitz. Initially, Luther explored the passages of Scripture pertaining to penance and immediately found the word "penance" and God's commands to be sweet. He then proceeded to the *dulcissimus*, the sweetest of them all: the savior, at which point he realized that Christ's call to penance is written as *metanoeite* in Greek[22]—literally "change the way you think!"[23] In this context, Luther then notes that he owes this understanding to the masters of the ancient languages, likely thinking about the Erasmus edition of the New Testament.[24]

If everything is correct so far, then the process in which he made the jump from the bitter word of penance to the sweetness of Christ must have taken place between his conversation with Staupitz on penance in the early summer of 1515 and his encounter with Erasmus's edition of the Greek New Testament in the spring of 1516.[25] That just happens to be the period in which most scholars place Luther's reading of John Tauler.[26] We

20. For more on the history of the concept "süß" or "sweet" in this period, see Friedrich Ohly, "Geistige Süße bei Otfried," in *Schriften zur mittelalterlichen Bedeutungsfroschung*, ed. Friedrich Ohly (Damstadt: Wissenschaftliche Buchgesellschaft, 1977), 93–127.

21. WA.Br 1,79,58–64: "Gusta ergo et vide, quam suavis est dominus, ubi prius gustaris et videris, quam amarus est, quicquid nos sumus."

22. He is literally speaking of studies by those who could read Greek and Hebrew, but he may well have been speaking of the Erasmus edition of the Greek New Testament which was published in 1516.

23. WA 1,530,20–21. This process was also a twofold one: The first step for Luther was to map *metanoia* to *post* and *mens*, then to *trans* and *mens*. The initial definition was thus: "after full discernment."

24. See, Wetzel, *Staupitz und Luther*, 81. Aland, *Weg*, 64, however thinks more generally about Luther's studies in Greek and comes to a much earlier date.

25. The Erasmus edition was published in Basel on March 1, 1516 (see Kurt Aland and Barbara Aland, *Der Text Des Neuen Testaments: Einführung in Die Wissenschaftlichen Ausgaben Sowie in Theorie Und Praxis Der Modernen Textkritik*, 2nd ed. [Stuttgart: Dt. Bibelgesellschaft, 1989], 13). Luther was using it for his explanations on Romans 9:19 at the latest (WA 56,400,15).

26. For the difficulties associated with dating this, cf. Leif Grane, *Modus loquendi theologicus: Luthers Kampf um die Erneuerung der Theologie (1515–1518)* (Leiden: Brill, 1975), 122, who assumes 1515/16 on p. 121; this is also true of Steven E. Ozment, *Homo spiritualis* (Leiden:

know he read Tauler because of his famous hand-written marginalia in the copy of Tauler's sermons which he used. In the same year, Luther came across excerpts of the *Theologia Deutsch.* He was struck so greatly by this text, which he believed to be a summary of Tauler's doctrine, that he sent it to the publishing house on December 4 for printing.[27]

As exhilarating as this all is, it is still challenging to understand. For Luther's intensive reception of mysticism is anything but straightforward. Many passages of Luther's marginalia contain only simple outlining aids[28] or definitions of words.[29] One significant indication of how Luther was reading Tauler can be found in the remark "*Hoc nota tibi*" ("remember this"). Luther emphasized the demand for a person to joyfully despise themselves. After calling on the reader to continually turn to God, Tauler wrote:

> Return to God so quickly and so sincerely that thy sins are pardoned thee even before thou hast time to tell them in confession. Let not thy sinful tendencies affright thee. Many a fault of thine is permitted by God, not so much to hurt thee as to help thee. For does it not cause thee to own to thyself that thou art but nothingness? Does not the shame of it lead thee to mortification and detachment?[30]

It is precisely at this point where Luther writes his little reminder.

The context in Tauler is one of true *contritio,* real regret about one's own sins and trespasses. It is a theology of penance, and Tauler commands his hearers (most of them were nuns) not to go immediately to their father

Brill, 1969), 185. Karl-Heinz zur Mühlen, *Nos Extra Nos* (Tübingen: Mohr Siebeck, 1972), 97, settles on the early phase of the Romans lectures. Regardless, Luther refers to Tauler as early as his occupation with Romans 8, before making reference to Erasmus (see WA 56,378,13).

27. This mapping of the "*scripturae*" to Tauler and the *Theologia Deutsch* makes all the more sense when we consider that Luther had made reference to this very text in a letter on March 31, 1518, addressed to Staupitz (as referenced at the beginning of this article).
28. WA 9,98,35–36.
29. See for example "*confiteri*" for "bejehen" WA 9,100,23.
30. Johannes Tauler, *Die Predigten Taulers aus der Engelberger und der Freiburger Handschrift sowie aus Schmidts Abschriften der ehemaligen Strassburger Handschriften*, ed. Ferdinand Vetter (Berlin: Weidmannsche Buchhandlung, 1910), 355, 36–356, 2; cf. also Johannes Tauler and Georg Hofmann, *Predigten: Vollständige Ausgabe* (Freiburg im Breisgau: Verlag Herder, 1961), 455: "Beeile dich . . . und dringe so ungestüm in Gott, daß dir die Sünden entfallen und du sie nicht mehr weißt, wenn du damit zur Beichte kommst. Dies darf dich nicht erschrecken; denn nicht zu deinem Schaden widerfährt dir das, sondern zur Erkenntnis deines Nichts und zur Verschmähung deines eigenen Selbst in Gelassenheit, nicht in Niedergeschlagenheit." Trans. after: John Tauler, *The Sermons and Conferences of John Tauler*, ed. and trans. Walter Elliott (Washington, DC: Apostolic Mission House, 1910), 696.

confessors. Here, Luther scribbled into the margins: "*utilissimum consilium*" (a most useful council).[31]

We can fully appreciate the meaning of Luther's comment only if we understand that what Luther is so enthusiastic about is not an isolated statement in Tauler's works. This theology of penance may even constitute the center of Tauler's mystical theology.[32] Tauler always describes a *necessary* self-deprecation as the precondition for mystical unification with God. True self-understanding leads a person to give themself up. Only when they have given themselves up can God fill the void left behind, or, to recall a mystical phrase explored earlier, only then can God be born in their soul. For both Tauler and his enthusiastic reader, the young monk Martin Luther, it is important to emphasize that this deprecation and humiliation of the human being is not destructive or obscure. The most effective way to create space for God is to be "closed off and in melancholy."[33]

Against this background, it becomes apparent that oral confession with a father confessor could become a secondary affair. A priest's mediation lost its absolute necessity. Thus, this passage of Luther's reception of Tauler appears to be the copy-proof of his first and second thesis on indulgence. Making penance a deeper, more internal experience implicitly and explicitly relativizes sacramental penance. Penance is decoupled from the punctual event of confession and becomes the central feature of Christian life.[34] Even the dramatic consequence drawn by Luther that the entire life of a faithful person is to be penance could have been inspired by Tauler. Just a few lines before where he wrote his reminders "*Hoc nota tibi*" and "*utilissimum consilium*" in the margins, Tauler writes: "To be made likeminded with that apostle is not the work of a day or two. Thou must set

31. WA 9,104,11–12.

32. For more on this understanding of Tauler, cf. Volker Leppin, "Tauler, Johannes (ca. 1300–1361)," in *Theologische Realenzyklopädie,* online (Berlin: De Gruyter, 2010); Also: Louise Gnädinger, *Johannes Tauler: Lebenswelt und mystische Lehre,* (Munich: C. H. Beck, 1993), 121.

33. Cf. as early as the "Resolutiones": "Nam per contritionem homo redit in gratiam" (WA 1,612,30–31) or "A man returns to the grace of God by means of contrition" (LW 31:224). The following address of Christ to the penitent demonstrates that a mystical transfer process was at work here much as in the *Freedom of a Christian*: "Omnia mea tua sunt." This is also true of the reference to Romans 8:32: "He who did not withhold his own Son, but gave him up for all of us, will he not with him also give us everything else?" It, therefore, does not seem sensible to assume that Luther had found what he was looking for in Tauler, but rather that Tauler gave him something genuine (as much as Grane, *Modus loquendi*, 123 would love to see it that way). Grane's warning *is* justifiable: we should not confront Luther with a reconstructed image of previous theologians. However, it is also true that Luther himself emphasizes the singular character of his turn in his theology of penance.

34. Müller, *Luther und Tauler*, 123, also makes reference to this similarity between Tauler and Luther.

thyself to constantly search thy soul and overcome thyself in all things."[35] What Tauler sees as the mystical context of encountering God becomes the decisive precondition for faith itself. The few lengthy passages jotted down by Luther in his Tauler marginalia point in this direction. In his sermon on Peter's great catch of fish in Luke 5, Tauler came to speak about the birth of God in the Soul. There, Luther wrote: "And even if we know that God is not working in us if we do not destroy ourselves and our own things (i.e., by crucifying the passions), we would still be stupid if we want to take such suffering upon ourselves which we choose based on us reading or seeing others suffer them."[36]

Luther understood Tauler properly with the idea that God must first destroy us and everything pertaining to us in order to deal with us. The idea comes up for Tauler again when he cites Psalm 42:8 in another passage: "*abyssus abyssum invocat*" / "Deep calls to deep."[37] Here we see the mystical *horor vaccui* of which Tauler (and later Luther) spoke in their hamartiological focus. For Luther, that meant: "Therefore, salvation consists entirely in resigning the will in all things, both spiritual as well as temporal. And in naked faith in God."[38]

Tauler's description of internal penance joins Luther's faith in God to become the center of the latter's salvation, or "*tota salus*." Luther is noted for his ceaseless usage of terms like humility and deprecation. These are not just expressions of uncompromising monasticism. They are the only possible path to salvation that Christ has opened.[39] As he wrote in his dedicatory letter to Staupitz, penance begins with loving Christ and can only be understood properly with this love as its root.

Against the background of such an understanding of penance, deeply focused on true regret and thoroughly soteriological in its disposition as was the case in the mystical tradition, the theology of young Luther

35. Tauler, *Predigten* (Vetter), 355,31–32; Tauler, *Predigten* (Hofmann), 455: "Das darf nicht an einem Tag sein und am andern nicht; es soll alle Tage sein; ohne Unterlaß sollst du dich selbst beobachten!" Trans. after: Tauler, *The Sermons and Conferences of John Tauler*, 696.

36. WA 9,102,10–13: "Et si sciamus, quod deus non agat in nobis, nisi prius nos et nostra destruat (i.e., per crucem et passiones), tamen adeo stulti sumus, ut eas velimus tantum suscipere passiones quas nos elegimus vel quas in aliis factas vidimus vel legimus." My translation.

37. Tauler, *Predigten* (Vetter), 176,7; Tauler, *Predigten* (Hofmann), 315.

38. WA 9,102,34–36: "Igitur tota salus est resignatio voluntatis in omnibus ut hic docet sive in spiritualibus sive temporalibus. Et nuda fides in deum." My translation. As early as the end of the same year, Luther formulates much more cautiously in a sermon on December 21: "*initium* salutis est nosse morbum et principium sapientiae timor Dei" / "The *first step* of salvation is our death and the fear of the Lord is the beginning of wisdom" (WA 1,114,40–41). My translation and italics.

39. This positive context makes all the more clear that Luther wanted to understand the Tauler sermons as an administration of Christ's sweetness.

takes on a positive tone against its frequent classification as a theology of humility. The Roman Catholic polemist Grisar picked up on this much better than the Protestant theologian Ernst Bizer[40] would centuries later. The moment when a person gives up their personal property in a broad, spiritual sense is the moment when they become free for God.[41] The mystical turn in Luther's theology becomes evident[42] when he writes: "In Romans ch. 1, Paul talks about how God's wrath and grace are revealed in the Gospel. Whoever hears that correctly is humbled and terrified . . . when that has taken place, then it is time for God to come."[43] With the help of mystical concepts which he enthusiastically adopted we suddenly see how his discovery of a new understanding of penance could become a "most pleasant game" for him.[44]

Luther's later self-interpretation from 1545 ought to convince us that these thoughts were not just a fad for him. They were at the very center

40. Cf. Hartmann Grisar, *Luther*, vol. 1, *Luthers Werden: Grundlegung der Spaltung bis 1530*, 3rd ed. (Freiburg im Breisgau: Verlag Herder, 1924), 176: "Luther repeatedly brings the attitude of despair under the concept of *humilitas* (a confession of humility and self-denial) not only as a mode of discernment for understanding God's ascribed grace (and thus the joyous state of being saved), but he also understands it as a means of salvation itself which can only lead to God's grace. He praises *humilitas* . . . in mystical tones as the ideal of the pious. For him, humility occupies the space of the justifying particular faith, which he would only discover later." My translation. It is sadly still broadly neglected that Bizer discovered Luther's theology of humility well before Grisar.
41. Cf. WA 1,272,33: "Nu kann keiner mehr haben, denn das er sich frey in gott gebe, es gehe wie es wolle und verzweivel an im selber," / "The fact is that nobody can do anything except freely surrender himself to God no matter what happens, and dispair if himself" and, just a bit later, and after having illustrated a fictitious counterpoint: "Ah du Narr, wenn du das empfindest, das in dir gewirckt ist, so ist die gnade schon da, folge du nur" / Ah, you fool, when you feel what has been affected within you, then grace is already there; just go on and follow." (Fastenpredigt von 1518, trans. after LW 51:43). Ernst Bizer, *Fides ex auditu: Eine Untersuchung über die Entdeckung der Gerechtigkeit Gottes durch Martin Luther*, 3rd ed. (Neukirchen Kreis Moers: Verlag der Buchhandlung des Erziehungsvereins, 1966), 44, has misunderstood this passage and ones like it as simple acts of voluntary acceptance: It has to do with a mystical process of unification. That is the only way to see how salvation flows through penance—it is positive and simultaneously automatic. Just how strongly Bizer builds the phase of humility theology into a theology of justification can be seen on p. 48, where he interprets the mystical passages in the sense of humility being "angerechnet" / "ascribed."
42. Cf. auch WA 1,85,20–21 (Predigt vom 21.9.1516): "Igitur veritas et iustitia, i.e., Christus, non venit, nisi ubi non est," / "Therefore, truth and justice, i.e., Christ, do not come anywhere where he is not present" or p. 115,2–3, after passages treating the discernment of one's own sinfulness which occurs after grace: "Gratia autem infundit amorem" / "Grace therefore pours into love" (Sermon on December 21, 1517). My translations.
43. WA 1,201,14–17 (Die sieben Bußpsalmen): "als Ro. 1 Paulus sagt, das im evangelio gottis gnaden und tzorn offenbart wird. Wer das heret recht, der wirt demutig und erschrecket. . . Wann das gescheen ist, ßo ists tzeit und eben, das got kome." My translation.
44. Brecht, *Luther 1*, 133, describes how Luther discovered only medieval obscurity and burden in this year but gives utterly no regard to Luther's self-perception in this time.

of his theological understanding.[45] It was not merely an isolated theological particle of penance per se that became sweet for him, but rather a new understanding of penance that led him straight to his sweet Savior, to salvation made manifest. Here we are not dealing with some abstract moment in a theological system. We are dealing with the entirety of Christian theology. In this period of Luther's life, penance had the same theological weight as justification had later. That in turn means that the Luther of 1516 had found a new center in mysticism.

When we take a look at Luther's edition of *Theologia Deutsch*, we once again see the tight relation between penance and mysticism, especially because he regarded this work to be a condensed form of Tauler's doctrine. That makes his reception of the *Theologia Deutsch* an important indication of how he understood Tauler. This is particularly helpful because the marginalia only provide us with insights into his reaction to isolated passages, not his general understanding. His copy of *Theologia Deutsch*, however, gives us precisely that.

The main thrust of his understanding is present in the text that Luther had printed on the title page of the 1516 edition. It concentrates on Adam's death: "A spiritual, noble little book on the proper distinction and understanding of what the old and the new human being is, what Adam's child and God's child are and how Adam must die in us and Christ arise in us."[46] Today's editions of this anonymous work locate the passages treating the death of the Old Adam and the resurrection of Christ in us in chapters 15 and 16.[47] The author really means a departure from self-centeredness, which the *Theologia Deutsch* regards as the first and central sin because it means detaching oneself from their creator.[48] In chapter 16, the author calls the turn away from this self-centered disobedience "*gebusset*"—repented

45. In contrast, it is a misunderstanding in light of an already formed theology of justification when Stracke, *Selbstzeugnis*, 119–120, attempts to diminish the value of the *poenitentia* testimony by claiming that this is only a *partial* aspect of penance, while *iustitia* supposedly has to do with the entire thing.

46. WA 1, 153: "Ein geistlich, edles Buchlein von rechter underscheid und vorstand, was der alt und neu mensche sei. Was Adams und was Gottes kind sei. Und wie Adam inn uns sterben unnd Christus ersteen soll." Cf. how the death of the inner Adam is the result of despair brought about by a foreign actor (opus alienum) in WA 1,112,33–36 (Sermon from 21.12.1516). In the following, Luther explains how the Opus alienum of the Poenitentiam agite is bound directly to the proclamation of the Kingdom of God as an Opus proprium (WA 1,113,28–31, Sermon from 21.12.1517): This is the vocabulary which enabled him to shed light on Staupitz's penitential tip.

47. Both chapters were contained in Luther's first edition which contained chapters 7–28.

48. "Der Franckforter" (*Theologia Deutsch*), ed. Wolfgang von Hinten, (Munich: C. H. Beck, 1982), 91,26.

or confessed.[49] The title page of the first edition shows that the center of this book is constituted by a process which the author described as penance.[50]

Accordingly, Luther regarded this little mystical text entirely through the lens of its theology of penance. And, just like Tauler's critical passages, its theological elements could take penance to a level far exceeding that of the church's Sacrament of Penance, now made obsolete by comparison.

LUTHER'S DEVELOPMENT OF HIS MYSTICAL INHERITANCE

Luther's intense occupation with the mystical authors of the fourteenth century probably lasted only a few months in 1516. But he had caught a mystical bug: on June 4, 1518, he started work on a new edition of the *Theologia Deutsch*, and this time it would be a complete edition.

But we cannot lose sight of the fact that mysticism was always a means to another end. Mysticism led to the Bible, and its relevance for Luther ended there. When he sent a copy of the *Theologia Deutsch* to his friend Spalatin, he sent a note with it in which he remarked that he knew of no other text that more fully captured the Gospel than this one.[51] His dedicatory text to Staupitz also speaks only of a deeper understanding of the *biblical* concept of penance.

If, however, mysticism was only a means to a better understanding of the biblical message, then one would expect that Luther would have articulated that understanding of penance beyond the context of his direct engagement with mysticism. If mystical penance theology really shaped Luther, then we *should* see its influence throughout his work in other areas as well. We do. An early sermon of Luther, usually dated to Lent of 1517,[52] clearly demonstrates how Luther was thinking about and receiving self-contained mystical penance theology. To explain penance, Luther first treated the distinction between the "*res*" and the "*signum*" of the Sacrament.[53] It would be a mistake to understand this distinction as a

49. Von Hinten, "Der Franckforter," 91,28. 32; 92,35.
50. Luther explicitly notes in the preface that the book was missing "title and name" (WA 1,153)
51. WA.Br 1,79,62–63.
52. Brecht, *Luther 1*, 183. WA 1,94, Footnote 1, is referring to 31.10.1516.
53. WA 1,98,24.

merely Augustinian element.[54] Here, a professor was working with general theological knowledge, for the distinction between "*res*" and "*signum*" had been taught to every master of theology by Lombard's *Sentences*. Luther took this general framework and filled it out in a unique fashion with the contents of penance.[55] The "*res*" became solely the internal regret of the heart or *contritio*. That is what Christ meant when he said "Repent!"[56] The scholarly transformation of Tauler's teaching was that internal contrition and a heartfelt confession to God could make external penance obsolete: the traditional three-fold penance of *contritio cordis, confessio oris*, and *satisfactio operis* now concentrated solely on the internal process. *Confessio* and *satisfactio* were now *only* external signs[57] and were certainly not what Christ had meant when he was talking about internal regret. This sermon from the spring of 1517 makes clear that Luther was not just sympathetic to Tauler and the *Theologia Deutsch*. The occasional marginalia had matured into theology fit to preach. What had started as a reader's fascination had become a positive application. Two things are of special note here. The first is that the content still aligned with Tauler. The second is that the very same sermon sees Luther using this matured concept of penance to attack indulgence: whoever trusts in indulgence trusts in external satisfaction instead of the satisfaction of the heart which is contained in self-accusation.[58]

As early as this sermon, Luther had armed himself with the arguments that he would later use in his struggle against indulgence. The following months and years would see them employed in a far riper form. But two important consequences had already been drawn that spring. In both of them, he followed an established medieval tradition. Both the idea of the first thesis—all a believer's life should be penance—and the idea of the second thesis—Christ's call to penance means something else than sacramental penance—are demonstrably consequences from what Luther had learned from mystical theology. Penance is an internal event constituted by true regret of the heart bound together with faith in Christ. It is so much more than just a punctual sacramental moment. The first and second theses on indulgence are the fruit of Luther's engagement with the mystical tradition in the previous years.

54. So, Brecht, *Luther 1*, 184.
55. After the Council of Ferrara-Florence, the material of the Sacrament had been determined as the threefold "*contritio*," "*confessio*," and "*satisfactio*" (DS 1323).
56. "*de qua Christus dicit: poenitentiam agite*" (WA 1,98,24–25).
57. WA 1,98,27–28.
58. WA 1,99,5–6.

CONSEQUENCES FOR UNDERSTANDING LUTHER'S THEOLOGICAL DEVELOPMENT

The *95 Theses* have a palpable mysticism to them, but Luther developed this much more clearly in the *Resolutiones.* His first thesis goes so far as to say that Christ is a "*Magister spiritus. . . , non literae*" (a spiritual master, not a scriptural/literary one).[59] The rest of the text sees him promoting the internal and demeaning the external with typically mystical concepts. He thus explains that Christ's call to repentance cannot be applied to sacramental penance because sacramental penance is "*externa tantum*" (*only* external). And anyway, it assumed internal penance for its efficacy. Therefore, the rite *per se* had no real integrity. The situation with internal penance was, however, vastly different because it was not directly dependent on the external act for just about anything. This was the clear conclusion drawn when one saw *contritio* as the central element of penance. *Contritio,* however, had always been more than merely a necessary precondition. It was always an essential component of sacramental penance.

However, we *can* see another moment of Luther's theology developing when we read the *95 Theses* and then let our gaze drift over to the *Resolutiones.* This moment is not nearly as prominent as the mystical one, but it is there. In one of the *95 Theses,* Luther explains: "Therefore, we are justified by faith, and by faith we also receive peace, not by works, penance, or confessions."[60] He adds just a few lines later: "not the sacrament, but faith in the sacrament, . . . justifies."[61]

A theology of justification, derived from Luther's mulling over Romans 1:17, has been layered upon the statements derived from an understanding of penance. The insights on penance remain, but Luther has started reformulating them in the language of a theology of justification. He apparently feels it necessary to relate his previous convictions to the new ones which will quickly form the famous center of his theology. But it is important to note that the old paradigm is not just thrown out and replaced. Instead, it is gradually molded into the new one.

Understanding that is a significant improvement in our understanding of how Luther discovered justification and started down his path to a full Reformational theology. Luther's discovery of justification theology was

59. WA 1,531,4–5.

60. WA 1,544,7–8: "*Igitur fide iustificamur, fide et pacificamur, non operibus neque poenitentiis aut confessionibus.*" Trans. after LW 31:105.

61. WA 1,544,40–41: "*Nicht das Sakrament, sondern der Glaube an das Sakrament rechtfertigt.*" Trans. after LW 31:107.

not just the product of his battle with the word *iustitia*. It was also filled with the fruits of his newly discovered concept of penance. The impulse for this new understanding of penance did not transpire because of his reading the Bible in the spring of 1515. We owe that to John of Staupitz, who was a good father-confessor who helped a soul entrusted to his care out of its despair.[62] Luther testifies to just that: "Staupitz is the one who started the teaching [of the gospel in our time]."[63]

And just like that, Luther found a theological polestar. It did not yet lie in the doctrine of justification, but he *did* experience it as new and liberating. He was helped along this path to a great extent by reading mystical texts, where he learned that giving up one's self was wholeness and salvation in itself. Mystical theology led him down a path on which he fully comprehended that a sinner is not lost, but in fact accepted in their sinfulness. The significance of mysticism for Luther's Reformational development must be assessed, therefore, as far more than merely a "confirmation," as Leif Grane and others have claimed.[64] As Luther himself testified, it had to do with a profound movement toward a positive understanding of attaining salvation through Christ.

It also primed him for the fight concerning indulgence. Just like Tauler two centuries before him, Luther would have his first major theological showdown within the framework of the existing church system. But he was closer to the system's boundaries, and the step to leave the church and blaze a new theological trail would be a relatively short one. He would commit to this trail once he shifted his theological center again, this time toward justification. The *Resolutiones* show how a topcoat of justification was being applied to the mystical-penitential painting. Somehow, a theological world rooted in mystical theology and integral penance was not enough. It needed a little "color correction." Paul's writings on justification gave him the technique and the pigment. The picture was improved so dramatically for him and others that he would look back upon this shift from the vantage of 1545 as being *the* decisive biographical development.

62. It is therefore insufficient when Bizer, *Fides ex auditu*, 20, allows for only a relativizing relation between Luther and Staupitz, speaking only of something going *against* the completed Reformational turn. Psychologically and biographically, it is clear that Luther's encounter with Staupitz led him to something new!

63. WA.TR 1,245 (Nr. 526, Jahr: 1533): "*Staupicius hat die doctrinam angefangen*." Trans. after LW 51:47. Luther refers to Staupitz advice for penance: "One must keep one's eyes fixed on that man who is called Christ." Trans. after: LW 51:97. This is exactly the point of the "Resolutiones," which really have to do with nothing other than a call to confession. When Aland, *Weg*, 81 classifies this in the "category of Luther's frequent overestimation of his peers" though, he underestimates its significance.

64. Grane, *Modus loquendi*, 125; also treated by Brecht, *Luther 1*, 137.

His discovery of penance with the help of mystical theology would become just one step on the way. But we should not forget (as, perhaps, did he) that he had previously worked very hard on preparing the canvas and the form of his theological painting, and that this work was conducted in a mystical studio with mystical techniques and mystical materials. Nevertheless, he would keep painting in the new way, and it would lead him to a lasting estrangement with the givens of late-medieval theological life.

4.

The Entanglement of Augustinianism and Mysticism in the Late Middle Ages and in the Early Reformational Movement

So far, I have tried to demonstrate that Luther developed his theology under the influence of mysticism.[1] If this is really the case, then we are faced with the question of how his indisputable Augustinianism related to this mystical influence. Both mysticism and Augustinianism had a long development in the Middle Ages, so we will have to examine this period. Scholars of the history of religion may well be surprised to discover that interdisciplinary medieval studies have long found a consensus in their conviction that Augustinianism and mysticism are closely related.[2] Medievalists are more or less on the same page that this connection was not created by Luther, but rather goes back to the fourteenth century. When I am referring to Augustinianism, I am of course not contesting that Augustine and his theology was *the* highest theological authority

1. See also Volker Leppin, *Die fremde Reformation. Luthers mystische Wurzeln*, 2nd ed. (Munich: C. H. Beck, 2016).
2. See for example, L. Grane, *Modus loquendi theologicus. Luthers Kampf um die Erneuerung der Theologie (1515–1518)* (Leiden: Brill, 1975), 122: Luther "reads Tauler not as one who knows what he wants but rather he discovers him as a comrade, which means that he understands him in the sense of his own Pauline and Augustinian theology." My translation. A special variety of this Augustinianism is the usage of Augustine by the Augustinian hermits. The extensive and profound study by E. L. Saak, *Highway to Heaven: The Augustinian Platform between Reform and Reformation*, Studies in Medieval and Reformation Thought, vol. 89 (Leiden: Brill, 2002), is very useful for understanding their usage of Augustine; for more on the usage of the *Erfurt* Augustinians, see the classic study by Adolar Zumkeller, "Erbsünde, Gnade, Rechtfertigung und Verdienst nach der Lehre der Erfurter Augustinertheologen des Spätmittelalters," *Cassiciacum*, vol. 35. (Würzburg: Augustinus-Verlag, 1984).

throughout the Middle Ages bar none.[3] Instead, my focus here is directed primarily toward the aspects of his theology that pertain to a theology of grace and justification.

MYSTICISM AND AUGUSTINIANISM IN THE LATE MIDDLE AGES

Recent scholarship in medieval studies—and here we need only refer to Bernard McGinn's peerless work on mysticism—has yielded the important insight that mysticism and Augustinianism are tightly related. While considering that mysticism is not a major theme in Augustine,[4] he nevertheless manages to use topics like the "ascendency of the soul to vision" and the "*Imago Trinitatis*" (image of the Trinity)[5] taken from the *Ennarationes in Psalmos*, *De Trinitate* and the commentary on John[6] to ultimately call Augustine the "founding father" of mysticism who exerted a "great influence on western mysticism."[7]

This is a corpus of Augustinian texts which has no direct connection to the conflict with Pelagius concerning grace. Adolar Zumkeller already pointed out that "mysticism provided particularly fertile ground for teachings on the insufficiency of human justice."[8] Karl Heinz Witte developed this idea with the help of observations made by Georg Steer.[9] Witte attributed the "Traktat von der Minne" ("Tract on Love," a text which does not appear to be well-known in English-speaking research at the moment), and those tracts normally attributed to the "Master of

3. For more details, see the contributions by R. Rieger, J. Doutre, U. Köpf, and V. Leppin in *Augustin Handbuch*, ed. V. H. Drecoll (Tübingen: Mohr Siebeck, 2007), 570–615.
4. Bernard McGinn, *The Presence of God*, vol. 1: *The Foundations of Mysticism* (New York: Crossroad, 1991), 230–231; however, it must be said that there is a very large spectrum of interpretation here; cf. E. Ephraem Hendrikx, *Augustins Verhältnis zur Mystik: eine patristische Untersuchung* (Cassiciacum. Würzburg: Rita-Verlag, 1936), whose investigations reach their climax in the sentence: "Augustine was a great enthusiast but he was no mystic"; the newer studies serve as a counterfoil, such as John Peter Kenney, *The Mysticism of Saint Augustine: Rereading the Confessions* (New York: Routledge, 2005).
5. McGinn, *The Presence of God*, 243.
6. McGinn, *The Presence of God*, 331–332.
7. McGinn, *The Presence of God*, 380; see also Herman Häring, "Eschatologie," in *Augustin Handbuch*, ed. V. H. Drecoll (Mohr Siebeck, 2007), 540–547, 544, who speaks of "a model of a hermeneutic-oriented mysticism" which has exerted an "enormous influence."
8. Adolar Zumkeller, "Das Ungenügen der menschlichen Werke bei den deutschen Predigern des Spätmittelalters." *Zeitschrift Für Katholische Theologie* 81, no. 3. (1959): 265–305, 273. My trans.
9. Georg Steer, *Scholastische Gnadenlehre in mittelhochdeutscher Sprache* (Munich: Beck, 1966).

the Disputation," the Basel Augustinian hermit Johannes Hiltalingen († 1392).[10] That allowed him to demonstrate that Augustinian hermits were working on adapting Eckhart's theology[11] already less than half a century after his death.[12] If Witte's identification is correct, then it yields the remarkable result that Hiltalingen presents us with an author whose Augustinianism is clearly structured by a theology of grace. His *Audi-filia* dialogue "Des menschen adel, val und erlösunge" (Humanity's nobility, fall and salvation)[13] undertakes a critical engagement with Meister Eckhart,[14] and ends up discussing the deep sinfulness of the human being and their utter dependence on grace. He adapts the structure of Anselm's *Cur Deus Homo* but then fills it with explicitly Augustinian terminology for grace. The student remarks: "The human being cannot bring forth that which they should give in due proportion for their sins."[15] They see themselves made entirely dependent on Christ:

> If I did not know the grace of Jesus Christ, then I would immediately despair by fear. Therefore, I want to reject [my trust in] my [own] justice and want to run into the light of Christian faith.[16]

10. Karl Heinz Witte, "Der 'Traktat von Der Minne', Der Meister Des Lehrgesprächs Und Johannes Hiltalingen von Basel. Ein Beitrag Zur Geschichte Der Meister-Eckhart-Rezeption in Der Augustinerschule Des 14. Jahrhunderts." *Zeitschrift Für Deutsches Altertum Und Deutsche Literatur* 131, no. 4 (Verlag, 2002): 454–87.
11. Witte, *Traktat*, 466–467.
12. For this person, Bernard McGinn, "How Augustine Shaped Medieval Mysticism." *Augustinian Studies* 31, no. 1 (2006): 21, has concluded: "Unlike Bernard, Eckhart shows little interest in the anti-Pelagian writings." According to McGinn, Eckhart's favorite texts from Augustine are: *Confessiones, De trinitate, Enarrationes in Psalmos, Tractatus in Ioannem*, and *De vera religione*; for more on the particularly important *Conefssiones* see Francesca Rita Alimonti, *Maître Eckhart et la tradition spirituelle: les "Confessiones" de Saint Augustin dans les sermons latins*. Analecta Augustiniana, vol. 58. (Nerbini International, 1995), 265–286.
13. *Der Meister des Lehrgesprächs, Der Audi-filia-Dialog: Des menschen val, adel vnd erlösunge. Nach der Handschrift CPC 1945 der Bibliothèque de Consistoire Colmar*, ed. and commented by K. H. Witte, unpublished manuscript. I thank Mr. Witte for providing me access to this manuscript.
14. Karl-Heinz Witte and Meister des Lehrgesprächs, *Der Meister des Lehrgesprächs und sein "In-principio-Dialog": ein deutschsprachiger Theologe der Augustinerschule des 14. Jahrhunderts aus dem Kreise deutscher Mystik und Scholastik: Untersuchung und Edition*. (Munich: Artemis, 1989), 172–173.
15. Witte, *Meister des Lehrgesprächs, Der Audi-filia-Dialog*, 76ra: "Der mönsch mag doch geleisten nùt, daz er zů rehter mässe sölte geben fur die sùnde." My translation.
16. Witte, *Meister des Lehrgesprächs, Der Audi-filia-Dialog*, 78ra: "wust ich nùt die gnäde Ihesu Christi, ich möhte uon vorhten verzwifeln. Dauon wil ich von miner gerehtigkeit lässen vnd wil fliehen in daz licht cristenliches glouben." My translation.; cf. Witte, *Meister des Lehrgesprächs*, 197.

With such statements, it is no wonder that Witte summarizes:

> The strict doctrine of predestination, the radical rejection of useful works, the unrestricted demand for manifest and coeffective grace all point to an Augustinian . . . who seems to be pointing to the [pre-Reformation] problem of justification which his brother in the order, Martin Luther, would wrestle with 200 years later.[17]

It is particularly remarkable that Hiltalingen adopts the Scholastic distinction between *meritum de condigno* and *meritum de congruo* in such a way that preserves the distinction but also moves it in a direction that would be central for Luther when he distinguished between the constitutive and consecutive function of works for salvation. Luther did this by translating *meritum de condigno* with the German word "*gelten*" (to be valid).[18] The thirteenth-century student interprets *meritum de condigno* as a "mode of thankfulness," also avoiding any sort of transactional terminology:

> Because grace and eternal reward are so good, no good work of an immaculate person can earn them. But the human being can become worthy [of these things] according to the manner of thankfulness such that God forgives them their penance for their sins out of grace and thankfulness makes them worthy for God to augment his grace and his crown in eternity.[19]

Previous debates about the relation between the Reformation and the Middle Ages have proven that structural analogies are not enough to overcome the deeply rooted reservations against interpreting the Reformation as a transformation of medieval concepts,[20] so I will not assume that people

17. Karl-Heinz Witte, and Meister des Lehrgesprächs. Der Meister des Lehrgesprächs und sein "In-principio-Dialog": ein deutschsprachiger Theologe der Augustinerschule des 14. Jahrhunderts aus dem Kreise deutscher Mystik und Scholastik: Untersuchung und Edition. (Munich: Artemis, 1989), 331–340: "Die strikte Prädestinationslehre, die radikale Ablehnung der verdienstlichen Werke, die uneingeschränkte Forderung der zuvorkommenden und mitwirkenden Gnade zeigen einen Augustiner (. . .), der sogar schon auf die (vorreformatorische) Rechtfertigungsproblematik seines etwa 200 Jahre jüngeren Ordensbruders Martin Luther vorzudeuten scheint." My translation.
18. Witte, *Meister des Lehrgesprächs, Audi-filia-Dialog*, 78rb.
19. Witte, *Meister des Lehrgesprächs, Audi-filia-Dialog*, 78va: "Wan gnäde vnd ewiger lon die sint als gůt, das sù keyn werk keins luteren mönschen mag verdienen. Aber nach der wise der danckbarkeit also mag der mönsch wùrdig werden, daz gott die bůsse der súnden uon gnaden ÿm vergit vnd die danckbe̊rkeit mag in wirdig machen, das gott sin gnäde vnd sine krone in ewigkeit meret." My translation.
20. At this point, it should be said that the mystical roots of the theses against indulgence, regardless of their controversial status within Lutheranism, can be counted among the philologically secure claims about them: even if we restrict our attention to Tauler and the *Theologia deutsch*, we see a chronologically proximate self-interpretation of Luther from March 31, 1518 (*Luther*

will be convinced by this one either. It cannot provide a watertight case for Luther's intellectual framework. A structural analogy *does* however become significant when we observe that Augustinianism and mysticism were amid a confluence in the late Middle Ages whose current propels us toward Luther. An example of this has been demonstrated by Mikhail Khorkov in his study on a fifteenth-century mystical manuscript in Salzburg where a statement from Meister Eckhart was interpreted and also lightly modified. Khorkov sees the central insight in the following passage:

> If the human being has God present in their mind, then their heart, mood and love will be drawn into God and unified with God and alienated from all creatures, for grace [is found] in God and not in creatures.[21]

As Khorkov has shown, the distance kept to the rest of the creatures remains close to Eckhart's way of thinking. Eckhart's favorite words such as "*ledic*" and "*blôzheit*" are still present, but the transformation can be seen in the emphasized usage of the word "*gnade*" (grace).[22] Augustinianism is present here, but not in high resolution. Gregory of Rimini and Thomas Bradwardine both articulated it more directly. It is a tradition, however, which will continue to move in the direction of Wittenberg's theology, something we cannot claim about these other two authors.

The tradition was relatively well-defined: Khorkov has demonstrated a considerable degree of association between the Augustinian transformation of Eckhart and the "Geestelike Bruolucht" by Jan van Ruusbroec.[23]

an Staupitz, 31. März 1518 [WA.Br 160 {Nr. 66,8–9}]), clear proof of a similarly proximate, hand-written Tauler reception in Luther's questioning about penance (Luther, *Randbemerkungen zu Tauler* [WA 9,104,11–12]), a summary of the further development of Luther's understanding of penance in his sermons; Volker Leppin, "'omnem vitam fidelium penitentiam esse voluit.' Zur Aufnahme mystischer Traditionen in Luthers erster Ablassthese," in *Transformationen: Studien zu den Wandlungsprozessen in Theologie und Frömmigkeit zwischen Spätmittelalter und Reformation* (Tübingen: Mohr Siebeck, 2015), 273–277; Volker Leppin, *Die fremde Reformation: Luthers mystische Wurzeln* (Munich: C. H. Beck, 2016) 55–60), and an indication of the way in which Tauler was received in the *95 Theses* (Leppin, *Fremde Reformation*, 55–60).

21. UB Salzburg, Ms. M I 476 f. 223v: "wenn der mensche hat got gegenwúrtig in siner meynung so wúrt sin hercz sin gemuet und sin minne in got gezogen und mit got vereint und entfroemdet allen creaturen und da ist gnade in got und nit in den creâturen." My translation.; cited after; Following quote: Michail L'vovič Chor'kov, "Unbekannter Eckhart Oder Unbekannter Ruusbroec?: Zum Augustinistischen Kontext Der Meister-Eckhart-Rezeption Im 15. Jahrhundert." In *Meister Eckhart in Erfurt*, ed. Andreas Speer and Lydia Wegener (Berlin: De Gruyter, 2005), 587–600, 590–591; Mikhail Khorkov, "Der Traktat 'Von Dem Ewigen Wort' Und Der Augustinische Kontext in Der Rezeption Der Lehre Von Der Gottesgeburt Am Oberrhein Im 15. Jahrhundert." University, Council, City (Brepols, 2007) 203–218.
22. Khorkov, "Der Traktat," 591.
23. Khorkov, "Der Traktat," 592–593.

Another field of transmission for the Augustinianism-mysticism connection can be found in the well-populated literature of the *Devotio moderna*, about which Luther was aware—he is known to have occupied himself with Rosetum and Zerbold of Zutphen.[24] Luther makes reference to the latter's *Tractatulus de spiritualibus ascensionibus* in his first lectures on the Psalms when treating Psalm 83 (84) because the *Tractatulus* opens with a citation from this Psalm.[25] Interestingly, he correctly identifies Gerhald Zerbold of Zutphen as the author here, but a few years later he would attribute the same text to Gerhard Groote and would do so with glowing praise for the (falsely identified) author.[26]

As the title conveys, the tract treats the ascension of the soul to God. Precisely, it is the return of the human person to the blessed status of paradise.[27] The goal is that the intellect moves "*ad intuitum divine speculationis*" (to an intuition of divine thought).[28] This is fostered by a spiritual life of meditation, the help of a spiritual advisor as well as by considering the passion of Christ. The Augustinian character of Zerbold's understanding of blessedness is unmistakable,[29] for every step toward God is only possible because of a *gratia specialis*,[30] a particular form of grace which goes beyond that of creation. It is even more than that given in baptism. The particular grace is therefore not to be confused with the pure grace in the sense of the later Reformation, as Zerbold explicitly remarks: "grace is not given to sleepers, to the negligent nor to them that will not work together with Him."[31] Zerbold assumes a sort of grace which assumes some form of cooperation on the part of the person, likely in the form of their disposition.

All that fits neatly into a mostly monastic, late-medieval world of spirituality. One can read this work as a sort of late-medieval spiritual guide for the soul with monastic individuals as the intended readers. The mystical

24. For more on the significance of Rosentum for Luther, see: Martin Elze, "Züge Spätmittelalterlicher Frömmigkeit in Luthers Theologie," *Zeitschrift Für Theologie Und Kirche* 62, no. 4 (Mohr, 1965): 383–394, of course with the period-correct emphasis on the tension between Luther and mysticism (Khorkov, "Der Traktat," 394–395).
25. Luther, *Dictata super Psalterium* (WA 55/2,638,242–244).
26. Luther, *Römerbriefvorlesung. Scholion zu Röm 5,14* (WA 56,313,13–16).
27. For more on this original state, cf. Gerard Zerbolt, *La montée du cœur / De spiritualibus ascensionibus II*, ed. and trans. Francis Joseph Legrand (Turnhout: Brepols, 2006), 102–108.
28. Zerbolt, *La montée du cœur*, 198.
29. For a general overview of the usage of Augustine, see: Zerbolt, *La montée du cœur*, 424–425.
30. Zerbolt, *La montée du cœur*, 198.
31. Zerbolt, *La montée du cœur*, 198, 200: "gracia tamen dormientibus, negligentibus et non cooperantibus non datur." Trans. after: Gerard Zerbolt, *The Spiritual Ascent: A Devotional Treatise* (London: Burns & Oates, 1908), 54.

notes are perceptible yet subtle. The book can generally be classified as "devotional literature."

The theology developed here thrived on a pairing between the positive path led by grace and a vivid depiction of humanity's sinfulness. The inverse of ascension, or more precisely the *necessity* of such ascension, was the profound fall from original grace. In chapters three to eight Zerbold waxes poetic about the deplorable status of having fallen from Paradise. Everything in the human person is now the opposite of what God had ordained so that, for example, our hopes are not directed to God but to *propria merita*, our own works.[32] According to Zerbold, the first step to changing this fate is to locate ourselves in this depravity with three exercises of self-awareness to prepare the foundation for our return to God and to enable our ascension to the lofty heights of his presence.[33]

We draw even closer to Luther and his potential connection to Augustinianism and mysticism when we examine those works that Luther had mentioned in his famous dedicatory letter to Staupitz on March 31, 1518: John Tauler and the *Theologia Deutsch*.[34] The *Theologia Deutsch* has been examined quite comprehensively in its treatment of Augustinianism and mysticism by Lydia Wegener. In her study, she has demonstrated that this text is to be understood entirely in the described traditions of an intensified Augustinian lineage. In fact, the *Theologia Deutsch* is *so* Augustinian that it is "alienated from the 'mystical discourse,'" meaning that it has a very distinct profile within the developments of mysticism.[35] Wegener argues this point, particularly with the help of chapters 15 and 16 of the *Theologia Deutsch* which embed the concept of the birth of God into an Adam-Christ typology. The birth of God is really the new birth after the total loss of divine accordance in Adam.[36] As the *Theologia Deutsch* puts it, the human being has lost all ability to be anything before God:

> This is how one can tell what disobedience is: the human being has a [high] opinion of themself and believes that they are, know and can do something, seeking themself and their own advantage in [all] things and love themselves and other such things.[37]

32. Zerbolt, *La montée du cœur*, 110.
33. Zerbolt, *La montée du cœur*, 198.
34. *Luther an Staupitz*, 31 März 1518 (WA.Br 160 [Nr. 66,8–9])
35. Lydia Wegener, *Der 'Frankfurter' / 'theologia deutsch': Spielräume und grenzen des sagbaren*, Frühe Neuzeit, vol. 201 (Berlin: De Gruyter, 2016), 172. My translation.
36. Wegener, *Der 'Frankfurter'*, 158–159.
37. 'Der Franckforter' ('Theologia deutsch'). Kritische Textausgabe, ed. Wolfgang von Hinten, 1982, 89,15–18; cf. Wegener, *Der 'Frankfurter'*, 159. "Hie bie magk man mercken, was vngehorsam sey. Das ist, das der mensche von ym selber etwas heldet vnd wenet, er sey vnd wisße

Wegener considers the negative anthropology of the *Theologia Deutsch* to be so well developed that it goes far beyond even Augustine. While Augustine's later years saw him see-sawing "between denigration and appreciation of the *natura humana*,"[38] the *Theologia deutsch* settled on a "demonization of human nature."[39] We can, of course, ask out of theological-historical interest if any proximity to Manichaeism (which Wegener identifies in the *Theologia Deutsch*)[40] must be considered when addressing its radicalism.[41] Regardless, the radicality only furthers the impression that this is a *very* Augustinian work. The issue with this statement, however, is that the *Theologia Deutsch* never actually cites Augustine explicitly. Wegener's reconstruction is based on a combination of known Augustine reception in other mystical sources and a systematic analysis of the *Theologia Deutsch*. Thus, when searching for mystical Augustinian influence on Luther, the *Theologia Deutsch* is substantially less valuable than John Tauler, who is just as important for Luther. Tauler cites Augustine several times. There is no space here to give a thorough analysis of this fascinating dependency, but we should take a look at the especially interesting question of divine grace and justice or human works in Tauler's writings.

In a sermon about the healing at the pool in Bethesda, Tauler mentions the necessity of remaining grounded: "Be assured, dear children, that whoever would engage in external works should keep a careful watch over his interior, earnestly inspecting his motives."[42] He justifies this with a citation of Augustine, which is somewhat tricky to identify as such due to its very general nature. He purportedly said: "St. Augustine tells us, that it sometimes happens that men who thus abandon a recollected life and unguardingly mingle with the joys of creatures, never more return."[43]

vnd vormuge etwas, vnd sich selbir vnnd das seyne suchte yn den dingen vnde sich selbir lip hat vnd dißen glich." My translation.

38. Wegener, *Der 'Frankfurter'*, 176–177. My translation.
39. Wegener, *Der 'Frankfurter'*, 176.
40. Wegener, *Der 'Frankfurter'*, 190.
41. See the review from Andreas Zecherle in: *Beiträge zur Geschichte der deutschen Sprache und Literatur* 139 (2017): 633–637.
42. Johannes Tauler, *Die Predigten Taulers aus der Engelberger und der Freiburger Handschrift sowie aus Schmidts Abschriften der ehemaligen Straßburger Handschriften*, ed. Ferdinand Vetter (Berlin: Weidmannsche Buchhandlung, 1910), 36,5–6: "Der mensche sollte in allen sinen werken und uzgengen sins grundes ein flissig warnemen haben." Trans. after: John Tauler, *The Sermons and Conferences of John Tauler*, trans. and ed. Walter Elliott (Washington, DC: Apostolic Mission House, 1910), 133.
43. Tauler, *Predigten* 36 (Vetter), 4, Trans. after: Tauler, *The Sermons and Conferences of John Tauler*, 133; cf. Augustine, *Enarrationes in Psalmos on Ps 119 Nr.* 7: "Multi enim et miseri sunt, et non gemunt, et peregrinantur, et redire nolunt" (PL 37, 1602) / "There are many others, just as

Tauler connected this citation of Augustine with a scathing critique of all things external—should they not emanate out of the spiritual foundation, then they are all in vain. One could perhaps interpret this as: works are not what make a person good, but rather it is the ground alone. That means being focused on God. Works must follow him.

We see exactly this sort of Augustine reception in another Tauler sermon, this time on the fourth Sunday after Easter, treating the text John 16:7–15. Tauler preaches on the text about the Paraclete revealing the final judgment in verses 8 to 11 and then expounds upon human sinfulness, which consists primarily of not discerning and confessing one's own faults:

> O, dear children, be assured that any so-called spiritual man who rests in total self-content, who is well pleased with his state of soul and his manner of living, is really in great danger and is committing offenses perilous to his salvation. He is a self-willed man from whom nothing good can be expected.[44]

Tauler used this grim depiction of humanity's sinful status before God to launch into an attack on any purported human justice. He used an Augustine citation to do this: "We and all of our justice depend on his mercy, [on him] not wanting to judge: I will exalt and take joy in your mercy."[45] We should note that God's justice and mercy are juxtaposed here. It is, however, clear that the judgment takes place according to his mercy and not according to uncompromising standards of justice. The sermon goes on to reach the poimenic pinnacle in its contention that humans in fact *cannot* do anything worthy of God's recognition. That is strongly Augustinian theology, and Tauler uses the same citations in other places.[46]

wretched, who do not grieve; they are exiles too, but have no desire to go home." Trans. after: Saint Augustine, "Expositions of the Psalms", vol. III/19. In *The Works of Saint Augustine (4th Release).* Electronic Edition, ed. John E. Rotelle, vol. 34 (Online publisher: Charlottesville, VI: InteLex Corp. 2014. Print Publisher: Hyde Park, NY: New City Press, 2003), 506. I am deeply indebted to Anja Bork, Philip Steinbach und Raphael Zager for helping me to identify the Augustine citations.

44. Tauler, *Predigten,* 73,20–21: "Kinder, die lúte den ir ding also wol gevellet und ander lúte tGn úbel, daz sint s=rgliche gebresten, und us den wurd niemer nút." Trans. after: Tauler, *The Sermons and Conferences of John Tauler*, 278.
45. Tauler, *Predigten,* 73,23–24: "wi und we aller gerechtigkeit obe sú Got noch sinre bermhertzekeit nút urteilen wil; exsultabo et jucundabor in tua misericordia«: 'non in mea justitia'." My translation; cf. *Augustine's Explanation of Ps. 30:8:* "exsultabo et jucundabor in tua misericordia": "non in mea justitia" (Augustin, *Enarrationes in Psalmos on Ps 30 Nr. 13*; PL 36,237); for Tauler's significance at this point, cf. Adolar Zumkeller, *Ungenügen der Werke*, 274 (his conclusions on Tauler's impact on Luther is, however, very conservative; see Zumkeller, *Ungenügen der Werke*, 304–305).
46. Tauler, *Predigten,* 215 (Vetter), 26–27.

It makes sense therefore that Tauler also employs Augustine to describe the proper attitude toward penance:

> St. Augustine says: "Man is formed of corrupt material, as if he were made of rotten wood and vile earth, and his end is eternal death." Then, for his salvation, there is granted him a life of penance, the same to which God has called you, by no merits of yours, but only by His free and loving gift And what is that life of penance in very truth and in its essential quality? Nothing else that a wholehearted turning away from all that is not God, and an equally sincere turning to all that leads to God and means God.[47]

Augustine has become a preacher of true penance, itself a change in the direction of life. Tauler's characteristic understanding of penance as a process much deeper and more fundamental than the sacramental event has at least been confirmed by Augustine. It may have even been entirely inspired by him. Tauler even joins Augustine in the idea of theosis when he uses him to describe the transformation of the elements: "You shall not change me into yourself, but into me you shall be changed."[48] This overview is eclectic, but I hope that it has demonstrated that Tauler is part of a late-medieval tradition that connected mysticism and Augustine. Chronologically, Tauler is right at the beginning of this tight association which would continue to think of these two concepts as being wrapped up in each other right up to the end of the Middle Ages. Wittenberg was no exception—its Augustinian hermits considered mysticism and Augustinianism to constitute a great harmony.

STAUPITZ'S MYSTICAL AUGUSTINIANISM

Henrik Otto has provided us with a thorough study of the Tauler renaissance in Wittenberg which has plausibly argued that John of Staupitz was

47. Tauler, *Predigten*, 58,26–33: "Sant Augustinus sprach: 'der mensche ist von einer fulen materien, stinckende und verderbende, ein klotz und ein ful ertrich, des ende ist der ewige tod; daz úberkummet man mit dem lebende der penitencien, und daz úch der minnencliche Got geladen und gerůffet hat von siner frigen lutern minen sunder alles verdienen'. Was ist daz leben der penitencien in dem wesende und in der worheit? Daz enist anders nút denne ein gantz wor abeker von allem dun daz Got nút enist, und ein gantz war zůkeren zů dem luteren woren gůte daz Got ist und heisset." Translation after: Johannes Tauler: *Sermons*, Classics of Western Spirituality, trans. Maria Shrady (Mahwah, NJ: Paulist Press, 1985). The Augustine citation contained therein is likely a summary of various statements made by Augustine.
48. Tauler, *Predigten*, 125 (Vetter), 20–21; cf. Augustine, *Confessiones 7, c. 10, Nr. 16*: "Nec tu me in te mutabis (. . .), sed tu mutaberis in me" (CSEL 33, 157).

at the forefront of rediscovering this Upper-Rhine mystic.[49] However, Staupitz was not limited to Tauler in his exploration of mystical concepts. As Markus Wriedt has convincingly demonstrated,[50] the *Libellus de exsecutione aeternae praedestinationis* only makes sense against the background of an Augustinian inquiry. For our purposes, it is enough to note that Staupitz develops his doctrine of justification in *De exsecutione* in such a way that demonstrates how he was formulating things in *as Augustinian a fashion as possible.* It is entirely clear to him that natural works cannot contribute to salvation in the slightest.[51] Instead, only that which Christ has given and effected can do so. The translation of the work made by Christoph Scheurl demonstrates this quite clearly:

> Therefore, all works come out of Christ and go into Christ and are therefore called particular "works of Christ," even though they are formally in human beings and are finite in and of themselves (and otherwise are not God's [works] except for an externally applied terminus).[52]

What Staupitz describes (again, very Augustinian in its manner) is a highly self-referential assurance of salvation which he connects with the core concept of Thomistic teaching on justification. The works are "works of formed faith" in which the faith sired by God takes form.[53]

Staupitz embeds this moderate version of Augustinianism in two mystical images. The first likely comes from Tauler and the second from Bernard of Clairvaux. He essentially copied the idea of the birth of God in the Soul from Tauler's first sermon. This sermon (regardless of its dubious authenticity, see chapter 1, first section) is especially prominent among Tauler's sermons because it was connected with four other sermons in a

49. Henrik Otto, *Vor-und frühreformatorische Tauler-Rezeption: Annotationen in Drucken des späten 15. und frühen 16. Jahrhunderts.* Quellen und Forshungen zur Reformationsgeschichte, vol. 75 (Heidelberg: Gütersloher Verlagshaus, 2003).
50. Markus Wriedt, *Gnade und Erwählung: eine Untersuchung zu Johann von Staupitz und Martin Luther.* Veröffentlichungen des Instituts für Europäische Geschichte Mainz, vol. 141 (Mainz: von Zabern, 1991).
51. Johann von Staupitz, *Sämtliche Schriften*, vol. 2, *Lateinische Schriften: Libellus de exsecutione aeternae praedestinationis*, ed. Lothar Graf zu Dohna and Richard Wetzel (Berlin: De Gruyter 1979), 120: "ideoque ad praemium aeternum nullo modo accedunt."
52. Johann von Staupitz, *Sämtliche Schriften*, vol. 2, *Lateinische Schriften: Libellus de exsecutione aeternae praedestinationis*, ed. Lothar Graf zu Dohna and Richard Wetzel (Berlin: De Gruyter, 1979), 125: "Darumb alle werk . . . geen aus von Christo und geen in Christum und sein also sunderliche werk Christi genant, wiewol sie formlich im menschen—und anders nit gots dann durch ein blosse außwendige benennung -, in inen selbst entlich gemessen und geschaffen sein." My translation.
53. Staupitz, *Sämtliche Schriften*, 123; the Latin reads: "opera . . . fidei formatae" (Staupitz, *Sämtliche Schriften*, 122).

1508 edition from Augsburg which was promulgated in Wittenberg at the time. Today's research has collected them in the "Birth of God Cycle" and attributed them to Meister Eckhart.[54] However, sixteenth-century readers did not know this; they read these sermons and their extensive depiction of the birth of God as statements from John Tauler. That included Staupitz, who went on the offense with them. He appears to have used an associative method, for the passages about rebirth are grouped within his passages on justification. He then brings the reader to the relation with Christ: "Where these things come together, then the Son of God is born there and makes both just and alive through faith which works through love."[55] That forming love makes faith alive, and the same love is the product of the birth of God, here not expressly bound to the soul. In any case, it is certainly the consequence and expression of a justification-centric relation to God. Staupitz then adds to this Taulerian birth image a Bernardian image of a mystical bride:

> The association between Christ and the church is perfect in the following way: "I take you to be mine, I take you for me, I take you into me." Conversely, the church or the soul says to Christ: "I take you to be mine, I take you for me, I take you into me." Therefore, Christ said: "The Christian is mine, the Christian is for me, the Christian is me" and the church says: "Christ is mine, Christ is for me, I am Christ."[56]

Staupitz uses this image to explain how Christ's justice gets transferred to sinful human beings. Christ takes on human sin, and sinners take on

54. The passages in question are (trans. after Meister Eckhart, *The Complete Mystical Works of Meister Eckhart*. Trans. and ed. Maurice O'C. Walshe. Foreword by Bernard McGinn [Crossroad Publishing, 2009].): "Dum medium silentium tenerent omnia et nox in suo" / "When all things lay in the midst of silence, then there descended down into me from on high, from the royal throne, a secret word." ([Pf 1, Q101, QT 57], 29) (Meister Eckhart, *Deutsche Werke. Predigten IV,1*, ed. George Steer, (Stuttgart: Kohlhammer, 2003), 334–367 [Nr. 101]), "Ubi est qui natus est rex iudeorum" (407–425 [Nr. 102]) / Where is he who is born king of the Jews?" ([Pf 2, Q102, QT 58], 39), "Cum factus esset Jesus annorum duodecim" (474–492 [Nr. 103]) / ". . . when our Lord was twelve years old[.]" ([Pf 4, Q103, QT59], 55); "In his quae patris mei sunt oportet me esse." ([Pf 4, Q103, QT59], 565–610 [Nr. 104b]) / "I must be about my Father's business." ([Pf 3, Q104], 46).
55. Staupitz, *Sämtliche Schriften*, 115: "Wo diese ding zusamenkummen, do wirdet geborn der sun gottes, gerechtfertigt und lebendig gemacht durch den glouben, der würkt durch die lieb." My translation.
56. Staupitz, *Sämtliche Schriften*, 145–147: "Die verbindung Christi und der kirchen ist volkumen, dergestalt: 'Ich nim dich zu der meinen, ich nim dich mir, ich nim dich in mich' und herwiderumb spricht die kirch oder die seel zu Christo: 'Ich nim dich zu dem meinem, ich nim dich mir, ich nim dich in mich'; domit Christus also sprech: 'Der christen ist mein, der christen ist mir, der christen ist ich'; und die braut: 'Christus ist mein, Christus ist mir, Christus ist ich'"; cf. Wriedt, *Gnade und Erwählung*, 63–67.

Christ's justice.[57] Mystical imagery leads to a process of justification which suddenly feels very Augustinian. Staupitz made it existential, weaving together traditions that can be read from two angles: mystical Augustinianism or Augustinian mysticism.

LUTHER'S MYSTICAL AUGUSTINIANISM

So far, we have demonstrated that medievalists have found a real conduit between mystical content and Augustinianism. As Luther emerged out of this tradition, we should be able to expect such compatibility to have also existed for Martin Luther. It did, as Lydia Wegener acutely observed:

> Having grown acquainted with the Anti-Pelagian Augustine, Luther incorporated Augustine's rigid teachings on grace and original sin into his own theological-anthropological concept. It would have been impossible for Luther to have anything positive to say about the preacher from Strassbourg [Tauler] (and he said *euphoric* things about him) if he had not read Tauler as being congruent with his understanding of Augustine.[58]

Another example of this connection can be found in Luther's thought as early as 1518 when he wrote in the preface to the second (and now complete) edition of Tauler:

> To boast with my old fool, no book except the Bible and St. Augustine has come to my attention from which I have learned more about God, Christ, man, and all things.[59]

This is a different look at Luther as a self-identifying Augustinian compared to how he had expressed it to John Lang on May 18, 1517. There, he had praised the progress of the *theologia nostra* (our theology) and Augustinian theology as they displaced Aristotelian theology in Wittenberg.[60] Luther pits Augustine against Aristotle, especially the latter's anthropology. He would make this same emphasis in a disputation against Scholastic theology by following Augustine's line of thought that a

57. Staupitz, *Sämtliche Schriften*, 147.
58. Wegener, *Frankfurter*, 79. My translation.
59. Luther, *Vorrede zur zweiten Ausgabe der Theologia deutsch* (WA 1,378,21–23): "Und das ich nach meynem alten narren rueme, ist myr nehst der Biblien und S. Augustino nit vorkummen eyn buch, dar auß ich mehr erlernet hab und will, was got, Christus, mensch und alle ding seyn." Trans. after LW 31:75.
60. Luther an Lang, 18 Mai 1517 (WA.Br 1, 99 [Nr. 41,8–13]).

bad-tree sort of person must also bring forth bad fruit.[61] He carried this out in his unabashed invective against Aristotle, including phrases such as "Indeed, no one can become a theologian unless he becomes one without Aristotle."[62] This point is valid for Luther's relationship to Aristotle and his followers almost exclusively at this point in time. He was then in the midst of a vigorous battle against Scholastic theology which he had broadly condemned as a representative of Aristotelian anthropology, and he believed that he had mystical theology on his side—not because of some misunderstanding on his part, but simply because Luther had good reasons to assume a possible alliance between mysticism and Augustine, again *because the connection already existed*.

The same is true of the statements made by Zerbold of Zutphen which we saw earlier. Luther richly praised the very passage we examined above in which Zerbold treats sin:

> I have not found so clear a discussion of the subject of original sin as in Gerard Groote's treatise Blessed Is the Man, in which he speaks not as an arrogant philosopher but as a sane theologian.[63]

The popular understanding of Luther portrays him as distinct from the mystical tradition because of his anthropology and his doctrine of sin.[64] This appreciation of Zerbold, however, casts another light on that image of Luther. It is found in a scholion on Romans 5:14, in the *Lectures on Romans*, and not too far after the decidedly long speech about *peccatum radicale* in his comments on Romans 4:7.[65] We can safely assume that the radicalizing concept of sin was still on his mind when he was writing glowing praise about Groote (we now know the author was Zerbold, but

61. Luther, *Dipsutatio Contra Scholasticam Theologiam* (WA 1,224,13–14).
62. Luther, *Dipsutatio Contra Scholasticam Theologiam* (WA 1,226,44). Trans. after LW 31:5–16
63. Luther, *Römerbriefvorlesung. Scholion zu Röm 5,14* (WA 56,313,13–16). Trans. after LW 34:300.
64. The standard work here is Steven E. Ozment, *Homo Spiritualis: A Comparative Study of the Anthropology of Johannes Tauler, Jean Gerson and Martin Luther (1509–16) in the Context of their Theological Thought* (Leiden: Brill, 1969); Interenstingly, even Leif Grane (*Modus loquendi theologicus: Luthers Kampf um die Erneuerung der Theologie (1515–1518)* [Leiden: Brill, 1975], 123), who tends toward a conservative estimate of Tauler's significance for Luther, relativizes Luther's juxtaposition to Tauler's anthropology—at least as concerns the question of whether Luther had discerned a tension to Tauler (as admitted by Grane) (Grane, *Modus loquendi theologicus*, 124). In a thorough study which is specially focused on image-teaching, Karsten Junk 9, *Der menschliche Geist und sein Gottesverhältnis bei Augustinus und Meister Eckhart. Augustinus,* Werk und Wirkung, vol. 5. [Paderborn: Ferdinand Schöningh, 2016]), has demonstrated that the anthropological differences between Eckhart and Augustine are not as great as is generally assumed (see his summary pp. 287–294).
65. Luther, *Römerbriefvorlesung. Scholion zu Röm 4,7* (WA 56,277,12).

that is not important here). That means in turn that Luther saw no tension between the Pauline-Augustinian radicality in his teachings on sin and the mystically informed tradition of the *Devotio moderna*. It makes sense for him because the latter was already deeply infused with Augustinianism.

For our purposes here, we can only take a few eclectic looks at the way Luther explored this connection between Augustinianism and the mystical tradition. One of them is in his edition of the *Theologia Deutsch*, which Luther edited but did not annotate with his own writing in any way. He *did*, however, elevate certain passages which betray a particularly well-defined reception of Augustinianism. One of them is chapter 16 of the first edition which he, much like Wegener, elevates as the center of the entire book (which was still incomplete at this point). Another indication is in the subtitle of the edition which read:

> A spiritual, noble little book on the proper distinction and understanding of what the old and the new human being is, what is Adam's child and what is God's child and how Adam must die in us and Christ arise in us.[66]

The Adam-Christ typology is what constitutes the anthropology of the *Theologia Deutsch*,[67] and Luther picks up on it quite acutely. Here he finds the answer to the issue occupying him at the time, and he adequately identifies the *Theologia Deutsch* as being *unique* in its ability to help him.

There are some obvious Augustinian aspects in Luther's reading of Tauler. After all, he *did* see the *Theologia Deutsch* as having been authored "almost entirely by the enlightened Doctor Tauler of the Order of Preachers [Dominicans]."[68] But there are other accents in which we can find evidence of his reception of Tauler. One of these is the demonstrable fact that the inspiration he garnered from Tauler can be clearly identified in his understanding of penance.[69] This was the very theological domain that Tauler had so tightly connected with Augustine in his own thought. While there is no trace of Luther's usage in his subtitle, we are nevertheless faced with what looks like a marked coincidence: Luther eagerly received that content of Tauler which he regarded to be properly Augustinian.

66. WA 1, 153: "Ein geistlich, edles Buchlein von rechter underscheid und vorstand, was der alt und neu mensche sei. Was Adams und was Gottes kind sei. Und wie Adam inn uns sterben unnd Christus ersteen soll." My translation.

67. In contrast to Wegener, *Der 'Frankfurter'*, 158n354, I do not think that we need to dispense with these concepts, but we *should* remember that the relation of Christ to Adam was primarily a negative one.

68. Luther, *Vorrede zur ersten Ausgabe der Theologia deutsch* (WA 1,153): "faßt nach der art des erleuchten doctors Tauleri, prediger ordens." My translation.

69. Leppin, *omnem vitam fidelium*.

That is also true of the statements mentioned above in which Tauler employs Augustine to support his own arguments pertaining to the priority of *metanoia* over the facts of life. Luther did not note a passage of Augustine that fits well to the idea, but he did mark a few passages of Tauler that go in such a direction. In his forty-fifth sermon, Tauler describes the end of the desired ascension to God: "Children, in this name do humans grow and ascend more so than they do with all external practices which the world cultivates for satisfaction.[70] Here, Luther adds a little comment: "The reason is that all of those things are the works of human beings, but this is the work of God."[71] That demonstrates clear agreement with Augustinian material in Tauler, and it does not stop there! Luther explicitly highlighted Tauler's references to Augustine and even attempted to match Tauler's Middle High German citations of Augustine to the Latin original. For example, when Tauler writes in his first sermon on the birth of God in the Soul: "Thus, as Saint Augustine says, we are just as good as God is."[72] Luther noted in the margins: "Aug[ustine:] Because God is good, so are we."[73] In so doing, Luther made clear that this was not a conditional but rather a causal clause in Augustine. Interestingly though, this is the only sentence among many Augustine references on these pages that Luther marks. It might be an indication that Luther was not actually as interested in the content as he was in the form when he made the correction, or it might be a further example of the phenomenon discovered by Jan Matsuura in the Erfurt Notations,[74] where Luther's humanistic pathos is made evident in a large collection of text-critical corrections.

Regardless of these possible explanations though, there are clear points of agreement with the Augustinian understanding of salvation. The most significant of them seems to be the marginal note which is also found in Tauler's Christmas sermon. Tauler's thought touches the core of mystical convictions here, especially the idea that an encounter with God demands

70. Sermones: des hochl geleerten in gnaden erleüchten dolctoris Johannis Thaulerii sannt | dominici ordens die da weißend | auff den nächesten waren weg im | gaist zů wanderen durch überswel bendenn syn. Von latein in teütsch | gewendt manchem menschenn zů | såliger fruchtbarkaitt, Augsburg: Hans Otmar 1508, f. O 7[v]: "Kinder in disem nåme der mensch mer zů. vnnd gienge mer auff. dann in allen den außwennigen ůbungen die alle welt mit ainander gethung mag." My translation.

71. Luther, *Randbemerkungen zu Tauler* (WA 9,103,16–17): "Et ratio est: qui illa omnia sunt opera hominum, hoc autem opus dei." My translation.

72. Tauler, *Sermones f. A 1*[v]: "Darumb / sprach sant augu. so got gůt ist / seind wir." My translation.

73. Luther, *Randbemerkungen zu Tauler* (WA 9,97,2): "Aug. Quia deus bonus est, sumus." My translation.

74. Luther, *Erfurter Annotationen 1509–1510/11*, ed. Jan Matsuura, et al. 2009 (AWA 9), LVIII-LXXX.

that one "denies everything of one's own" for God to be born in them and to arrive at a unification: "When two things become one, then the first must comport itself passively and the second actively."[75] This is where Luther was apparently interested and noted in the margins:

> Note that the divine suffers more than they act, therefore it is natural for both the senses as well as the intellect that this is also a passive virtue. As the Apostle says: "He gives me desire but I cannot find perfection," which means that we are a pure matter, God is a creator of the form and therefore everything in us has been operated by God.[76]

This is exactly the point at which Tauler leads the reader into a citation of Augustine,[77] and it is the very same point where Luther scribbles in a citation from Paul.[78] That makes it clear that the deeply mystical statements dwelling on the ideas of *unio* and the birth of God lead directly into a Pauline-Augustinian head space. The theology of grace and the theology of mysticism have incorporated each other and become one. Luther prominently uses the word *passivus* (passive)[79] to point to an Augustinian approach to grace. This all sheds helpful light on Luther's 1545 account of his Reformational discovery which he described as the discovery of *iustitia passiva—passive* justice.[80] The secondary interpretation also makes clear that passivity remained a decisive criterion for the later Luther in his development of Pauline-Augustinian teaching on grace. The idea derived from Aristotelian philosophy that the human being is *pura materia* is found in thesis 35 of the famous *disputatio de homine*: "Therefore, man in this

75. Tauler, *Sermones A 2*ʳ: "verlaugnen aller aygenschafft" / "wann wenn zway sollnn ains werden / so můß sich dz ain haltnn leidend / daz ander wirckent."
76. Luther, *Randbemerkungen zu Tauler* (WA 9,97,12–16): "Nota, quod divina pati magis quam agere oportet, immo et sensus et intellectus est naturaliter etiam virtus passiva. Et Apostolus: 'Velle mihi adjacet, perficere non invenio' i.e. Nos materia sumus pura, deus formae factor, omnia enim in nobis operatur deus."
77. Tauler, *Sermones A2*ʳ: "Geüß vß daz du mo̊gest ervollet werden" (cf. Augustin, *In Ioannem tratctus 20*, Nr. 12: "Effunde super te animam tuam" [PL 35, 1563]).
78. Tauler, *Sermones A2*ʳ, (WA 9,98,3).
79. For the earlier usage, see the study of rather limited use by Emanuel Hirsch, "Initium theologiae Lutheri," in *Der Durchbruch der reformatorischen Erkenntnis bei Luther*, ed. Bernhard Lohse (Darmstadt: Wissenschaftliche Buchgesellschaft, 1968), 73–75; The point made by Oswald Bayer, "Vita Passiva: Luther Und Die Mystik," in *Die Kirchenkritik Der Mystiker*, vol. 2, Frühe Neuzeit, ed. Mariano Delgado and Gotthard Fuchs (Fribourg: Academic Press, 2005), 104, is very important to Luther's statements about the vita passiva in the *Operationes in pslamos* belong in the context of his comments on Tauler and other *expertii*. See Luther, *Operationes in pslamos* (AWA 2,301, 17–20; 303, 5–19). Bayer has even argued that *iustitia passiva* and has even postulated that this *vita passiva* is identical with *iustitia passiva* (Bayer, "Vita Passiva, 105).
80. Luther, *Vorrede zu Bd.1 seiner Lateinischen Werke* (WA 54,186,3–8).

life is the simple material of God for the form of his future life."[81] Here we see that the marginal comment of a mystical author from the fourteenth century is an idea that Luther never forgot. He would retain it as one of his central anthropological insights for Reformational theology.

That looks like radical Augustinianism which negates *any* human participation. There *are* however statements from Luther which pick up on the form of Augustinianism shared by Tauler and Staupitz in which human persons *do* participate in salvation. For example, we read in the fourth sermon of the Tauler collection:

> God has decided that he will reward nothing other than his own works. He will crown nothing in heaven for eternity except for his own work, and not yours.[82]

The emphasis on grace here is connected with the idea that God *supports* human efforts and does not fully reject them. Luther immediately discerned a saying veiled in this Tauler citation which likely goes back to Albertus Magnus. He had employed this saying in his commentary on Lombard's *Sentences* and repeated it here as well: "Whatever you have of merit the preempting grace has given to you, [for] God crowns nothing in us except for his gifts."[83] When we take a quick look at the *Sentences,* we see that Luther did in fact identify this passage as a condensed version of Augustine. He does not use this verse but rather one from Augustine which is very similar:

> What merit, then, does a human being have before grace so that by that merit he may receive grace, since only grace produces in us every good merit of ours and since, when God crowns our merits, he only crowns his own gifts?[84]

81. Luther, *Disputatio de homine* (WA 39/1, 177,3–4): "homo huius vitae est pura materia Dei ad futurae formae suae vitam." Trans. after: Martin Luther, "The Disputation Concerning Man. 1536," in *Luther's Works*, vol. 34, *Career of the Reformer IV*, trans. Lewis W. Spitz, ed. Helmut T. Lehmann and Lewis W. Spitz, 133–144 (Philadelphia: Muhlenberg Press, 1960), 139n35; Gerhard Ebeling, "Luthers Psalterdruck vom Jahre 1513." In *Lutherstudien*, vol. 1 (Tübingen: Mohr, 1971), 489, has provided a very accurate theological characterization of this thesis, which, however, did not pick up on the connection of the early Tauler marginalia.
82. Tauler, *Sermones B* [2r]: "got hate sich des beraten. das er nicht lone dann seinen aigen wercken. in dem himelreych kr=net er nichts in der ewikait. Dann sein werck. vnnd nit die deinen." My translation with altered punctuation for clarity.
83. Luther, *Randbemerkungen zu Tauler* (WA 9, 99,28–29): "Quicquid habes meriti praeventrix gratia donat, Nil deus in nobis praeter sua dona coronat"; cf. the quotation in the commentary on Lombard's sentences in *Erfurter Annotationen* (AWA 9), 470,10–11.
84. Petrus Lombardus, *Sentenzen l. 2 d. 27 c. 6* (Petri Lombardi, *Sententiae in IV libros distinctae. Bd. 1*, Quaracchi 1971, 484, 14–15). Trans. after: Saint Augustine, "Letters 156–210," in *The Works of Saint Augustine*, Vol. II/3 (4th Release). Electronic Edition, ed. Boniface Ramsey, vol.

Luther could sense a harmony between Augustine and the mystic John Tauler, but he did not yet extend it to those domains which we identify with the doctrine of justification.[85]

Thus, it should not surprise us that Luther integrated mystical notes into his interpretation of Pauline texts. We see them in his treatment of the Mary-Martha pericope, long cherished as a story allegorizing active and passive forms of life:[86] he refers to it in his Tauler marginalia.[87] His lectures on Galatians, which he began on October 27, 1516 (right after finishing reading Tauler) also smack of mysticism.[88] Here, his occupation with mysticism went so far that Luther described justification in clearly mystical language when he conceived of a faith-oriented *unio*:

> Therefore, whoever believes in Christ does not only satisfy all things through Christ but also satisfies all things which he or she should do, for all things are made through one faith with Christ.[89]

This notion of becoming one with Christ apparently had deeper roots in Luther's own thought, going back to the beginning of his work with Tauler in 1515/16.[90] As I have described above, there are Augustinian-mystical

17 (Online publisher: Charlottesville, VI: InteLex Corp. 2014. Print Publisher: Hyde Park, NY: New City Press, 2004), 296, 5, 19. Cf. Gabriel Biel, *Collectorium circa quattuor libros Sententiarum. Liber secundus*, ed. Wilfridus. Werbeck and Udo Hofmann (Tübingen: Mohr Siebeck, 1984), 508,11: "cum Deus coronat nostra merita, sua coronat munera"; this passage is based on Augustine, *Epistola 194*: "Quod est ergo meritum hominis ante gratiam, quo merito percipiat gratiam, cum omne bonum meritum nostrum non in nobis faciat nisi gratia et, cum deus coronat merita nostra, nihil aliud coronet quam munera sua?" (CSEL 57, 190,12–15).

85. Wolfgang Enderlein, "Rechtfertigungslehre Und Mystik: Zum Mystischen Kern Der Rechtfertigungslehre Bei Luther." *Theologische Zeitschrift* 70, no. 2 (2014): 118–141, https://doi.org/10.5169/seals-877743 has provided a very nice presentation of the interdependence between mysticism and justification, which has given broad consideration to current literature in church-history and systematics with his conclusion being that Luther had a "mysticism of trust" (Enderlein, "Rechtfertigungslehre Und Mystik," ,141), which is, of course, oriented toward the idea of fiducia; cf. also Klaus Hägele, "Luther Strikt Mystisch Verstehen!: Ein Zwischenruf Zum Reformationsjubiläum." *Deutsches Pfarrerblatt* 113, no. 10 (Verlagshaus Speyer, 2013): 586–588.
86. Dietmar Mieth, *Die Einheit von vita activa und vita contemplativa in den deutschen Predigten und Traktaten Meister Eckharts und bei Johannes Tauler: Untersuchungen zur Struktur des christlichen Lebens. Studien zur Geschichte der katholischen Moral-theologie* (Regensburg: F. Pustet, 1969).
87. Luther, *Randbemerkungen zu Tauler* (WA 9,98,17–18).
88. WA 57/II, V.
89. Luther, *Galatervorlesung* (WA 57/II, 69,23–25): "Ideo qui in Christum credit, per Christum non solum omnibus satisfacit, sed eciam facit, ut omnia sibi debeant, cum per fidem efficiatur unum cum Christo." My translation.
90. Since the mention of Tauler in the context of Romans 8:26 took place at the end of the winter semester (see WA 56, p. XXIX), I have parted ways with Karl-Heinz Zur Mühlen, *Nos Extra Nos: Luthers Theologie Zwischen Mystik Und Scholastik.* Beiträge Zur Historischen Theologie,

notes in the references to Zerbold of Zutphen in the *Dictata super Psalterium*—and it is precisely here that we see evidence of a mystically shaped reading of Augustine, right in the *Enarrationes in Psalmos*, described by Bernard McGinn as characteristically mystical. Luther repeatedly develops the idea of Christ dwelling in the faithful through faith[91] as "*fides Christi*."[92] While summarizing Psalm 113, he argued that this interpretation was harmonious with Augustine's own explanation of that Psalm:

> However, according to Saint Augustine, this Psalm is spoken in the person of the Church and of any faithful who is snatched out of death and spiritual dangers. This does by no means contradict that whatever Christ as their head has effected and suffered shows in a spiritual sense how faith in Christ acts and suffers from sin in his faithful. And this is the moral sense.[93]

With that, it seems pointless to try to pit Augustine and mysticism against each other after all. Even before Luther had come into intensive contact with German-language mystical theology through his reading of Tauler, he had deeply engaged with Augustine—and, in fact, much of the Bible—in a monastic context profoundly shaped by mysticism.[94] He did not need

vol. 46 (Tübingen: Mohr, 1972), 97, who dates Luther's reading of Tauler to spring of 1515 (see Volker Leppin, "Johannes Tauler," in *Das Luther-Lexikon*, ed. Gury Schneider-Ludorff, [Regensburg: Bückle & Böhm, 2014], 675–676), but have chosen instead to place it in spring of 1516.

91. See Luther, *Dictata super psalterium, Glossa on Ps 23,7*: "Non enim 'Intrauit' Christus vt 'rex glorie' nisi in celum ascendendo, et in animam, que est spirituale celum, per fidem ingrediendo" / "Therefore, Christ did not 'enter' as the 'King of Glory' except ascending into heaven, and also entering through faith into the soul, which is a sort of spiritual heaven." (WA 55/1, 214, 18–20); *Scholion on Ps 71,5*: "Tamen in vtruque permanet nunc ineternum, tam scil. Deus quam homo permanens in seipso, et in fidelibus suis talis per fidem" / "Therefore he remains in both forever, as God remains, so does also the human in themselves, and [God remains] in his faithful through faith." (WA 55/2, 441, 225–226); My translations.
92. Luther, *Dictata super psalterium, Glossa on Ps 123,1*: "Ita Quilibet Christianus, licet moriatur et occidatur, tamen propter fidem Christi in ipso semper viuit" / "Therefore, any Christian can die or be killed but will live forever in Christ because of their faith in Christ." (WA 55/1, 319, 2–4). My translation.
93. Luther, *Dictata super psalterium, Glossa on Ps 113 Summarium* (WA 55/1, 753,1–754,5): "Sed secundum B. Augustinum dicitur psalmus in persona Ecclesie et cuiuslibet fidelis de morte et periculis spiritualibus erepti. Nihil autem hoc discordat, quia quecunque Christus caput egit et passus est, significant spiritualiter, quomodo fides Christi agit et patitur in suis fidelibus a peccatis. Et iste es intellectus Moralis."; An author as early as Adolf Hamel, *Der junge Luther und Augustin. Ihre Beziehungen in der Rechtfertigungslehre nach Luthers ersten Vorlesungen 1509–1518 untersucht. 1.Teil: Der Sententiar von 1509/10 und Exeget der Psalmen von 1513–15 in seinem Verhältnis zu Augustin* (Gütersloh: Bertelsmann, 1934), 203n3, has remarked that Luther based his arguments "for these thoughts on Augustine."
94. Thus, my heavy focus on Tauler while searching for Luther's mystical roots in Leppin, *Die fremde Reformation*, can be considered one-sided. Future research in this matter will have to have a broader focus and take into consideration Augustine and the *Devotio moderna*.

anyone to explain to him that Augustinianism and mysticism were a coherent, mutually affirming complex in his time.

* * *

At this point, we should summarize what we have been working on. First, a retrospective look at the two medieval traditions of mysticism and Augustinianism shows us that Augustinianism *did* impact Luther more than mysticism did[95]—as concerns *authority*, but not *content*! He referred to Augustine as a matter of fact and an academically indispensable authority, seen most poignantly in the *Disputatio contra scholasticam theologiam.*[96] At the same time, we find rhapsodic statements about the theological significance of mystical theologians in texts such as the recommendation to Spalatin[97] or the famous preface to the *Theologia deutsch*, where he says that he has not found anything comparable "in the Latin or the Greek or the Hebrew tongues"[98] to what was contained in this German text. These

95. See the critical objections from Wegener, *Frankfurter*, 85, which one can indeed accept in a modified form if the mystical roots become disproportionate, as I have done in Volker Leppin, *Die fremde Reformation: Luthers mystische Wurzeln*, 2nd ed. (Munich: C. H. Beck, 2017), (cf. however my reference to the general complex of thought from Tauler, *Augustine and Paul*, in Leppin, *Die fremde Reformation*, 25 et al.).
96. See especially the first thesis in Luther, *Disputatio contra scholasticam theologiam*: "Dicere, quod Augustinus contra haereticos excessive loquatur, Est dicere, Augustinus fere ubique mentitum esse." (WA 1, 224,7–8) / "1. To say that Augustine exaggerates in speaking against heretics is to say that Augustine tells lies almost everywhere." Trans. after: Martin Luther, "Disputation against Scholastic Theology, 1517," in *Luther's Works*, vol. 31, *Career of the Reformer*, trans. Harold J. Grimm, ed. Helmut T. Lehmann and Harold J. Grimm, 3–16 (Philadelphia, PA: Fortress Press, 1958), 9n1.
97. *Luther an Spalatin*, 14 Dezember 1516, (WA.Br 1,79 [Nr. 30,58–64]: "Gusta ergo et vide, quam suavis est dominus, ubi prius gustaris et videris, quam amarus est, quicquid nos sumus." / "Taste it and see how sweet the Lord is after you have first tried and realized how bitter is whatever we are." Trans. after: Martin Luther, "To George Spalatin. Wittenberg, December 14, 1516," in *Luther's Works*, vol. 51, *Letters I*, trans. Gottfried G. Krodel, ed. Helmut T. Lehmann and Gottfried G. Krodel, 32–36 (Philadelphia, PA: Fortress Press, 1959), 36.
98. Luther, *Vorrede zur zweiten Ausgabe der Theologia deutsch* (WA 1, 379, 10). Franz Posset, "Goldene Worte: Augustinus Und Bernhard in Der Sicht Des Alten Luther (1531–1546)," *Catholica Münster* 54, no. 3 (2000): 220–239 (Münster: Aschendorff, 2000), 220–221, has rightly pointed out similar phenomena concerning Augustine and late Luther. For example, in the Mathesius variant of a Table Talk from 1533, it reads: "Patres antiqui venerandi. Doctores et patres ut Augustinus, Hieronymus, Hilarius, Ambrosius, Bonaventura etc. venerandi sunt et magno honore habendi propter testimonia fidei, quod videmus in his ipsis ecclesiam primitivam credidisse in Iesum Christum. Bernhardus in suis praedicationibus excellit omnes alios doctores, vel ipsum etiam Augustinum, quia pulcherrime praedicavit Christum; in disputationibus vero suis plane sui dissimilis est et praedicationibus plane contrarius. Post Bernhardum secundas obtinet Bonouentura." (WA.TR 3, 295,3–10 [Nr. 3370b]); cf. Luther, *An die Ratherren*: "Sanct Bernhart ist eyn man von grossem geyst gewesen, das ich yhn schier thuerst uber alle lerer setzen, die beruembt sind, beyde allte und newe." (WA 15,40,30–32) / "St. Bernard was a man so lofty in spirit that I almost venture to set him above all other celebrated teachers both ancient

documents testify to the existential significance of mysticism for Luther's development and that he saw no difference between mysticism and his developing Augustinianism. Today, we distinguish them, but they were still one and the same for him.

Our second insight is slightly more provocative: Luther saw the commonalities in the anthropology depicted by these systems. Whoever is searching for a distinction between Reformational theology and mysticism will have to admit that it is precisely in matters of anthropology that Luther perceived mysticism to be the same as his own theology. We should add, of course, that in the case of the *Theologia deutsch*, this is not just because of sloppy or tendentious reading on the part of Luther. Instead, we must assume that Luther is a member of a long genealogy that combined Augustinian teachings on grace and anthropology with mystical spirituality. This tight connection was just the thing that made the Wittenberg movement so powerful.

and modern." (LW 45:363). A different tack is to be seen in the statement from Luther (also identified by Posset) in Luther, *Genesis-Vorlesung*: "ac antefero omnibus Bernhardum: habuit enim religionis optimam cognitionem" (WA 42, 453,41–42) / ". . . and I prefer Bernard to all the others, for he had the best knowledge of Religion[.]" (LW 2:269)—read in context, then *religio* is understood to be situated in monastic life; Cf. also the remark from Posset, "Goldene Worte," 224, that Luther occasionally did criticize Augustine in matters of justification. Ultimately, Posset reaches the provocative conclusion: "One cannot escape the impression that Luther appreciated the preacher Bernard more than he did Augustine in the later years of his life" ("Goldene Worte," 239, my translation). While this verdict may be one-sided in its own right, it might be a beneficial impulse for a research tradition which has tended to find one-sidedly Augustine in Luther.

5.

Luther's Passion Mysticism*

The scene is May 22, 1516, the feast of Corpus Christi:[1] a large procession wends its way through Eisleben. The Augustinian hermits were consecrating their new cloister. The Vicar General of the order's observant branch, John of Staupitz,[2] as well as the District Vicar, Martin, were among the celebrants. At the time, the latter still went by the last name "Luder."[3] Many years later, having changed his name to "Luther" and having become a famous renewer and reformer of the church, he reminisced about this event:

> What happened in my case? I was once terrified by the sacrament which Dr. Staupitz carried in a procession in Eisleben on the feast of Corpus Christi. I went along in the procession and wore the dress of a priest. Afterward I made a confession to Dr. Staupitz and he said to me, "Your thought is not of Christ."[4]

* I thank Herrn Jonathan Reinert for having carefully proofread my German manuscript of this chapter.

1. For more on the dating question, see Wilhelm Ernst Winterhager, "Martin Luther Und Das Amt Des Provinzialvikars in Der Reformkongregation Der Deutschen Augustiner-Eremiten," in *Vita Religiosa Im Mittelalter* (Berlin: Duncker u. Humblot, 1999), 736.
2. For more on the title of Staupitz, see Hans Schneider, "Staupitz' Ausschreiben zum Kapitel der deutschen Augustinerkongregation in Heidelberg 1518. Ein Quellenfund," in *Blätter für pfälzische Kirchengeschichte und religiöse Volkskunde* 74 (Grünstadt: Verein für Pfälzische Kirschengeschichte, 2007) 361–372, 363; Berndt Hamm, "Johann von Staupitz (ca. 1468–1524)—spätmittelalterlicher Reformer und 'Vater' der Reformation," *Archiv für Reformationsgeschichte—Archive for Reformation History* 92, no. jg (2001): 10.
3. See Bernd Moeller and Karl Stackman, *Luder, Luther, Eleutherius, Erwägungen zu Luthers Namen/ Bernd Moeller; Karl Stackmann. Nachrichten der Akademie der Wissenschaften zu Göttingen 1981*, vol. 7 (Goettingen: Vandenhoeck & Ruprecht, 1981), 7.
4. WA.TR 1,59,8–12 (Nr. 137): "Wie geschah mir? Ich erschrak ein mal fur dem sacrament, das Doctor Staupiz zu Isleben in der procession trug corporis Christi. Da gieng ich auch mit und

Today, I think we might be able to see just what was going on here with a bit more clarity than the people in Luther's time did. Two late-medieval types of spirituality collided with each other, one more exterior, focused on the Sacrament, and one more interior, searching for intermediate relation to God.[5] Corpus Christi is all about Christ, celebrating the still-valid self-sacrifice of Christ on the cross. The accent of the festival is a visual one; it has *following*—both visually and spatially—as the key external form of participation. Luther, however, did not remember finding peace for his spirit. His lasting memory was one of terror, as can be seen in the other recollection of Staupitz's counsel: "It is not Christ who is terrifying you, for Christ does not terrify but consoles."[6] Consolation comes from Christ and Christ alone, not from the despairing obsession plaguing young Luther, which in turn was shaped by the Augustinian focus on predestination. Was Luther counted among the elected or the damned? Staupitz told him to look away from this question and instead to regard Christ and especially his suffering.

> I once went and consulted my Staupitz about the sublimity of predestination. He responded to me: "Predestination is to be understood and found in the wounds of Christ and nowhere else, for it is written: Listen to him: The Father is too high [for you to reach], but the Father says: I give to you a path which leads to me, none other than Christ. Go, believe, cling to that Christ. In that way will you discover who I am in his time. We do not do that, therefore God is incomprehensible and unintelligible to us. He cannot be understood, he does not want to be conceived apart from Christ."[7]

hett ein priester kleyd an, beichtets darnach Doctor Staupiz, et dicebat mihi: Vestra cogitatio ist nit Christus." Translation after: Martin Luther, "Table Talk Recorded by Viet Dietrich, 1531–1533." Transl. after LW 54:19.

5. For more on the polarities of the late Middle Ages, cf. Volker Leppin, "Die Wittenberger Reformation und der Prozess der Transformation kultureller zu institutionellen Polaritäten," in *Transformationen: Studien zu den Wandlungsprozessen in Theologie und Frömmigkeit zwischen Spätmittelalter und Reformation* (Tübingen: Mohr Siebeck, 2015), 31–68.
6. WA.TR 2,417,14f (Nr. 2318a). My translation.
7. WA.TR 2, Nr. 1490 (112,9–16) "Ego semel conquerebar de sublimitate praedestinationis Staupitio meo. Respondit mihi: In vulneribus Christi intelligitur praedestinatio et invenitur, non alibi, quia scriptum est: Hunc audite. Der Vater ist zu hoch, sed dixit Pater: Ego dabo viam veniendi ad me, nempe Christum. Ite, credite, hengt euch an den Christum, so wirts sichs wol finden, quis sim, suo tempore. Das thun wir nicht, ideo Deus est nobis incomprehensibilis, incogitabilis; er wirt nicht begriffen, er will ungefast sein extra Christum." My translation.; cf. WA.TR 1,512,18–20 (Nr. 1017); 2,227,20–29 (Nr. 1820); 2, Nr. 2654. As Rudolf Mother ("Leiden und Weisheit in der protestantischen Mystik" in *Leiden und Weisheit in der Mystik*, ed. Bernd Jaspert [Paderborn: Bonifatus, 1992], 243–270, 249–250) has pointed out it is notable that Luther could channel 1 Cor 12:1–5 to describe the terrors of his own experience of sin with mystical-visionary imagery and to also describe the necessity of experience for full discernment: "Sed et ego novi hominem, qui has poenas saepius passum sese asseruit, brevissimo quidem temporis intervallo, sed tantas ac tam infernales, quantas nec lingua dicere nec calamus

The wounds of Christ as the real comfort. That is an idea true to the late-medieval spirituality of the passion, conveyed to us with words and in the moving images of the Man of Sorrows or the *Schmerzensmann*.[8] Luther

scribere nec inexpertus credere potest, ita ut, si perficerentur aut ad mediam horam durarent, immo ad horae decimam partem, funditus periret et ossa omnia in cinerem redigerentur. Hic deus apparet horribiliter iratus et cum eo pariter universa creatura. Tum nulla fuga, nulla consolatio, nec intus nec foris, sed omnium accusatio. Tunc plorat hunc versum: Proiectus sum a facie oculorum tuorum, nec saltem audet dicere: Domine, ne in furore tuo arguas me. In hoc momento (mirabile dictu) non potest anima credere, sese posse unquam redimi, nisi quod sentit nondum completam poenam. Est tamen aeterna, neque potest eam temporalem existimare, solum relinquitur nudum desiderium auxilii et horrendus gemitus, sed nescit unde petat auxilium. Hic est anima expansa cum Christo, ut dinumerentur omnia ossa eius, Nec est ullus angulus in ea non repletus amaritudine amarissima, horrore, pavore, tristicia, sed hiis omnibus non nisi aeternis. Et ut dem simile utcunque: si sphaera transeat super lineam rectam, quilibet punctus lineae tactus totam fert sphaeram, non tamen comprehendit totam sphaeram, Ita anima in suo puncto, dum tangitur a transeunte inundatione aeterna, nihil sentit et bibit, nisi aeternam poenam, sed non manet, iterum enim transit. Igitur si viventibus contingit illa inferorum poena, id est intolerabilis ille pavor et inconsolabilis, multo magis animarum in purgatorio videtur talis esse poena, sed continua. Et hic est ignis ille internus multo atrocior quam externus. Quod siquis ista non credit, non contendimus, sed id tantum effecimus, quod illi veniarum praecones multa dicunt, quae vel ignorant vel dubitant, nimis audacter. Magis enim credendum est expertis in hiis quam illis inexpertis." (Luther, *Resolutiones Concl. 15* [WA 1,557,33–558,18]) / "I myself 'knew a man' [2 Cor 12:2] who claimed that he had often suffered these punishments, in fact over a very brief period of time. Yet they were so great and so much like hell that no tongue could adequately express them, no pen could describe them, and one who had not himself experienced them could not believe them. And so great were they that, if they had been sustained or had lasted for half an hour, even for one tenth of an hour, he would have perished completely and all of his bones would have been reduced to ashes. At such a time God seems terribly angry, and with him the whole creation. At such a time there is no flight, no comfort, within or without, but all things accuse. At such a time as that the psalmist mourns, 'I am cut off from thy sight' [Cf. Ps 31:22], or at least he does not dare to say, 'O Lord, . . . do not chasten me in thy wrath' [Ps 6:1]. In this moment (strange to say) the soul cannot believe that it can ever be redeemed other than that the punishment is not yet completely felt. Yet the soul is eternal and is not able to think of itself as being temporal. All that remains is the stark-naked desire for help and a terrible groaning, but it does not know where to turn for help. In this instance the person is stretched out with Christ so that all his bones may be counted, and every corner of the soul is filled with the greatest bitterness, dread, trembling, and sorrow in such a manner that all these last forever. To use an example: If a ball crosses a straight line, any point of the line which is touched bears the whole weight of the ball, yet it does not embrace the whole ball. Just so the soul, at the point where it is touched by a passing eternal flood, feels and imbibes nothing except eternal punishment. Yet the punishment does not remain, for it passes over again. Therefore if that punishment of hell, that is, that unbearable and inconsolable trembling, takes hold of the living, punishment of the souls in purgatory seems to be so much greater. Moreover, that punishment for them is constant. And in this instance the inner fire is much more terrible than the outer fire. If there is anyone who does not believe that, we do not beg him to do so, but we have merely proved that these preachers of indulgences speak with too much audacity about many things of which they know nothing or else doubt. For one ought to believe those who are experienced in these matters rather than those who are inexperienced." (LW 31, 130–131)

8. John of Paltz expressed very clearly the centrality of the passion for late-medieval spirituality in Paltz, *Coelifodina*: "passio Christi est quasi summa totius sacrae scripturae" (13,11) / "The

accepted this consolation and developed it in his own way. Staupitz's gentle advice formed his understanding of Christ cast in the form of Christ's wounds. He would meditate on them for his entire life.

LATE-MEDIEVAL PASSION MYSTICISM AMONG AUGUSTINIAN HERMITS

Staupitz's passion-focused Christology as pastoral care was an expression of his deeply rooted piety. Only a few years earlier in Lent of 1512, he held a series of sermons between the March 23 and the April 7 in the city church of Salzburg on the suffering of Jesus Christ.[9] The texts have been

Passion of Christ is almost all of Holy Scripture."; cf. Berndt Hamm, *Frömmigkeitstheologie am Anfang des 16. Jahrhunderts.* Studien zu Johannes von Paltz und seinem Umkreis. Beiträge zur historischen Theologie, 0340–6741; vol. 65 (Tübingen: Mohr, 1982), footnote 262, 273. One can indeed say that meditation on the passion constituted "the heart of late medieval piety" (Graham Tomlin, "The Medieval Origins of Luther's Theology of the Cross." *Archiv für Reformationsgeschichte*, vol. 89 [Gütersloh: Gütersloher Verlagshaus, 1998], 23). Of course, the wounds of Christ as the real source of comfort goes back all the way to Bernard, who was received by Luther; see Bernhard, *Sermo 61*: "Et revera ubi tuta firmaque infirmis requies, nisi in vulneribus Salvatoris?" (Bernard von Clairvaux, "Sermo 61," in *Sämtliche Werke. Lateinisch/deutsch*, vol. 6, ed. Gerhard B. Winkler (Innsbruck: Tyrolia, 1995), 314, l.7–8. Luther used this idea precisely in his first lectures on the Psalms: "Quia secundum Bernardum anima non habet requiem nisi in vulneribus Christi." (WA 3,640,40–41; for more on this context see Theo Bell and Bernard of Clairvaux. "Divus Bernhardus: Bernhard Von Clairvaux in Martin Luthers Schriften." *Veröffentlichungen Des Instituts Für Europäische Geschichte Mainz*, vol. 148 [Mainz: Von Zabern, 1993], 60; Tomlin, *Origins 33*; Volker Stolle. "Wortglaube Und Passionsmystik: Zwei Seiten Des Lutherischen Verständnisses der Realpräsenz Im Breslauer Vorbereitungsgebet." *Lutherische Theologie Und Kirche*, vol. 25, no. 3/4 (2001): 131–156, 142–143; see Stolle, "Wortglaube Und Passionsmystik," 143–146 for the later effect of the wound-motive in Protestantism).

9. See Hamm, "Johann von Staupitz," 19; Johann von Staupitz, *Salzburger Predigten. Eine textkritische Edition,* ed. Wolfram Schneider-Lastin (Tübingen: Mohr, 1990), 5. For information on the further effect of passion mysticism for Staupitz, see Rudolf K. Markwald, ed., *A Mystic's Passion: The Spirituality of Johannes von Staupitz in his 1520 Lenten Sermons.* Renaissance and Baroque Studies and Texts, vol. 3 (New York: Lang, 1990); for more on these Lenten sermons from 1520, see Hamm, "Johann von Staupitz," 22. Between 1512 and 1520, Staupitz substituted for the preacher in the Stift of Salzburg and occasionally also preached in his later cloister, St. Peter's (Hamm, "Johann von Staupitz," 14); Franz Posset, "Preaching the Passion of Christ on the Eve of the Reformation," *Concordia Theological Quarterly* 59 (1995): 279–300, has given special prominence to the significance of these sermons in the cities for the Salzburg Lenten Sermons. Along with the spirituality particular to the Augustinian hermits, Luther's Passion spirituality had many different influences. It included the *"Rosetum"* from Johannes Mauburnus, which Luther explicitly mentioned in the context of passion meditation (Luther, *Sermo II de passione* [WA 1,341,35–36]), in tit. 21 and 22 its own sections *"Schala passionis"* and *"De passione"* (*Rosetum exercitiorum spiritualium| et sacrarum meditationum: Jn quo etiam habant materia predi=| cabilis per totum anni circulum* (Basel: Wolff, 1504), f. 141v-166r); Martin Elze, *Züge spätmittelalterlicher Frömmigkeit in Luthers Theologie*, ZThK 62 (Tübingen: Mohr

preserved thanks to an attentive nun who transcribed them.[10] They illustrate the great pains taken by Staupitz to make Christ's suffering relevant for his listeners and to help them to identify with the suffering Christ. His sermons walked their way with Christ from Bethany to the tomb.[11] He wanted to make one thing in particular clear in his twelve sermons: "All of our suffering and all of our sickness is entirely bound up in and overcome by his suffering."[12] For Staupitz, the suffering of Christ is the basis of all salvation. This, however, can only be received if the person relates to Christ by means of identification, penetrating his body and soul, and making their way to divinity, until they are ultimately made divine themselves.[13] When the believer suffers with Christ, they end up stumbling into the mercy of God.[14] They thus discover the "sweetest Jesus Christ,"[15] apart from whom there is "no consolation at all" for people.[16] In his intensive meditation on the wounds of Christ, Staupitz comes to address Christ directly: "All virtue, all grace is in you alone."[17] The *Sola gratia* of the later Reformation did not have to fight against such

Siebeck, 1965), 381–402, 390–393, has demonstrated the significance of the Rosetum, which greatly aided Luther in his understanding of *Devotio Moderna.*

10. Staupitz, *Salzburger Predigten*, 9.
11. For more information concerning the distribution of material, see Staupitz, *Predigten*, 13; Franz Posset, *The Front-Runner of the Catholic Reformation: The Life and Works of Johann von Staupitz* (Burlington, VT: Ashgate, 2003), 136. On the same page, Posset points out that Staupitz generously expanded the life of Jesus with nonbiblical material.
12. Staupitz, *Salzburger Predigten*, 25,9–10.
13. Staupitz, *Salzburger Predigten*, 25,15–26,21; Posset, *Front-Runner*, 139, has rightly emphasized that Staupitz remained skeptical toward ecstatic forms of spirituality and recommended meditation as an appropriate path. The Athanasian idea of theosis can be found repeatedly by Luther, as the Mannermaa School has made evident, see *Luther und Theosis. Vergöttlichung als Thema der abendländischen Theologie*, eds. Simo Peura and Antti Raunio, Schriften der Luther-Agricola-Gesellschaft A 25 (Helsinki: Erlangen, 1990). Remarks about how rare this statement is (see Albrecht Beutel, "Antwort und Wort. Zur Frage nach der Wirklichkeit Gottes bei Luther," in *Protestantische Konkretionen* (Tübingen: Mohr Siebeck, 1998), 28–44, 30–32) do make their relative value for understanding Luther's thought clear, but they should not lead us to avoid the task of understanding just how this idea could be integrated into Luther's thought as well.
14. Staupitz, *Salzburger Predigten*, 26,33–27,53. The idea of *compassio* had become so significant around 1500 that, according to Heike Schlie, "Exzentrische Kreuzigungen um 1500. Zur Erfindung eines bildlichen Affektraums," in *Golgotha in den Konfessionen und Medien der Frühen Neuzeit*, ed. Johann Anselm Steiger and Ulrich Heinen (Berlin: De Gruyter, 2010) (Arbeiten zur Kirchengeschichte 113), 63–91, 69, they even acquired their own artistic expression: the "eccentric crucifixions," in which "the cross and the Christ figure are both pushed to the side of the image" and create a "homogenous affective space."
15. Staupitz, *Salzburger Predigten*, 34,7. For more on the relation between sweetness and passion, see Friedrich Ohly, "Süsse Nägel der Passion: Ein Beitrag Zur Theologischen Semantik" in *Saecula Spiritalia*, vol. 21 (Baden-Baden: Koerner, 1989), especially 425–432.
16. Staupitz, *Salzburger Predigten*, 39,139.
17. Staupitz, *Salzburger Predigten*, 43,53.

late-medieval spirituality. Its way had already been paved, along with that of *Solus Christus*. Luther likely thought of just this when he recalled in 1533: "Staupitz is the one who started the teaching [of the gospel in our time]."[18] It is also obvious, however, that Staupitz is much less concerned with hamartiological anthropology than would be Luther.[19] Staupitz sees the human person as sinful contra to Christ, but by facing Christ, all of their sins are transferred to him. Interestingly, Staupitz avoids the second person in these statements, restricting himself to the third person or even "quoting" Christ's own words directly (placing his theology into Christ's mouth).[20] The listeners are invited primarily to self-identify with Christ. Identification with the sinful person is briefly hinted at but never fully developed. The decisive moment occurs when God descends in human form and appears as an appeal to identification: "Look my Lords, he is lying here as a human being in the pains of death."[21]

Staupitz was not alone in his order when he preached such a methodological spirituality of the passion. He was joined by John of Paltz, who, in 1490 at the request of brothers Friedrich the Wise and John the Steadfast[22] (who would become the consecutive princes of Luther), collected several sermons into the "*himmlische Fundgrube*" (*Heavenly Treasure*). By 1521, its printings numbered eighteen in Early Modern German and three in Low German[23] (excluding the version from 1501/2[24] with its extensive passages in Latin), thus being counted among the "most popular devotional text[s] of the Late Middle Ages."[25] Two-thirds of the text consists of passion meditation[26] and it also contained passages about blasphemy, an *ars moriendi,* and a depiction of final unction.[27] Evidently it is supposed

18. WA.TR 1,245,11–12 (Nr. 526): "Staupicius hat die doctrinam angefangen." Translation after: Martin Luther, "Table Talk Recorded by Viet Dietrich, 1531–1533." In *Luther's Works*, vol. 54, *Table Talk*, trans. John W. Doberstein, ed. Helmut T. Lehmann and Theodore G. Tappert, 3–115 (Philadelphia, PA: Fortress Press, 1967), 97n245.
19. Cf. Volker Leppin, "Aristotelisierung, Immediatisierung Und Radikalisierung: Transformationen Der Sündenlehre Von Thomas Von Aquin Bis Martin Luther." In *Transformationen* (Mohr Siebeck: Tübingen, 2018), 323–332.
20. Staupitz, *Salzburger Predigten*, 43,55–56. 59–60
21. Staupitz, *Salzburger Predigten*, 45,110–111: "Secht an meinen herren, da ligt er als ain mensch in todesnötten!" My translation.
22. See the dedicatory writing to both in Paltz, *Opuscula*, 202, 1–15; cf. Johannes von Paltz, *Werke. Bd. 3: Opuscula* (Berlin: De Gruyter, 1989), 158; Hamm, *Frömmigkeitstheologie*, 112.
23. Paltz, *Opuscula*, 3, 170–183.
24. Johannes von Paltz, *vol. / Band 1: Coelifodina, vol.2 Spätmittelalter und Reformation*, ed. Christoph Burger and Friedhelm Stasch, preface by Heiko A. Oberman (Berlin: De Gruyter, 1983).
25. Hamm, *Frömmigkeitstheologie*, 111. My translation.
26. For more on the significance of the passion for Paltz see Hamm, *Frömmigkeitstheologie*, 262.
27. For more on the content, see Paltz, *Opuscula*, 164.

to help people who are plagued by their impending death. Paltz vividly portrays self-identification with Christ and summarizes:

> There is nothing which is more useful for a healthy body, protecting the soul or honor, for overcoming the world and the flesh and the evil spirit and to protect against all dangers of the body and soul than is meditation on the Passion of Christ.[28]

The concept of the titular "Fundgrube," the heavenly treasure, is really derived from mining, with the connotation of *striking* gold.[29] The soul must pass through many "tunnels" or passages before it ends up with Christ. The first layer is that of the five wounds of Christ.[30] In his introduction, Paltz recommends meditating on a crucifix and taking refuge "with your thoughts in the holy five wounds, especially that in His side."[31] This meditation should then lead into a prayer with the Lord's Prayer repeated many times, deepening the soul's intimacy with Christ.[32] The supplicant places their wicked works and thoughts into the negative, left side of the body. The right side takes on the good thoughts and works. According to the standard paradigm of late-medieval spirituality, the good works were presented both as an act of thanks as well to receive Christ's "confirmation" of them.[33] The meditator reaches their true goal, however, only when they plunge into the side wound with the request "that you would open my heart and inflame it in your body."[34] The next layer varies this theme a bit, focusing on the *beating* of Christ and emphasizing the relation of guilt between the faithful and Christ—after thanking the first blow that hits Christ, it requests forgiveness for sins.[35] This is then taken

28. Paltz, *Opuscula*, 203,11–14: "Auch ist kein nutzer ding zu gesuntheit des leibes, zu bewarunge der sele und der ere, zu uberwindung der welt und des fleisch und des bosen geistes und vor aller ferlichkeit leibs und sele als die betrachtung des leidens Christi."
29. Hamm, *Frömmigkeitstheologie*, 113.
30. Paltz, *Opuscula*, 204,4f.
31. Paltz, *Opuscula*, 205,1–2. Hamm, *Frömmigkeitstheologie*, 263, correctly points out that Paltz clearly understood regarding something not merely as a consequence but at least also a preparation for the effect of God's grace; see especially Paltz, *Opuscula*, 203,6–8: "Darzu als man aus vil leren mag versten, so ist kein nutzer ding, guts hult zu erwerben zu gunst der muter gots und aller heiligen und aller engel, dann die betrachtung ds heiligen leidn Cristi." Hamm has identified this as not only a difference to Luther but also to Staupitz.
32. Paltz, *Opuscula*, 205,9–206,5.
33. Paltz, *Opuscula*, 205,18–20: "Darnach danke ich dir des rechten fuß, den du hast lassen durch graben. Ich opher dir all mein gute werk und begird darein und dank dir der und bitte dich, das du die wellest bestetigen." ("Therefore, I thank you for your right foot which you permitted to be pierced through. I offer to you into it all of my good works and my desires and thank you for it and ask that you would confirm them.") My translation.
34. Paltz, *Opuscula*, 205,22–23.
35. Paltz, *Opuscula*, 207,3–4.

up by the third "passage" through the Seven Words of Christ from the cross, especially the phrase (Luke 23:34): "Father, forgive them; for they do not know what they are doing." The supplicant is, of course, expected to apply these words entirely to themself.[36] Paltz emphasizes counter-identification more than Staupitz does, encouraging the supplicant sinner to focus on being the *counterpart* to Christ and the source of his suffering, not so much to identify *with* him. Nevertheless, much like Staupitz, the Christological center is found in the last of the Seven Words: "Father, into your hands I commend my spirit." Here, the supplicant recasts these words as: "O dear Lord Jesus, into your hand I commend my body and soul, goods and honor and especially my spirit 'at my final hour.'"[37] This moment of counter-identification was an established part of the world of late-medieval piety, as the "Pomegranate," a pseudonymous collection of sermons (later attributed to Geilers of Kaysersberg) demonstrates:

> Lift up the inner eyes of your reason and of your soul's power, perceive, look at Jesus Christ your spouse hanging in suffering on the Cross in such great, bitter pains and sufferings with outstretched arms, with an inclined head, with weeping eyes, with an opened heart, with a fearful and sad face, his beautiful, tender body all torn up, a pleasing offering to God his heavenly Father for the sake of the world's sins. Oh regard who he is and consider whose will it was that he died. It is the innocent little lamb that carries all of the world's sins. And you, poor creature, are a cause of his suffering, [so] consider how and where this pertains [to you].[38]

For Paltz, the supplications lead into the next passage, which focused on Christ's words to John and to Mary respectively:[39] "Here is your mother," and "Woman, here is your son" (John 19:26–27). It then shifts

36. Paltz, *Opuscula*, 208,8–12.
37. Paltz, *Opuscula,* 210,2–4.
38. *Das buch Granatapfel.* im la-| tein genant Malogranatus . . . Merers teyls gepredigt durch den hoch-| gelerten doctor Johannem Geyler vonn Keysersberg etc., Straßburg: Johann Knobloch 1516, D 5[r]: "Heb vff die innwendigen augen deiner vernunfft vnnd deiner sel krefft / nym wol war / blick an Jesum cristum deinen gemahel hangen i(merlich an dem creütz in grossem bittern schmertzen vnnd leyden / mit vßgespannen armen / mit geneygtem haupt / mit weinenden augen / mit vffgethnem hertzen / mit angstlicher vnnd trauriger geb(rd / sein sch=ner zarter leyb aller zerrissen / ein wolgefelligs opffer got seinem hymlischen vatter vmmb aller welt sünd. Eya vernym wer er sey, vnnd bedenck durch wes willen er gestorben sey. Es ist dz vnschuldig lemlein / dz aller welt sünd vff im getragen hat. Vnd du arme creatur ein vrsach gewesen bist seines sterbens / vnnd gedenck wo dz hin treff." My translation.
39. This is not the right place to explore the meaning of Mary in passion mysticism. It can be seen in Suso's *Hundred Regards* (see Seuse, *Deutsche Schriften,* 318,24–319,20; 322,7–20) as well as in the *stabbat Mater*, popular since the thriteenth century, which leads the faithful into identification with Mary and subsequently to the suffering Christ (see Schlie, *Kreuzigungen*, 69–71).

to a brief supplication to Mary[40] which foreshadows the fourth passage of the "*Von der muter gots kreuz stehen*" / *Stabat mater.*[41] The fifth passage returns to a holistic look at the suffering of Christ, "that a person can discern themself day and night in the suffering of Christ, be they clerical or layperson."[42] The meditative guide takes the person through a whole day (corresponding to the office prayers of a monk) from the Last Supper through the Garden of Gethsemane, the trial, and the death on the cross.[43] Thus, Christ's suffering shapes Christian everyday life in such a way that oscillates between the distance of the supplicant and the mystical nearness of the passages through Christ's suffering. The final passage for Paltz is the Book of Life, which is presented open on the cross which serves as a lectern.[44] Here, Paltz challenges his readers to try to understand a deeper theological level, attempting to use the form of the cross to explain the Trinity and the doctrine of cardinal virtues.[45]

As is well known, these guidebooks did not always line up with the practiced spirituality of the time. In fact, we might even deduce from the sheer variety of the approaches that Paltz may have assumed that not everything was going to be carried out. He makes an explicit distinction

40. Paltz, *Opuscula,* 208,22–209,5.
41. Paltz, *Opuscula,* 210,5.
42. Paltz, *Opuscula,* 218,12–13.
43. Paltz, *Opuscula,* 218–227. In his investigations into the effect of Suso's *Hundred Regards* in the third part of the *Little Book of Eternal Truth,* (Seuse, *Deutsche Schriften,* 314–322) in various religious milieus, especially among the *mulieres religiosae,* José van Aelst, "Vruchten Van De Passie: De Laatmiddeleeuwse Passieliteratuur Verkend Aan De Hand Van Suso's "Honderd Artikelen." In *Middeleeuwse Studies En Bronnen,* 129 (Hilversum: Verloren, 2011), 23–25, 40, emphasizes the celebration of the Eucharist as the daily actualization of the Passion. The portrayal from Paltz points out that this does not exhaust all of the possibilities of daily *Passion memoria.* Suso's regards constitute their own basic text for late-medieval Passion mysticism: He starts with Jesus walking through the Garden of Gethsemane and his arrest and trial (Seuse, *Deutsche Schriften,* 315,1–22), before working through every step of his suffering in an identificatory fashion. see for example Seuse, *Deutsche Schriften,* 316,33–317,2: "Ach, minneklicher herre, also beger ich, daz ich in lieb und in leide unbeweglich zů dir werde genegelt, alles min vermugen liebes und sele an din krúz zerspennet, min vernunft und min begirde zů dir geheftet." ("Oh dear Lord, I desire that I would be nailed to your body and suffering, that all of my bodily and spiritual faculties be suspended on your cross, that my reason and desire are attached to you.") My translation. These texts enjoyed an enormous reception, in translation and allegory (see the overview provided by van Aelst, Vruchten, 40) and thus shaped a broad current of late-medieval Passion mysticism. For more on the effect of Suso on the preacher Stephan Fridolin (who was especially active among the Clarissen), see Petra Seegets, *Passionstheologie und Passionsfrömmigkeit im ausgehenden Mittelalter: der Nürnberger Franziskaner Stephan Fridolin (gest. 1498) zwischen Kloster und Stadt,* Spätmittelalter und Reformation 10 (Tübingen: Mohr Siebeck, 1998), 107–108.
44. Paltz, *Opuscula,* 228–236.
45. Paltz, *Opuscula,* 230,6–231,8.

between the monks and the laypersons and admits that it is enough for the latter if they contemplate the Last Supper before going to sleep and the rest of the passion after waking up.[46] The monks, however, *were* to meditate throughout the day with the office prayers. Perhaps the great plentitude of instructions indicates that his readers would only practice what suited their fancy. In any case, it still testifies to the fact that going deeper into the suffering of Christ was firmly anchored in the practiced faith around 1500. Paltz uses the visual world of the late Middle Ages with his references to the crucifix and the general form of the cross to support meditation, which only further emphasizes this passion-focus in the sixteenth century. Cruciform spirituality did not yet exclude the world of the saints. That tension would emerge with the Reformation's *Solus Christus*. But medieval spirituality does make the focus of faith a simultaneous identifying and counter-identifying relation to Christ. The believing person experiences themself in their sinfulness as the cause of Christ's suffering, but also locates in it the path to their salvation, and is consequently taken into, and identifies themselves with, the suffering: "I ask of you that you would forgive me all my sins which I have committed with my head, and that you would give me everything which you have intended with the Crown of Thorns[,] and that you would crown me with your grace."[47]

Martin Luther grew up in this religious world, which informed not only the counsel he received from Staupitz as a father confessor but also the passion-focused consolation that he is said to have given to another before the Corpus Christi procession we mentioned at the beginning of this chapter. On April 15, 1516, Luther wrote to Georg Leiffer, an Augustinian brother in Erfurt, advising him to consider in the midst of his temptations that the cross of Christ is honored abundantly simply because it was touched by Jesus Christ. Therefore, injustices, persecutions, and suffering (points of common experience with Christ) must be regarded all the more as "*sanctissimae. . . reliquiae*" (most sacred relics).[48]

We can see this same passion-focus some years earlier in his first lectures on the Psalms. Already in the 1513 printed copy of the Psalms which he would use for his lectures,[49] he interpreted the entirety of Psalm 6 as "a prayer of Christ for his sufferings."[50] The Christological interpretation

46. Paltz, *Opuscula,* 227,16–20.
47. Paltz, *Opuscula*, 207,4–6 (Commas added to help better convey the sentence structure).
48. *Luther an Georg Leiffer, 15. April 1516* (WA.Br 1,37–8 [Nr. 12,15–34]). My translation.
49. Cf. Gerhard Ebeling, "Luthers Psalterdruck vom Jahre 1513," in *Lutherstudien*, vol. 1, (Tübingen: Mohr, 1971), 69–131.
50. Luther, *Dictata super Psalterium* (WA 55/I,38,3–4). *"oratio Christi pro suis passionibus"* My translation.

of the Psalm is thus legitimized by the fact that Christ used verse 9 in Matthew 7:23.[51] Luther read it as if he heard it directly from the mouth of Christ: any Christian—monk or a layperson—praying it spoke and prayed it with Christ and identified with his suffering.[52] This is the hermeneutic which allows Luther to interpret the Psalm as the prayer spoken by Christ in Gethsemane. Luther directly references Psalm 6:7 to Luke 22,[53] likely thinking about verses 39–46.[54] The participation of the faithful, however, occurs in the mode of counter-identification as we saw with Paltz, with the faithful discerning themselves as the cause of Christ's suffering who is burdened with "your sins and those of the whole world."[55] As the source of Christ's suffering, the faithful is drawn into the passion. They weep with the weeping Christ (v. 7).[56] In his explanation of Psalm 38 (37 Vg.), where it reads "a complaint of our mediator in [his] passion for the sake of our sins,"[57] Luther explains the hermeneutical basis for his process in a very similar fashion:

> For according to the Apostle, Christus "became" "cursed for us," [cf. Gal 3] and "sin" [cf. 2 Cor 5], and "he carries" our "sins" [cf. Isa 53]. Therefore, this Psalm is spoken in his person in whom "he remembers" and he [Jesus] carries our sins for us before God the Father and desires his liberation (i.e., ours) for his sake and in him. Therefore, whoever wants to pray this Psalm in a fruitful manner should not pray it in themself but in Christ and should also hear him praying and thereby will connect their affects to him and will say "Amen."[58]

51. Luther, *Adnotationes Quincuplici Psalterio adscriptae* (WA 4,474,7f).
52. See Volker Leppin, "Exegese und reformatorische Theologie: Beobachtungen zur Deutung des Alten Testaments bei Luther," in *Ex Oriente Lux: Studien Zur Theologie Des Alten Testaments; Festschrift Für Rüdiger Lux Zum 65. Geburtstag*, ed. Angelika Berlejung, Rüdiger Lux, and Raik Heckl, Arbeiten Zur Bibel Und Ihrer Geschichte 39 (Leipzig: Evangelische Verlagsanstalt, 2012), 687–710.
53. Luther, *Dictata super Psalterium* (WA 55/I,42,13–14).
54. This is certainly the object of the explanation of vol. 4 through "*tristis vsque ad mortem*" / "sorrowed to the point of death" (Luther, *Dictata super Psalterium* [WA 55/I,42,4]), a word-for-word citation from Mark 14:34 or Matthew 26:38.
55. Luther, *Dictata super Psalterium* (WA 55/I,40,4–10): "*peccatis tuis et totius mundi*" My translation.
56. Luther, *Dictata super Psalterium* (WA 55/I,40,9–10).
57. Luther, *Dictata super Psalterium* (WA 55/I,328): "*querela mediatoris nostri in passione propter peccata nostra.*" My translation.
58. Luther, *Dictata super Psalterium* (WA 55/I,328–329n3,1–8): "Quia secundum Apostolum Christus 'factus' est 'pro nobis maledictum', Galatians 3, et 'peccatum', 2 Corinthians 5, Et 'peccata' nostra 'ipse tulit' Esaie 53., Ideo hic Psalmus in persona eius dicitur, in quo 'commemorat' et confitetur pro nobis Deo patri peccata nostra et querit liberationem sui, i.e., nostram per ipsum et in ipso. Ideo quicunque vult illum Psalmum fructuose orare, debet eum non in se, Sed in Christo orare et tanquam eum audire orantem, et sic ei suum adiungere affectum et dicere Amen." My translation.

We can draw one important conclusion from all this: By the time Staupitz told Luther to meditate on the wounds of the savior in Eisleben, Luther had been deeply infused with Passion-mysticism for quite some time.

He would deepen said mysticism while reading John Tauler in 1515 or 1516.[59] In a lengthy passage, Luther developed the idea that God works in us by destroying everything in us "*per crucem et passiones*"[60] (by means of the cross and suffering), and added that it is a typical form of human idiocy to choose the form of suffering themselves instead of expecting it from God "*mera fide*" (purely by faith).[61] Here, suffering has a central function for the attainment of salvation and corresponds to a purity of faith made evident by its passivity and acceptance. Luther would later write of a "*nuda fides in deum*" (a naked faith in God).[62] While occupied with late-medieval devotional literature, Luther had already reached a deeper understanding of the soteriological significance of Christ's suffering when he received his counsel from Staupitz. Staupitz reinforced Luther's orientation more than providing it. In any case, one can speak of Luther on the eve of the great Reformational events of 1517 as a monk who deeply resonated with late-medieval passion-mysticism and knew how to appropriate it for his own theological-existential purposes.

THE DEVELOPMENT OF PASSION-MYSTICISM IN THE EARLY STAGES OF THE REFORMATIONAL MOVEMENT

In March or April of 1517,[63] about half a year before the *95 Theses*, Luther published an interpretation of the seven penitential Psalms, which naturally included an explanation of Psalm 6. He does not stress the point about a prophet being the speaker of the Psalms,[64] but does persist in the idea that the sinful speaker of the Psalm ultimately speaks "through Christ."[65] Thus,

59. For more on the difficulties of dating this (it certainly took place during the *Lectures on the Romans*), see Leif Grane, *Modus loquendi theologicus: Luthers Kampf um die Erneuerung der Theologie (1515–1518)* (Leiden: Brill, 1975), 121–122; Steven E. Ozment, *Homo Spiritualis: A Comparative Study of the Anthropology of Johannes Tauler, Jean Gerson and Martin Luther (1509–16) in the Context of Their Theological Thought* (Leiden: Brill, 1969), 185; Karl-Heinz Zur Mühlen, *Nos Extra Nos: Luthers Theologie Zwischen Mystik Und Scholastik. Beiträge Zur Historischen Theologie*, vol. 46 (Tübingen: Mohr, 1972), 97.

60. Luther, *Randbemerkungen zu Tauler* (WA 9,102,11).

61. Luther, *Randbemerkungen zu Tauler* (WA 9,102,11–16).

62. Luther, *Randbemerkungen zu Tauler* (WA 9,102,35–36).

63. WA 1,155.

64. Luther, *Sieben Bußpsalmen* (WA 1,159,18–19); for the further development during the second lectures on the Psalms, see Leppin, "Exegese und reformatorische Theologie," 696–698.

65. Luther, *Sieben Bußpsalmen* (WA 1,159,33).

counter-identification gets subsumed by self-identification with Christ. Luther interprets the psalmist's plea that God would return, as the mutual relation of an internal rejection of God, and the experience of God's own consolation.[66] The turn is made when the external person is destroyed. Luther describes this person with a high degree of identification as the crucified one:

> However, it only is resurrected in the crucified, dead old person. The external ways of the person, regardless of their worldliness or the appearance of holiness, will all be destroyed and only the best will remain, as Christ says [cf. Matt 5]: Blessed are those who mourn and hunger and thirst for justice, for this life will be no different than hatred for the old person and a search and longing for the life in the new person.[67]

Luther's first-ever publication, published just a few months earlier, makes clear that he was thinking about a mystical process of transformation. The first edition of the *Theologia deutsch* came out with Luther as editor in 1516.[68] The title page describes its central contents as "what is Adam's child and what is God's child."[69] The image on the title page makes the Christological and staurological connections more than obvious.[70] It shows a small crucifixion group, the soldiers (Longinus is discernable by his lance) on one side, and Jesus's mother Mary with John on the other (see figure 5.1). Below the cross, Mary Magdalene kneels before a skull symbolizing Adam and Golgotha. Adam and Christ explain each other,

66. Luther, *Sieben Bußpsalmen* (WA 1,161,9–14). This is where we see the structure of destruction and reconstruction which was extensive in late-medieval mysticism and which Luther gradually transformed into Law and Gospel (see Volker Leppin, "Transformationen spätmittelalterlicher Mystik bei Luther," in *Transformationen*, 399–417, 408–412)—in the *Seven Penitential Psalms*, Luther is still moving within the thought structures of the late-medieval mystics.
67. Luther, *Sieben Bußpsalmen* (WA 1,162,36–163,5): "Sundern es steet nur yn eynem creutzigen und todten des alten menschen, alßo das des eußern menschen wandel, es sey nach der werlt adder nach der scheynend heyligkeyt soll zu nichte werden, und alleyne das besten, [Matt 5] das Christus sagt, Selig seyn die do weynend und hungern und dursten nach der gerechtigkeit, dan ditz leben soll nit anders seyn, dan ein haß uber den alten menschen und eyn suchen und vorlangen des lebens yn dem newen menschen."
68. For more on this see: Andreas Zecherle, "Die 'Theologia Deutsch.' Ein spätmittelalterlicher mystischer Traktat," in *Gottes Nähe unmittelbar erfahren: Mystik im Mittelalter und bei Martin Luther, Spätmittelalter und Reformation neue Reihe*, vol. 36, ed. Berndt Hamm and Volker Leppin, in collaboration with Heidrun Munzert (Tübingen: Mohr Siebeck, 2007), 1–95. In approximately the same time as the publication of the *Theologia deutsch*, there are two short Passion meditations also attributed to Luther (Luther, *Passionsbetrachtungen* [WA 59,211–212]).
69. WA 1,153.
70. Eyn geystlich edles Buchleynn.| von rechter vnderscheyd | vnd vorstand. was der | alt vnnd new mensche sey. Was Adams | vnnd was gottis kind sey. vnd wie Adam | ynn vns sterben vnnd Christus | ersteen sall. Wittenberg: Rhau-Grunenberg, 1516 (VD 16 T 890).

Eyn geyſtlich edles Buchleynn:
von rechter vnderſcheyd
vnd vorſtand. was der
alt vñ new menſche ſey. Was Adams
vñ was gottis kind ſey. vñ wie Adã
ynn vns ſterben vnnd Chriſtus
erſteen ſall.

Figure 5.1 Title Page from First Edition of *Theologia Deutsch.*

the old and the new creation are made visible in this mystical text. This is the idea which Luther adopts in his explanation of the seven penitential psalms. He uses this mystical-identificatory scheme to sketch out a model of living "according to the cross of Christ,"[71] which he places in remarkable contrast to other forms of living:

> For it has never had, nor has, nor will have an enemy other than those who want to be right and desire to destroy the just for the sake of justice, living with great efforts to enjoy peace, quietness, honor, comfort and prosperity and must never experience the cross or a disquieting life. They are no different from the other crude sinners—some search for satisfaction in their lust for things of the flesh, others search for the same satisfaction in spiritual goods, wisdom, reason, and piety. The deeper and more superfluous they go into this desire for such things, the more they sin in the flesh.[72]

The cross invites identification, but it also distinguishes two ways of living. Luther rejects the life of "honor," a passion-mystical move which Luther would repeat at the Heidelberg Disputation a year later where he would distinguish between a theology of glory and a theology of the cross.[73] For Reformation studies, this is an important and humbling result; the search for Luther's genuine innovations has tended to oversee the late-medieval background of passion mysticism which forms such basic decisions like this one. When we read Luther in the lineage of Tauler, then we see him juxtaposing human works and suffering:

> This is clear: He who does not know Christ does not know God hidden in suffering. Therefore he prefers works to suffering, glory to the cross,

71. Luther, *Sieben Bußpsalmen* (WA 1,164,12–13).
72. Luther, *Sieben Bußpsalmen* (WA 1,164,33–165,4): "dan sie hat nach nie ander feynd gehabt, nach hat, nach haben wirt, dan die do recht haben wollen, und umb ungerechtickeyt willen vormeynen die gerechten zuvortilgen, ßo sie doch mit allem fleyße also leben, das sie nur yn ruge, frid, ehr, gemach, gnugde, und nit ym creutze ader unruge leben muegen, und von den andern groben sundern keyn ander underscheid tragen, dan das jhene in fleyschlichen dingen lust suchen, und diße yn yren geistlichen gutern, weyßheyt unnd vornunfft und frumickeyt, ja hoffertiger und tiffer yn lust der selben stecken, dan die groben sunder ym fleysch." My translation.
73. Luther, *Heidelberger Disputation* 21 (WA 1,354,21–22). Now the point made by Mihreteab Gebrehiiwet, *Christ-Mysticism in the theology and Spirituality of Martin Luther*, Diss. Chicago 1977, 125, *is* justifiable that Luther turns his theology against Pseudo-Dionysius the Areopagite because of the speculative character of the latter's theology. But the main thrust of the argumentation (which Gebrehiiwet directly connects to the *Heidelberg Disputation*) is less directed to a specific form of mysticism as it is toward the scholastic epistemological path against a broader mystical background (cf. in much the same vein Mohr, Leiden 251. 253; the mystical background is also identified by Dennis Ngien, *The Suffering of God According to Martin Luther's 'Theologia Crucis,'* (New York: Lang, 1995) [American University Studies VII, 181], 27–35).

> strength to weakness, wisdom to folly, and, in general, good to evil. These are the people whom the apostle calls "enemies of the cross and of Christ" [Phil 3:18].[74]

Luther is riffing on Philippians 3:18, which calls for a new way of living and opens up the ethical horizon that Luther spoke of in his explanation of the seven penitential psalms. The joy in the "things of the flesh" which he talks about there also finds its correspondence in Philippians 3:19: "their God is the belly." There is a direct path from the passion-mystical explanations of Psalm 6 in the lectures on the Psalms via the explanation of the seven penitential psalms to the Heidelberg Disputation. And that path leads through a forest of late-medieval passion theology and mysticism.[75]

At right about the same time, in 1518, Luther wrote two sermons about the Passion in which he developed the idea of Christ as *sacramentum et exemplum*,[76] and placed a special accent on the sacramental character. As the believer discovers themselves in and through Christ, it is not enough to simply feel compassion for Christ's suffering.[77] One must discern the wounds of Christ in the wounds of one's own soul:[78] "It is not necessary for the human person to mourn about Christ in His Passion but rather in

74. Luther, *Heidelberger Disputation 21 probatio* (WA 1,362,23–26): "Patet, quia dum ignorat Christum, ignorat Deum absconditum in passionibus. Ideo praefert opera passionibus et gloriam cruci, potentiam infirmitati, sapientiam stulticiae, et universaliter bonum malo. Tales sunt quos Apostolus vocat Inimicos crucis Christi." Trans. after LW 31:53.
75. For more on the corresponding classification of Staupitz, cf. Hamm, "Johann von Staupitz," 16; for more on the term "Frömmigkeitstheologie" see Berndt Hamm, "Was ist Frömmigkeitstheologie? Überlegungen zum 14. bis 16. Jahrhundert," in *Praxis Pietatis: Beiträge zu Theologie und Frömmigkeit in der frühen Neuzeit*, ed. Wolfgang Sommer, Hans-Jörg Nieden, Marcel Nieden, and Elke Axmacher (Stuttgart: Kohlhammer, 1999), 9–45.
76. Luther, *Sermo I de passione / Quomodo Christi passio sit consideranda* (WA 1,337,14; 339,17–21; Martin Elze, "Das Verständnis der Passion Jesu im ausgehenden Mittelalter und bei Luther," in *Geist und Geschichte der Reformation: Festgabe Hanns Rückert zum 65. Geburtstag*, ed. Heinz Liebing and Klaus Scholder (Berlin: De Gruyter, 1966), 127–151, 135, has revealed that these texts are not notes taken during a sermon but rather a copy of Luther's own preparatory notes; for more on this pairing of concepts, cf. Eberhard Jüngel, *Das Opfer Jesu Christi Als Sacramentum Et Exemplum* (Stuttgart: Diakonie-Verlag d. Gustav Werner Stiftung zum Bruderhaus, 1986/87), 6–25; Magnus Löhrer, "Das augustinische Binom 'Sacramentum et exemplum' und 'die Unterscheidung des Christlichen' bei Gerhard Ebeling und Eberhard Jüngel," in *Mysterium Christi: Symbolgegenwart und theologische Bedeutung: Festschrift für Basil Studer*, ed. Magnus Löhrer and Elmar Salmann (Rome: Pontificio Ateneo S. Anselmo, 1995), 377–403.
77. Luther, *Sermo I de passione* (WA 1,338,12–14). Hamm, *Frömmigkeitstheologie*, 263, also sees a separation from this *compassio*-concept as early as Paltz and Staupitz. It would thus be a grave reduction to interpret this as a distinguishing feature of Luther in comparison to medieval spirituality. Elze, *Verständnis*, 143, Sees this very markedly in Luther's *Sermones De passione* in WA 1,336–345
78. Luther, *Sermo I de passione* (WA 1,338,37–39).

Christ."[79] Thus, Luther can interpret the events of the passion allegorically: Christ represents the *old Adam* who is subjected to God's judgment,[80] from which only faith can help.[81] The meditation on this event is the best path for Christians and must have priority over all other prayers and works.[82]

Luther did not publish these sermons immediately, but in April 1519[83] he did publish a classical tract on passion mysticism: the "*Sermon von der Betrachtung des Leidens Christi*" ("Meditation on Christ's Passion"). Luther put the word "Sermon" in the title, which indicates that he understood it to be preached. However, we have no evidence that it actually was preached, and given Luther's announcement, it likely was not.[84] Luther had recently discovered the effect of having a sermon published and the success of the text confirms Bernd Moeller's thesis that Luther started his writing career with devotional literature.[85] The editors of the Weimar Edition rightly contend about the sermon: "The frequent reprintings of the text testify to how much he handled the needs of the people."[86] Twenty-two editions had appeared by 1524 and it was also translated into Latin.[87] The first edition used exactly the same sort of image as Luther's previous text (see figure 5.2). It showed a Golgotha scene including the skull of Adam at the foot of the cross, but now entirely focused on the figures of Mary and John.[88] The Nurnberg reprint, which appeared very soon thereafter,

79. Luther, *Quomodo Christi passio sit consideranda* (WA 1,339,16–17): "Homini non est necessarium, ut Christum in ipsius passione[m] deploret, sed maghis seipsum in Christo." This passage is not actually part of the sermon but is rather from a small text titled "Quomodo Christi passio sit consideranda," which is possibly understood as "a written summary of the just-heard sermon." (WA 1,335, my translation).
80. Luther, *Sermo I de passione* (WA 1,339,2–4). An interesting take on the phenomenon of the allegorical sermon has been provided by Wiesenhütter, *Passion Christi 32*: "As much as the Protestant sermon fought against the allegorical travesty of the Middle Ages and sought for a textual, objective explanation, the allegorical and typological interpretation remains one of its most essential basic features." My translation.
81. Luther, *Sermo I de passione* (WA 1,339,12–14).
82. Luther, *Sermo II de passione* (WA 1,342,9–16).
83. WA 2,130.
84. In a letter to Spalatin from 13 March, Luther mentions that he has the sermon *"in mente"* (*Luther an Spalatin, 13. März 1519* [WA.Br 1,350 {Nr. 161,26}]), on April 5 he sent the text to Spalatin (*Luther an Spalatin, 5. April 1519* [WA.Br 1,367 {Nr. 166,9–10}]):
85. Bernd Moeller, "Das Berühmtwerden Luthers," in *Luther-Rezeption. Kirchenhistorische Aufsätze zur Reformationsgeschichte*, ed. Johannes Schilling, (Göttingen: Vandenhoeck & Ruprecht, 2001), 23–24.
86. WA 2,130. My translation.
87. WA 2,130–135.
88. Eyn Sermon von der Betrach | tung des heyligen leydens | Christi D. Martini Luther zu | Wittenberg: Rhau-Grunenberg 1519 (VD 16 L 6519). The printing shop Rhau-Grunenberg had already published the *Theologia deutsch*. Their press had been set up close to the Augustinian cloister, which is why it was common parlance to speak of a text from the Augustinians (cf.

Eyn Sermon von der Betrach-
tung des heyligen leydens
Christi D. Martini Luther zu
Wittenberg.

Figure 5.2 Title page from Luther's 1519 *Meditation on Christ's Passion.*

adopted the idea of Christ-meditation all the more intensely with an *ecce Homo* type (see figure 5.3): Christ sitting on a stone surrounded by the arms of Christ.[89] The "needs of the people" follows the patterns of late-medieval piety; Luther only undertakes a light transformation of the contemporary culture, picking up the present "needs" and leading them to a solution that radically emphasized the emptiness of all human works.

At the beginning of the Meditation, Luther listed out the forms of piety which he approved of and those of which he did not. In so doing, he placed himself right on the boundary between external and internal spirituality.[90] He condemned the sort of passion meditation that culminated in a deep hatred of the Jews and Judas as well as those who sought to find personal advantage by using the images of the passion like magic charms.[91] Much in line with the sermons of the previous year, he rejected those who wailed on about Christ's suffering[92] without giving the slightest regard to their own guilt,[93] hoping that hours-long masses might be considered a worthy work.[94] This last group lumps together several different societal strands,

for more on this Bernd Moeller, "Thesenanschläge," in *Luthers Thesenanschlag—Faktum oder Fiktion, Schriften Der Luthergedenkstätten In Sachsen-anhalt*, ed. Joachim Ott and Martin Treu (Leipzig: Evangelische Verlagsanstalt, 2008), 9–31, 25)—which means conversely that it is likely that Luther's personal influence on how the title page was laid out was comparatively great.

89. Eyn sermon von der | betrachtung des heyligen leydens christi. | Doctor Martini Luther Augustiner zu Wittenbergk. Nürnberg: Jobst Gutknecht, 1519? (VD16 L 6516).
90. However, Tomlin, *Origins*, 24–25, rightly points out that certain spiritual forms rejected by Luther belong to the internal type. Luther thus was a proponent of a special form within this current of late-medieval spirituality which can be seen in the *way* in which self-identification with Christ took place.
91. Luther, *Sermon von der Betrachtung des Leidens Christi* (WA 2,136,11–20).
92. At this point we can detect a significant difference from Staupitz, whose passion-contemplation was greatly shaped by "mitleiden" or "suffering with" (Staupitz, *Salzburger Predigten*, 26, 34).
93. Luther draws attention to this opposition later in the text when he speaks about Christ's lament: Luther, *Sermon von der Betrachtung des Leidens Christi* (WA 2,138,4f).
94. Luther, *Sermon von der Betrachtung des Leidens Christi* (WA 2,136,21–137,9); Luther attacked this form of spirituality in his Commentary on Hebrews: "Unde sequitur, quod hi, qui meditantur Christi passionem tantum, ut compatiantur aut aliud quam fidem inde consequantur, prope infructuose et gentiliter meditantur. . . . Sed eo studio debet eius passio cogitari, ut fides augeatur, scilicet ut quo frequentius meditetur, eo plenius credatur sanguinem Christi pro suis peccatis effusum. Hoc est enim bibere et manducare spiritualiter, scilicet hac fide in Christum impinguari et incorporari" / "Therefore it follows that those who meditate solely on Christ's passion to suffer with him or to attain something other than faith reflect upon him in a fruitless and heathenly manner. . . . But you should think about his passion to grow in faith, for it is obvious that whoever meditates more frequently [on Christ's suffering] also believes more fully in the blood of Christ being poured out for their sins. This is spiritual drinking and eating, namely being incorporated and christened into Christ." (WA 57,209,15–22; cf. Tomlin, *Origins*, 25). My translation.

Eyn sermon von der
betrachtũg des heyligen leydens christi.
Doctor Martini Luther Augustiner zu Wittenbergk.

Figure 5.3 Title Page from the Nurnberg Reprint of *Meditation on Christ's Passion.*

but that does not stop Luther from attacking them and their merit-driven understanding of the mass with gusto. Luther really cared about those people who placed their hope in gaining grace through their own works, even if this work consisted of an intensive lamenting about Christ's suffering.[95] He countered this model with the following words:

> They contemplate Christ's passion aright who view it with a terror-stricken heart and despairing conscience. This terror must be felt as you witness the stern wrath and the unchanging earnestness with which God looks upon sin and sinners, so much so that he was unwilling to release sinners even for his only and dearest Son without his payment of the severest penalty for them. Thus he says in Isiah 53 [:8], "I have chastised him for the transgressions of my people."[96]

Luther embraced the form of piety that he had received from Paltz (with a certain distinction to that of Staupitz), a counter-identificatory posture in which a sinner is aware of their distance to God and their guilt. The internalization, the counter-identificatory exploration of Christ's suffering goes so far that the sinner recognizes themself as "the one who is torturing Christ thus, for your sins have surely wrought this."[97] That language has been lifted almost directly out of Paltz and is made very central to the piety of mapping one's own sin to Christ's suffering. Just like in

95. These passages are part of the reason why the sermon (despite its deep roots in late-medieval spirituality) could be considered as "the classical document of the conflict between new and old forms of spirituality," as Alfred Wiesenhütter, *Die Passion Christi in der Predigt des deutschen Protestantismus von Luther bis Zinzendorf* (Berlin: Furche-Verlag, 1930), 20, described it (Similarly Mager, *Passionslied*, 412, who actually uses the conformity idea from Staupitz to emphasize the Reformational character of Luther's thought), while also referring to its intensive transfer of medieval content. The "countless" reprints mentioned by him resulted in the sermon being collected in the Church Postille however, there were isolated prints based on the Church Postille see z.B. SERMON | D: Martin Luthers /| von der | Betrachtung | des | Leidens Christi /| In der Kirchen-Postill /| und | Im ersten Jenischen Theile | befindlich, (Leipzig: Heinrich, 1693) (VD 17 14:670203B); for more on the effect of this sermons within Lutheranism, cf. Johann Anselm Steiger, "Zorn Gottes, Leiden Christi und die Affekte der Passionsbetrachtung bei Luther und im Luthertum des 17. Jahrhunderts?" in *Passion, Affekt und Leidenschaft in der Frühen Neuzeit*, ed. Johann Anselm Stiger (Wiesbaden: Harrassowitz, 2005), 179–201, 183–184; Steiger, "Zorn Gottes," 186, points out the terrible lack of interconfessional studies on passion sermons, which he rightly accepts as a "common spiritual communicative space" given the many and various common roots of the confessions in this area. Steiger's approach has paved an important way for future work.
96. Luther, *Sermon von der Betrachtung des Leidens Christi* (WA 2,137,10–16). Trans. after: LW 42:8–9.
97. Luther, *Sermon von der Betrachtung des Leidens Christi* (WA 2,137, 23). Trans. after: Martin Luther, "A Meditation on Christ's Passion 1519," in *Luther's Works*, vol. 42, *Devotional Writings I*, trans. Gottfried G. Krodel, ed. Helmut T. Lehmann and Gottfried G. Krodel (Philadelphia, PA: Fortress Press, 1969), 9n5.

high-medieval mysticism,[98] a sinner's self-discernment[99] serves as the true sense of meditation[100] as well as for Luther's sermon of 1518. Luther follows the medieval tradition of switching between counter-identification and self-identification with Christ in this sermon, for one's own guilt implies that everything that Christ had suffered should also afflict the sinner:

> For every nail that pierces Christ, more than one hundred thousand should in justice pierce you, yes, they should prick you forever and ever more painfully! When Christ is tortured by nails penetrating his hands and feet, you should eternally suffer the pain they inflict and the pain of even more cruel nails.[101]

This meditative journey follows the instruments of Christ's immolation, just as Paltz had recommended in the *Himmlische Fundgrube* and as Luther also discovered in Bernard of Clairvaux.[102] All of these authors employ the same inversion: because Christ was wounded for our sake, our inner being and our conscience must be wounded for his.[103] Luther would have known this particularly well from John Tauler, whose Corpus Christi sermon (which, incidentally, also refers to Bernard) inverts the consumption of the Eucharist into Christ consuming the inner being of the sinner.[104] Luther's dialectical rhetoric is best understood as participation in late-medieval culture of proclamation and of spirituality in general.[105] He makes that

98. S. Alois Maria Haas, *Nim din selbes war: Studien zur Lehre von der Selbsterkenntnis bei Meister Eckhart, Johannes Tauler und Heinrich Seuse* (Freiburg, Switzerland: Universitätsverlag, 1971).
99. Luther, *Sermon von der Betrachtung des Leidens Christi* (WA 2,138,15–17).
100. *Meditatio* is the Latin term which Luther uses for "betrachtung" (often translated as "regard"); see *Luther an Spalatin, 13 März 1519* (WA.Br 1,350 [Nr. 161,26]).
101. Luther, *Sermon von der Betrachtung des Leidens Christi* (WA 2,137,30–33). Transl. after: Martin Luther, "A Meditation on Christ's Passion 1519." In *Luther's Works*, vol. 42, *Devotional Writings I*, trans. Gottfried G. Krodel, ed. Helmut T. Lehmann and Gottfried G. Krodel, 3–14 (Philadelphia: Fortress Press, 1969 [3rd ed. 1983]), 9n6.
102. Luther, *Sermon von der Betrachtung des Leidens Christi* (WA 2,137,37–138,4): "Zcum siebenden, eyn solchen erschrecken nam sanct Bernhard dar auß, da er sprach: Ich meynet, ich were sicher, wiste nichts von dem ewigen urteyl, das yhm hymell uber mich gangen war, Biß das ich sach, das der eynige gottis sun sich meyn erbarmet, erfurtritt unnd yn das selb urteyll sich fuer mich ergibt. Awe, es ist myr nit mer zu spielen und sicher zu seyn, wan eyn solcher ernst dahynden ist." Here, we are not dealing with an excerpt from a Bernard text but rather a story told about him (see Theo Bell, *Divus Bernhardus. Bernhard von Clairvaux in Martin Luthers Schriften* (Mainz: von Zabern, 1993) (VIEG 148), 263). This idea is connected to the frequently portrayed type of the Christ Love (Christusminne) from Bernard of Clairvaux.
103. Luther, *Sermon von der Betrachtung des Leidens Christi* (WA 2,138,20–22).
104. Tauler, *Predigten* (Vetter), 294, 23–25: "Sprach S: Bernhardus: 'wenne wir Got essen, so werden wir von ihm gessen; so isst er uns.'" / "As Saint Bernard said, 'when we eat God, then we are eaten by him, he eats us.'"
105. For the exact details about how antithesis and dialectic functioned in late-medieval mysticism, cf. Albert Auer, *Leidenstheologie im Spätmittelalter. Kirchengeschichtliche Quellen und Studien. vol.2* (St. Ottilien: Eos Verlog der Erzabtei, 1952), 128–129.

all the more apparent when he speaks of the death of the Old Adam in the context of the Eucharist. That figure, of course, was derived from the seven penitential psalms and from the *Theologia deutsch*.[106] He could talk about this process of consumption and death as being made into Christ's own form,[107] thus employing one of Staupitz's favorite figures.[108] Taking on the form of Christ did not quite complete the journey from counter-identification to self-identification with Christ, though. Luther brings the listener back from Good Friday to Easter and describes another inversion point in the seven penitential psalms. That brings us back to the pure passivity of the human with a strong accent on justification: where the traditional Sacrament of Penance would have spoken of *satisfactio* in the sense of performing some work, Luther advises the person to cast all of their sins on Jesus Christ and—very much in the sense of Staupitz's counsel as a confessor—to regard his wounds and to trust "that his wounds and sufferings are your sins, to be borne and paid for by him."[109] Luther finds the basis for all of these late-medieval moments of passion theology in the Pauline statement that people who belong to Christ have crucified their flesh with him (Gal 5:24).[110] Paul's message of justification is not seen by Luther as a countermeasure to late-medieval internal piety but rather as the first and fundamental step toward it.

Read this way, the Meditation on Christ's Passion demonstrates impressively that Luther was a proponent of late-medieval piety in the year 1519, even though he could also zealously attack other forms such as indulgence at the same time. He stuck to passion mysticism, heavily emphasizing counter-identification with Christ's suffering and blaming a person's own sin for being the cause of Christ's suffering. The doctrine of justification was therefore not distinct from late-medieval mysticism. It was mysticism's highest realization. This passion-mystical explanation would become the

106. Luther, *Sermon von der Betrachtung des Leidens Christi* (WA 2,139,15–18): "Hie wircket das leyden Christi seyn rechtes naturlich edels werck, erwurget den alten Adam, vortreybt alle lust, freud und zuvorsicht, die man haben mag von creaturen, gleych wie Christus von allen, auch von got vorlaßen war" / "Here the passion of Christ performs its natural and noble work, strangling the old Adam and banishing all joy, delight, and confidence which man could derive from other creatures, even as Christ was forsaken by all, even by God." Trans. after LW 42:11.

107. Luther, *Sermon von der Betrachtung des Leidens Christi* (WA 2,138,20. 35–36).

108. Markus Wriedt, *Gnade und Erwählung: eine Untersuchung zu Johann von Staupitz und Martin Luther.* Veröffentlichungen des Instituts für Europäische Geschichte Mainz, vol. 141 (Mainz: von Zabern, 1991), 145–186.

109. Luther, *Sermon von der Betrachtung des Leidens Christi* (WA 2,140,7–8). Translation after LW 42:12.

110. Luther, *Sermon von der Betrachtung des Leidens Christi* (WA 2,1141,36–37).

main content of the *Fastenpostille* from 1525, meaning that it had lasting effect in the emerging church of the Reformation.

HISTORICAL AND MYSTICAL APPROACHES TO THE PASSION IN THE SERMONS OF THE REFORMATION

The passion of Christ is one of the most common topics for sermons, and Luther wrote a lot of sermons treating it. They can be found in the *Postilles*, both those for Lent in 1525 as well as the *House Postille*. He wrote many other passion sermons besides these though, and we find one almost every year in the 1530s.[111] That is the decade of Luther's Reformational maturity and vitality, and these sermons can be considered among his best theology. The passion sermons vary in their focus, length, and content throughout the years. Some lack almost any mystical vocabulary and follow a pattern of historization, tending toward a more abstract formulation of the faithful's relation to the cross than did the earlier sermons.

The historicizing and distancing sermons are more numerous than those which preserve and transform the mystical tradition by means of identificatory texts. The passion cycle from 1531 is the most extensive one of mystical character: over the course of seven sermons between Wednesday of Holy Week and Easter Saturday (April 5–8, 1531), Luther explained the passion in all of its theological detail to his listeners. The sermons were recorded in notes taken by Georg Rörer[112] and Friedrich Myconius.[113] They are quite long, something which can be explained by Luther's desire to tell the story in its full content and also to explain every detail.[114] In this period, Luther was clearly devoting an enormous amount of attention to the events of the passion themselves, also seen in the fact that his *Little Prayer Book*

111. 1530: WA 32,28–39; 1531: WA 34/I,189–271; 1533: WA 37,21–23; 1534: WA 37,352–358; 1536: WA 41,525–531; 1537: WA 45,60–68:1538: WA 46, 285–313; 1539: WA 47,716–721; 1540: WA 49,84–97. We do not have a sermon explicitly devoted to the passion from 1532. Kurt Aland, Ernst Otto Reichert, and Gerhard Jordan. *Hilfsbuch zum Lutherstudium*, 4th ed. (Bielefeld: Luther-Verlag, 1996), 241, lists a sermon from March 24, 1532 (WA 36,134–137), which is a Palm Sunday sermon which ends with a few passages on suffering and sympathy (WA 36,136,34). Both a Maunday Thursday (WA 36,153–158) and an Easter sermon (WA 36,159–164) were provided for this year. In 1535, the transmission appears to have gotten muddled: *The sermons for the Sunday Judica* (WA 41,41–46) and the *Festival of the Annunciation* (WA 41, 47–51) contain some material from the Passion story, which, however, is not sufficient for more extensive interpretation.

112. WA 34/II,570.

113. WA 27, XVIIf.

114. Luther, *Predigten des Jahres 1531* Nr. 20 (WA 34/I,190,1 R ["historiam praedicare velimus"]; Luther, *Predigten des Jahres 1531*, Z. 20N ["Ideo hic nudum textum volumus proponere"]).

from 1529[115] includes an appendix with a passional which vividly depicts the passion story with images and texts.[116] Luther did occasionally interrupt the course of the passion story with his own excurses on the sacraments (good examples can be found in the sermons for Maundy Thursday).[117] In 1531, however, he had to stay relatively focused in order to cover all of the content. The notes from Rörer indicate that he treated faith (*verus usus passionis*) on Good Friday as preferable to a purely historical narrative[118] and preached about the wounds of Christ healing us.[119] However, there are no passages which feel like passion mysticism.[120] As the Good Friday sermon from 1534 demonstrates (also included in Rörer's notes), such historization could fathom the same depths of hamartiology that the early Meditation on Christ's Suffering had reached. In 1534, Luther remained in late-medieval currents and explained the words of Jesus on the cross. In his explanation of "Father, forgive them," he stated: "Now

115. For more on the original edition, see Michael Beyer, "Martin Luthers Betbüchlein," in *Lutherjahrbuch*, vol. 74 (Göttingen: Vandenhoeck & Ruprecht, 2007), 29–50.
116. Ein bet-|bůchlin/ mit | eym Calender vnd | Passional/ hůbsch | zugericht.| Marti.Luther., Wittenberg: Hans Lufft 1529 (Cited as VD16 L 4100). The earliest edition available as a scan on the internet (1538) can be found at https://gateway-bayern.de/VD16+L+4100 (accessed February 16, 2024): Ein | Betbuchlin/| mit eim Calender vnd | Passional/ hůbsch | zu gericht.| D.Mart. Lut, Wittenberg: Hans Lufft 1538 (VD 16 L 4104), the passional contained within can be found on f. c. iii^{r}—i V^{r}. Luther justified this expressly with the mnemotic function: "Ich habs fur gut angesehen das alte Passional buechlin zu dem bettbuechlin zu thun, allermeist umb der kinder und einfeltigen willen, welche durch bildnis und gleichnis besser bewegt werden, die Goettlichen geschicht zu behalten, denn durch blosse wort odder lere, wie Sant Marcus bezeuget, das auch Christus umb der einfeltigen willen eitel gleichnis fur yhn prediget habe. Ich habe aber etlich mehr geschicht aus der Biblia dazu gethan, und sprueche aus dem text dabey gesetzt, das es beides deste sicher und fester behalten werde." / "I thought it good to append the old Passional book to the book of prayers, mostly for the sake of children and simple people who are better moved by the images and parables to keep the divine things in order than they are moved by words or doctrines alone, as Saint Mark testifies that Christ preached in parables for the sake of the simple people. However, I have taken much more out of the Bible and have added more verses from the text so that both are understood and remembered all the better." My trans. (WA 10/II,458,16–22). The mention of the "old Passional" should give us cause for caution concerning the occasional idea that this can be seen as the first "children's Bible edition": Luther was using an old medieval technique of combining words and images. The content of Luther's passional went far beyond that of the biblical passion story: It began with the creation story, then went through the stations of the banishment from paradise, the flood, the exodus, Isaiah 7 before making a great leap and landing at the Annunciation (Luther, VD 16 L 4104, d vii^{v}—e^{r}).
117. Luther, *Predigten des Jahres 1531 Nr. 21–22* (WA 34/I,200–222).
118. Luther, *Predigten des Jahres 1531 Nr. 23* (WA 34/I,231,7–8).
119. Luther, *Predigten des Jahres 1531 Nr. 23* (WA 34/I,232,8–9).
120. We see something similar in the very sparse material from 1533, in which Luther preached mostly only within his own house, including on Good Friday, April 11, 1533 (Luther, *Predigten des Jahres 1533 Nr. 8* [WA 37,21–23]).

this is our comfort and our sermon, that he is a priest not only for me or you, but also for those who crucified him, for this prayer means the entire world."[121] In this case, Luther intensifies the degree of participation *until* reaching those who crucified Christ, allowing him to distinguish his listeners from those who actually committed the historical act and assure them that their participation is less severe. The homiletic device employed in 1518/19, which draws the believer into the presence of the crucifixion through active mystical participation, is missing. The loss of this mystical dimension really does constrain the possibilities for the sermon's statement. Luther then expounds upon the necessity of a confession of sin, drawing on the example of the criminals at Christ's side. He then reformulates it as an attack on the papacy.[122]

Did Luther grow past his mystical early years? This sermon from his mature period might convey that impression. There are sermons, however, in which the mystical vocabulary continues to thrive.[123] One of them is the Easter Saturday sermon from 1530, Luther's first sermon in Coburg.[124] It is full of passion mysticism, recycling words from the Meditation in 1518 like *sacramentum* and *exemplum* in order to refute the accusation that the doctrine of justification leads to a disdain for a life of following the cross.[125] That, of course, does not mean that an active life is the only possibility. Luther's concept remains true to its early mystical roots, which allowed Luther to explain that God has "appointed that we should not only believe in the crucified Christ, but also be crucified with him."[126] Such suffering leads a believer to the hope "that we may be conformed

121. Luther, *Predigten des Jahres 1534 Nr. 25*, April 5, 1534 (WA 37,354,18–19). The pattern employed here to explain the Seven Words on the Cross echoes the *Good Friday Sermon* from 1539 in a similarly historicizing-distancing way (Luther, *Predigten des Jahres 1539 Nr. 16*, April 4, 1539 (WA 47,716–721): "Das ist nu unser trost et nobis praedicatus, quod is sacerdos non solum pro me, te, sed etiam pro crucifixoribus suis, quia ista oratio ist gangen super totum mundum."

122. Luther, *Predigten des Jahres 1534 Nr. 25*, April 5, 1534 (WA 37,356,26–33). The ascription of sin to the entirety of humanity is somewhat more intensive in Luther, *Predigten des Jahres 1536*, April 14, 1536 (WA 41,530,12–13) (despite the claim to be only telling the story the way it was; WA 41,525,25), but even this takes place only in an abstract third person.

123. My usage of two categories broadly matches the three-fold classification of *historia*, *vis*, and *usus* as well as the simplification of *historia* and *usus* undertaken by Hans-Martin Barth, "Historie Und Identifikation: Über Luthers Passions- Und Osterpredigt," in *Pastoraltheologie*, 70–80 (Germany: Vandenhoeck & Ruprecht, 1966), 71n10, which itself refers to WA 27, 124, 31–32: "Hodie audivimus de resurrectione Christi, qui facta, qui distributa et capienda." / "Today we have heard of the resurrection of Christ, which was done, distributed and which must be understood."

124. WA 32, XXVIII.

125. Luther, *Sermon vom Leiden und Kreuz*, April 16, 1530 (WA 32,29,2–3).

126. Luther, *Sermon vom Leiden und Kreuz*, April 16, 1530 (WA 32,29,6–8). Trans. after: Martin Luther, "Sermon at Coburg on Cross and Suffering. April 16, 1530." In *Luther's Works*, vol.

to him"—a clear riff on the Staupitz-shaped vocabulary from the early period.[127] The general thrust of the sermon places even more emphasis on self-identification with Christ than did the Luther of 1518/19. With phrasing that is an almost word-for-word citation from his Tauler marginalia, Luther adds: "Beyond this, it should be the kind of suffering which we have not chosen ourselves."[128] Just like in the Meditation, a clear emphasis is placed on the insistence that this suffering cannot be seen as a work or merit before God.[129] The connection between mysticism and justification remains in Luther's thought as long as mysticism is understood as a passive, God-given posture. In this sermon, we also see the early thought of transforming suffering into elevation:

> This is true. When the suffering and affliction is at its worst, it bears and presses down so grievously that one thinks he can endure no more and must surely perish. But then if you can think of Christ, the faithful God will come and will help you, as he has always helped his own from the beginning of the world; for he is the same God as he has always been.[130]

What is interesting about the *consistency* of the passion-mystical tone in this sermon is that it demonstrates how Luther's occupation with a theology of the word of God amidst the spiritualist controversies[131] of the early 1520s did not lead to a complete erasure of the mystical-existential dimension of his theology.[132] Concentration on the Word—which manifests

51, *Sermons I*, trans. John W. Doberstein, ed. Helmut T. Lehmann and John W. Doberstein, 197–208 (Philadelphia, PA: Fortress Press, 1959), 198.

127. Luther, *Sermon vom Leiden und Kreuz*, April 16, 1530 (WA 32,29,5–8). Trans. after: Martin Luther, "Sermon at Coburg on Cross and Suffering. April 16, 1530." In *Luther's Works*, vol. 51, *Sermons I*, trans. John W. Doberstein, ed. Helmut T. Lehmann and John W. Doberstein, 197–208 (Philadelphia, PA: Fortress Press, 1959), 198.
128. Luther, *Sermon vom Leiden und Kreuz*, April 16, 1530 (WA 32,29,22–23), trans. after: LW 51:198; cf. Luther, *Randbemerkungen zu Tauler* (WA 9,102, 11–13): "tamen adeo stulti sumus, ut eas velimus tantum suscipere passiones quas nos elegimus vel quas in aliis factas vidimus vel legimus."
129. Luther, *Sermon vom Leiden und Kreuz*, April 16, 1530 (WA 32,30,16–17).
130. Luther, *Sermon vom Leiden und Kreuz*, April 16, 1530 (WA 32,31,14–19). Trans. after: Martin Luther, "Sermon at Coburg on Cross and Suffering. April 16, 1530." In *Luther's Works*, vol. 51, *Sermons I*, trans. John W. Doberstein, ed. Helmut T. Lehmann and John W. Doberstein, 197–208 (Philadelphia, PA: Fortress Press, 1959), 200.
131. See Leppin, *Transformationen spätmittelalterlicher Mystik*, 412.
132. Unnuanced conceptions of Luther "removing all unbiblical elements which had found their way into Passion spirituality during the Middle Ages" (Inge Mager, "Weshalb hat Martin Luther kein Passionslied geschrieben?" in *Passion, Affekt und Leidenschaft in der Frühen Neuzeit*, ed. Johann Anselm Steiger, (Wiesbaden, 2005), 405–422, 408n21), do not help us to reach a better understanding of how spirituality developed in this period; for more on this experiential dimension, cf. the already strongly existential text in the *Dedication to Staupitz* from May

as trusting in the consolation of Scripture[133]—does not necessarily mean that suffering disappears from the Reformational life of faith. The Coburg was clearly one place of many where the Reformer experienced suffering, and he utilized familiar language from the mystical tradition at this time.

Rörer's notes on the Good Friday Sermon from March 20, 1537 show that a theology of suffering never fully disappeared from Luther's sermons in the following years.[134] In that sermon, he takes up the idea of the exemplum[135] (example) of Christ's suffering, now, however, emphasizing that Christ's suffering is far more than the example of the exemplary suffering of the Saints because it took place entirely *pro nobis*—for us.[136] Luther describes the method of this salvation with the same idea of exchange that comes up in the early passion sermons and the Freedom of a Christian:[137] Christ has taken all human sins upon himself[138] and has destroyed them in his body.[139] As in the Meditation, the pro nobis is paired with a confession of one's own sins being the cause Christ's suffering.[140] A similar emphasis on the hamartiological relation of the faithful to Christ shows up in the following year as well. In that year, both Rörer and Johann Stolz took notes, and the latter reports how the image of the crucified Christ in the soul of the faithful should induce them to cry out: "Oh dear! Am

30, 1518: "Ita enim dulcescunt praecepta dei, quando non in libris tantum, sed in vulneribus dulcissimi Salvatoris legenda intelligimus" (Luther, *Resolutiones* [WA 1,525,21–23]).

133. Luther, *Sermon vom Leiden und Kreuz*, April 16, 1530 (WA 32,35,30–31).
134. Ronald Rittgers, *The reformation of suffering: pastoral theology and lay piety in late medieval and early modern Germany* (New York: Oxford University Press, 2012), has shown that we can reconstruct Reformational theology and its transformation of late medieval spirituality through the lens of suffering.
135. Luther, *Predigten des Jahres 1537 Nr. 9* (WA 45,61,4–5).
136. Luther, *Predigten des Jahres 1537 Nr. 9* (WA 45,61,1). It is worth considering if Luther's recent adoption of an internalized interpretation of the crucifixion may have also had to do with his personal situation at the time: After lengthy battles with kidney-stones, he felt close to death at the close of February of this year before his urinary tract normalized itself (Luther writes quite frankly about this to his wife: *Martin Luther an seine Frau, 27. Februar 1537*, right after passing his kidney-stone [WA.Br 8, Nr. 3140]). Both the usage of an *exemplum* idea as well as the Christophorus theme (Luther, *Predigten des Jahres 1537 Nr. 9* [WA 45,63,4–5]; cf. Luther, *Sermon vom Leiden und Kreuz*, April 16, 1530 [WA 32,32,18–33,6]) make it plausible that Luther felt inspired by his sermon from 1530 in 1537.
137. When this transfer event is degraded to the status of a parable, even along with the idea of merging into one dough with Christ (Mager, *Passionslied* 410, on WA 12,486,8–4871), then the weight of these statements is misunderstood in a modern interest in watering-down of Luther.
138. Luther, *Predigten des Jahres 1537 Nr. 9* (WA 45,61,8–9).
139. Luther, *Predigten des Jahres 1537 Nr. 9* (WA 45,61,17–18).
140. Luther, *Predigten des Jahres 1537 Nr. 9* (WA 45,62,3–6).

I the one who has such grave sins that Christ must carry them with his bitter death?"[141] That is a very explicit counter-identificatory moment like the one we saw in his early explanations. Once again, Luther pivots back to consolation:[142] "I am terrified and I am consoled."[143] On Easter Saturday, Luther returned to the Adam-typology. Being crucified with Christ means that the *vetus Adam*—the Old Adam—is now dead and buried.[144] This is entirely in line with earlier statements and refutes the thesis that Passion mysticism was only a phase in his younger development. Luther continued to draw on the vocabulary of passion mysticism, and so did the generations following his. Ultimately, the Meditation would make its way into the *Fastenpostille*, ensuring its influence on generations to come.

* * *

There are many reasons to believe that late-medieval mysticism exerted a major influence on Luther's development into a Reformer. One of them is his usage of passion mysticism. Luther focuses the mystical tradition entirely on Jesus Christ and provides us with clear evidence of how great of an influence Staupitz exerted on him and that his influence was tightly connected to mysticism.

If we take Luther's memories at face value, then Stauptiz's advice to regard the wounds of Christ was a crucial moment in his spiritual life, so it should come as no surprise that Luther returned to these roots in some way for his further theological development. He made a very important contribution to Passion mysticism when he intensified its counter-identificatory moment, vastly elevating it in comparison to previous mystical texts. The sinner discerns themself as being *distant* from Christ and therefore the source of Christ's suffering. Paltz had started musing about this idea, but Luther made it the center of passion mysticism and spent the rest of his life establishing the connection between it and justification.

Counter-identification was not all, though. There were other areas where Luther developed in continuity with late-medieval spirituality. The 1530s saw counter-identification still alive in his thought, but Luther

141. Luther, *Predigten des Jahres 1538 Nr. 27*, April 19, 1538 (WA 46,286,23: "Aw we, bin Ich der, der so schwere sunde hat, Das sie Christus mit seinem bittern tode mus tragen?" My translation; cf. the very similar notes taken by Rörer, WA 46,286,11–12).
142. Luther, *Predigten des Jahres 1538 Nr. 27*, April 19, 1538 (WA 46,287,1–2; WA 46,286,28–31S).
143. Luther, *Predigten des Jahres 1538 Nr. 27*, April 19, 1538 (WA 46,287,4): "Et sic terreor et tamen consolor." My transl.
144. Luther, *Predigten des Jahres 1538 Nr. 29*, April 20, 1538 (WA 46,301,1–5R; cf. WA 46,23–27S).

tended to develop it toward self-identification with Christ, accompanied by a strongly distancing, historicizing, dogmatic approach to the Passion. This would form the basis of his preaching on the passion for many years. Nevertheless, Luther's passion sermons preserved a substantial amount of mystical content, providing his listeners with the possibility of relating to the crucifixion in their own lives.

6.

The Transformation of Late-Medieval Mysticism in Reformational Theology

If the ideas developed in this book are correct so far, then they describe a Luther who was deeply rooted in late-medieval mysticism. Now we need to ask how that mystical home shifted throughout his life. Those developments have garnered a lot of attention over the previous century: the psychological concept of a breakthrough to explain Luther's development has lost a lot of its plausibility and we are increasingly committed to a paradigm described by Otto Pesch as a process taking place "via various steps" on the path toward a broader "theological reorientation."[1] How does this apply to transformations of the mystical experiences of his early years? How did he distinguish himself from what he had received? What amount of mystical thought remained in his spiritual identity?

To really answer these questions, we must examine Luther's entire body of work. We have only scratched the surface of it, however, so we cannot yet dream of making a definitive statement about Luther's transformation, and certainly not in a single book chapter. Here we will stick to an eclectic approach to the transformation processes in Luther's mystical thought. In an attempt to be representative of his thought in general, we will first look at some concepts that unquestionably show a genuine Reformational character: the polarity of Law and Gospel, the doctrine of justification, and the priesthood of all believers. Taken together, these three elements ought to be enough to profile Reformational theology against other forms.

1. Otto H. Pesch, "Zur Frage nach Luthers reformatorischer Wende," 500.

LAW AND GOSPEL

The dialectic of Law and Gospel is well-known as genuine Lutheran thought.[2] Luther developed its fullest form during the Antinomian Disputations, but he was already experimenting with it in his early lectures, although there it lacked the definition that it would take on later.[3] The texts from the 1520s can be considered largely Reformational in their theology; they consistently present us with two major topics that occupied Luther intensely during this time. The first starts in the hamartiological classification of the Law and its effects. This period is where Paul's Letter to the Romans (Rom 5:20; 7:7–10.) develops special significance for Lutheran theology. We see such challenging statements such as: the Law somehow augments or multiplies sin. In the clear distinction between Law and Gospel, which he had developed in his Latin *Epistle and Gospel Postille* from 1521, Luther repeatedly and extensively worked on this line of reasoning.[4] Luther intensively develops the juxtaposition of these concepts but never loses sight of their intrinsic relation.[5] The tension between Law and Gospel is an old one, also presented to us in Augustine's *De spiritu et littera*: "The Law was therefore given in order that grace might be sought: grace was given in order that the Law might be fulfilled."[6] Much in this

2. See WA 7,502,34–35; 36,9,224–31; 39/I,361,1–6; 40/I,207,3–5. A similar emphasis is given to this distinction in the modern treatments of Luther's theology, such as: Paul Althaus, *Die Theologie Martin Luthers* (Gütersloh: Gütersloher Verlagshaus Mohn, 1962), 218–219.; Bernhard Lohse, *Luthers Theologie in ihrer historischen Entwicklung und in ihrem systematischen Zusammenhang* (Göttingen: Vandenhoeck & Ruprecht, 1995), 283–294; Oswald Bayer, *Martin Luthers Theologie: eine Vergegenwärtigung* (Tübingen: Mohr Siebeck, 2003), 53–70; Albrecht Beutel, "Theologie als Unterscheidungslehre," in *Luther Handbuch*, ed. Albrecht Beutel (Tübingen: Mohr Siebeck, 2005), 451–453.
3. For more, cf. Lohse, *Luthers Theologie*, 284–287.
4. WA 7, 503,4–504,5.
5. See the explicit connection undertaken in the *Obrigkeitsschrift* (WA 11, 250,29–31) (*Temporal Authority: To What Extent It Should be Obeyed*, LW 45:75–129): "Datzu gibt S. Paulus dem gesetz noch eyn ampt Ro: .7. unnd Gal: .2. das es die sund erkennen leret, damit es den menschen demütigt zur gnad unnd zum glawben Christi. 136–142" / "In addition, Paul ascribes to the law another function of Romans 7 and Galatians 2, that of teaching men to recognize sin in order that it may make them humble unto grace and unto faith in Christ . . ." Trans. after: Martin Luther, "Temporal Authority: To What Extent it Should be Obeyed, 1523," in *Luther's Works*, vol. 45, *Christian in Society*, trans. J. J. Schindel, ed. Helmut T. Lehmann and Walther I. Brandt, 75–130 (Philadelphia, PA: Fortress Press, 1962), 90.
6. Augustin, *De spiritu et littera*, 19, 34 (Corpus scriptorum ecclesiasticorum Latinorum 60, 187,22–23): "Lex ergo data est, ut gratia quaereretur, gratia data est, ut lex impleretur." Trans. after: Saint Augustine of Hippo, *St. Augustine: On the Spirit and the Letter*, trans. W. J. Sparrow-Simpson (London: Society for Promoting Christian Knowledge, 1925), 77.

vein of classification, the *Church Postille* from 1522 describes the Law as a sort of path to Jesus Christ:

> The second [usage] is that the human discerns by means of the law how wrong and unjust their heart is, how distant they are from God, how their nature is worth nothing, so that they detest their body and understand how it is in no way suited to satisfying the demands of the law. They are thereby humbled, they crawl to the cross and wail to Christ and yearn for his grace, despair before him and find all of their comfort in Christ.[7]

This passage brings together far more than merely the Augustinian legacy. The concept of humiliation is clearly building upon the humiliation idea from the earlier lectures[8] and the portrayal of Christ as the sole consolation appears to reflect Luther's own history of consolation with Staupitz when Staupitz told him that Christ does not terrify but rather consoles (see chapter 3). This passage from the *Reformational Church Postille* thus shows us how Luther began to weave different strands of medieval theology into his own well-defined theological concept. It shows, quite remarkably, how Luther emphasizes the futility of human deeds.[9] The message of the Law is intended to demonstrate how utterly worthless a person's property and works are before God. During the *Antinomian Disputation*, Luther summarizes this with a further concept from the context of monastic life: *desperatio*.[10] We find it as early as the first lectures on the Psalms where it is used as the precondition for justice,[11] thus constituting a protoform of the Law and Gospel dialectic developed in the *Antinomian Disputation*.

7. WA 10/1/1, 455,5–11: "Das ander, das der mensch sich alßo durchs gesetz erkenne, wie falsch und unrecht seyn hertz sey, wie fern er noch von gott sey, wie gar die natur nichts sey, das er seyn erber leben vorachte und erkenne, wie es nichts sey gegen dem, das tzu des gesetzes erfullunge gehoret. Und alßo gedemuettigt werde, tzum creutz krieche, Christum erfeufftze und sich nach syner gnaden sehne, an yhm selbs gar vortzage, alle seynen trost auff Christum setze." My translation.
8. See the standard text Ernst Bizer, *Fides ex auditu: Eine Untersuchung über die Entdeckung der Gerechtigkeit Gottes durch Martin Luther*, 3rd ed. (Neukirchen Kreis Moers: Verlag der Buchhandlung des Erziehungsvereins, 1966).
9. For more on the relation between nothingness and discernment of sin, mostly treating the lectures on the Psalms, but giving plenty of attention to 1518–1523, see Sammeli Juntunen, *Der Begriff des Nichts bei Luther in den Jahren von 1510 bis 1523* (Helsinki: Luther-Agricola-Gesellschaft, 1996), 371–378.
10. WA 39/I,50,36–37; 40/I,368,12. 32–33; cf. for more on despair in a monastic context, cf. WA 4,665,21–22; 56, 266,25–28.
11. AWA 2, 182,4–8; For more on this cf. Hubertus Blaumeiser, "Martin Luthers Kreuzestheologie: Schlüssel Zu Seiner Deutung Von Mensch Und Wirklichkeit; Eine Untersuchung Anhand Der Operationes in Psalmos (1519–1521)," in *Konfessionskundliche Und Kontroverstheologische Studien 60* (Paderborn: Bonifatius, 1995), 154.

We can establish this link very clearly because *desperatio* takes on a central role in Luther's argumentation there; in the *Disputation*, Luther uses *desperatio* as a precondition for justice in conjunction with the idea: "God only considers the humble."[12] The basic structure and spiritual vocabulary remain the same, but the framework was being recast into a theology of the Word. The term *desperatio* shows up again in the *Heidelberg Disputation*, still functioning as the pivot point between humility and an orientation toward God and salvation. There it is cast in the language of the *opus alienum* (the alien/other work of God).[13] A startling proximity to this is found in the *Resolutiones* to the *95 Theses* when Luther terms true *contritio cordis* as an *opus alienum*. The deeply felt contrition has been sifted out from the classical triad of penance (*contritio, confessio, satisfactio*) and has taken a place of its own, parallel with humility, and the work of God's Word in the human spirit. In sum, these facets convey the impression that Luther's theology of the Law goes beyond the Pauline and Augustinian tradition(s) and has a monastic/mystical dimension as well. For the mystic, the first step of self-discernment was purification, something expressed by those mystical authors held in high regard by Luther such as John Tauler.[14] An example is found in Tauler's sermon on John 5:1–2:

> The third portico is repentance for sin, deep and true. It is turning away in all sincerity from everything that is not God, or that does not come from God. The very marrow of true contrition consists in this—that a sinner returns absolutely to God with all that he is inwardly and outwardly.[15]

Such emphasis on true, internal contrition shows up early in Luther's thought, during the period of Luther's intensive reading of Tauler. As we have pointed out earlier in this book (see p. 47–48), a brief notice "*Hoc nota tibi*" is found at one of the passages of Tauler where this recognition of one's own worthlessness is profiled over against the ritualized, external act of Confession, relativizing the Sacrament of Penance by a claimed true internal contrition:

12. AWA 2,197,25. "*deus humiles solum respiciat.*" My translation.
13. WA 1,357,6–8.
14. See Johannes Tauler, *Die Predigten Taulers aus der Engelberger und der Freiburger Handschrift sowie aus Schmidts Abschriften der ehemaligen Straßburger Handschriften*, ed. Ferdinand Vetter (Berlin: Weidmannsche Buchhandlung, 1910), 65, 22–27.
15. Tauler, *Die Predigten*, 36,10–14: "Die dirte porte von disen daz ist ein war wesenlicher ruwe der súnden. Welicher ist daz? Das ist ein gantz war abeker von allem dem daz nút luter Got enist oder des Got nút ein ware sache enist, und ein war gantz zuoker zuo Gotte mit allem dem daz man ist." Trans. after: John Tauler, *The Sermons and Conferences of John Tauler*, trans. and ed. Walter Elliott (Washington, DC: Apostolic Mission House, 1910), 133.

> Return to God so quickly and so sincerely that thy sins are pardoned thee even before thou hast time to tell them in confession. Let not thy sinful tendencies affright three. Many a fault of thine is permitted by God, not so much to hurt thee as to help thee. For does it not cause thee to own to thyself that thou art but nothingness? Does not the shame of it lead thee to mortification and detachment?[16]

This statement is even more radical than the above-cited one from Luther concerning the effect of the Law and provides us with a glimpse into the transformation Luther was undertaking in his own theology. The early Luther regards contrition very highly within the set of late-medieval penitential elements with his estimation actually going beyond the parameters established by medieval discussion surrounding Attritionism and Contritionism,[17] (despite what Luther's later recollections might suggest). It is largely a mystical tradition, most of it received via Tauler. Luther's comprehension of the mystical-contritional way continues as he reads mystical literature, but it is recast by his rapid discovery of the Word in his theology. The structure of the mystical way, however, never gets entirely removed. The mystical way leads from the destruction of the human being in a comprehensive spiritual sense to an opening for God to fill the resulting vacuum (see p. 21–22).[18] The above-cited Tauler sermon continues:

> The very marrow of true contrition consists in this that a sinner returns absolutely to God with all that he is inwardly and outwardly. That a man is wholly absorbed in trustfulness of God's goodness, that he ardently longs to possess Him and Him only, that he is resolutely determined to cleave to Him forever in all love, that he has the purpose clear and distinct to do God's will alone to the utmost of his power: My dear children, this is what repentance essentially is.[19]

16. Tauler, *Die Predigten*, 355,36–356,2: "Beeile dich . . . und dringe so ungestüm in Gott, daß dir die Sünden entfallen und du sie nicht mehr weißt, wenn du damit zur Beichte kommst. Dies darf dich nicht erschrecken; denn nicht zu deinem Schaden widerfährt dir das, sondern zur Erkenntnis deines Nichts und zur Verschmähung deines eigenen Selbst in Gelassenheit, nicht in Niedergeschlagenheit." Trans. after: Tauler, *The Sermons and Conferences of John Tauler*, 696.; cf. *Luthers Randbemerkungen hierzu* WA 9,104,11–14; cf. for more on the argumentation Leppin, *Omnem vitam*, 15–17.
17. WA 40/2,411,39–412,20. Cf. Volker Leppin, *Sola: Christ, Grace, Faith, and Scripture Alone in Martin Luther's Theology* (Minneapolis: Fortress, 2024), p. 56–58.
18. See Tauler, *Die Predigten*, 305,23–306,4.
19. Tauler, *Die Predigten*, 36,14–18. "und daz ist alleine der kerne und daz marg des ruwen; und dan mit einer versaster getrúwunge versinken in das minnenkliche luter guot das Got ist, und an ime und in ime iemer zuo blibende und anzuohangende mit minnen und mit luterre meinunge in eime vollen bereiten willen, den liebsten willen Gottes zuo tuonde also verre also er mag." Trans. after: Tauler, *The Sermons and Conferences of John Tauler*, 133.

The return described by Tauler is reflected in the soteriological categories of Law and Gospel for Luther; here we see despair leading to the destruction of human works, and it does not just precede the word of promise[20] but in fact, leads directly to it and prepares it. As the *Antinomian Disputation* unfolds, the human person experiences that "the world becomes too small for that person" and is pushed toward Christ.[21] That is a clear parallel between Luther's doctrine of Law and Gospel and the mystical description of the path to salvation. God's works of grace (for the mystic, it is a mystical union with God) is always preceded by a form of preparation which the human perspective perceives as destructive. That parallel is no coincidence; the overlap of the semantic fields and the vocabulary of the early lectures on the doctrine of the Law in the 1520s leave no doubt about that. Both the medieval mystics and Luther adhere to a theology of humility, but in Luther's case, that theology is gradually transforming its basic theological coordinates. Luther associates the preceding *destruction* of human life much more clearly *with God* than do the mystics. Late-medieval mystics *did* see God as the subject of all human salvation,[22] but Luther adhered to this idea to the point of crowding out virtually all alternatives. This likely corresponds to the point in Luther's development when the *Via moderna* with its very strong image of God[23] deeply shaped Luther's own image of God. His transformed use of humility and destruction bears its mark.

There is a second and equally important development that Luther undertakes: he resettles mystical structures into the theology of the Word. Luther received a tradition of mystical thought (including what Bizer has identified as a theology of humility) and then vastly expanded and improved it with the theology of the Word because it describes the *origin* of the processes in the soul as *extra nos*[24] and does so far more precisely

20. For more on the prommisorial character, see the standard work Oswald Bayer, *Promissio: Geschichte Der Reformatorischen Wende in Luthers Theologie* (Darmstadt: Wissenschaftliche Buchgesellschaft, 1989).
21. WA 39/1,456,7–8: "die weite welt zu enge." Translation after LW 73:142.
22. Tauler, *Die Predigten*, 305,16–19: "Die nechste und die aller höchste bereitunge in ze enphahende die muos er selber bereiten und wúrken in den menschen. Er muos die stat selber bereiten zuo im selber und muos sich selber och enphahen in dem menschen."
23. See William J. Courtenay, *Capacity and Volition. A History of the Distinction of Absolute and Ordained Power* (Bergamo: Lubrina, 1990) (= Quodlibeta 8); Volker Leppin, "Does Ockham's Concept of Divine Power Threaten Man's Certainty in His Knowledge of the World?" *Franciscan Studies* 55 (1998), 169–180; Hubert Schröcker, *Das Verhältnis der Allmacht Gottes zum Kontradiktionsprinzip nach Wilhelm von Ockham*, Veröffentlichungen des Grabmann-Institutes 49 (Berlin: Akademieverlag, 2003).
24. For more on how Luther broke this mystical formula see Karl-Heinz Zur Mühlen, *Nos Extra Nos: Luthers Theologie Zwischen Mystik Und Scholastik. Beiträge Zur Historischen Theologie*, vol. 46 (Tübingen: Mohr, 1972).

than did the late-medieval texts. Those did, of course, live in a profoundly biblical world and assumed the effect of external action, but they rarely put them into such clear categories as Luther. This is the strength of the Lutheran transformation and would prove to be decisive for the later boundaries drawn around *Lutheran* theology.

THE DOCTRINE OF JUSTIFICATION

Luther's teachings on justification were not simply born out of late-medieval mysticism. The story everybody knows is that Luther (re)discovered justification through his study of Paul and Augustine, and that model goes a long way in explaining how and why Luther increasingly lived and thought in the paradigm of justification throughout his life. He made justification the key to understanding the person faced with God. Nevertheless, in Luther's thoughts on justification, there are structural analogies to certain aspects of mystical thought that would have made a mystically influenced thinker like Luther far more receptive to the message of undeserved grace. Mystical theologians such as John Tauler or the author of the *Theologia deutsch* belonged to the spiritual currents of the late Middle Ages which Berndt Hamm has described with the concept of "proximate grace":[25] God (usually Jesus Christ) draws near to the mystics in such a manner that relativizes the usual, gradualist forms of sacramental mediation in the late Middle Ages,[26] though never entirely making them obsolete.[27] Of special note, the *clerics* as administrators of the *steps to salvation* are no longer the focal point of a person's relation to God because the whole process has been made *immediate*.[28] Here, at least, we see Christ and God as "proximate grace," standing over and against the sacramental mediation as a way of direct access to salvation. The late-medieval mystics never launched an assault on the mediating structures.[29] But authors such as Tauler could describe salvation as: "not ever com[ing]

25. Hamm: "Die nahe Gnade" (proximate grace).
26. For more on gradualism, see Berndt Hamm, "Einheit und Vielheit der Reformation—oder: was die Reformation zur Reformation machte," in *Reformationstheorien. Ein kirchenhistorischer Disput über Einheit und Vielfalt der Reformation*, ed. Bernd Moeller and Dorothea Wendebourg, (Göttingen: Vandenhoeck & Ruprecht, 1995), 69–70.
27. See Volker Leppin, "Mystische Frömmigkeit und sakramentale Heilsvermittlung im späten Mittelalter," in *Zeitschrift für Kirchengeschichte 112* (Stuttgart: Kohlhammer, 2001), 189–204.
28. See Volker Leppin, *Wilhelm von Ockham: Gelehrter, Streiter, Bettelmönch* (Darmstadt: Primus, 2003), 169–170.
29. See Leppin, *Mystische Frömmigkeit.*

from human effort or deserving, but purely from the grace and merits of our Lord Jesus Christ flowing from God into our souls."[30]

Tauler's formulation has a lot in common with Augustinian terminology. Being steeped in this language certainly made its proponents receptive to the Augustinian teachings on justification. It likely had a strong effect on Luther, which we see in the very unique way he bound together three various strands of the late-medieval theology of immediacy. These had been developing since the early fourteenth century and were by no means always coherent with each other. They were: (1) the papalism of John XII, (2) the mystical theology of Meister Eckhart, and (3) the *potentia* theology of William of Ockham. All were in conversation with each other in Avignon at the same time, the last two of them being accused of heresy by the first.[31] Two of these currents come together in Luther: the mystical immediatization of a relation to God joins with the then-new and revolutionary *Via moderna* of William of Ockham which he discovered in Erfurt. It was not necessarily a given that William of Ockham was regarded as a great teacher by Biel in Tübingen as well as by Luther's teachers in Erfurt.[32] Regardless of the reasons for the peculiarly strong fascination that Ockham exerted on scholars of Luther's time, Luther learned about him from fascinated teachers and later classified himself as an adherent to Ockham's "sect."[33] What he learned from Ockham, Biel, and his Erfurt teachers was that God can influence human affairs directly and actually does so in the context of salvation. In his *Quodlibeta die potentia Dei*, Ockham treated Paul, a man who was chosen by God entirely unexpectedly and without any disposition for God's work.[34] Ockham thus stood in a broader current of theology which Werner Dettloff (focused on Franciscan doctrinal development)[35] has presented as a direct act of God for human salvation in its *acceptatio divina*. And there *are* two possible conclusions to be drawn from the strong emphasis on the *potentia*

30. Tauler, *Die Predigten*, 123,7–8: "niemer von menschlichen werken noch von verdiende, sunder von luttere genaden und von dem verdiende unsers herren Jhesu Christi." Trans. after Tauler, *The Sermons and Conferences of John Tauler*, 387.
31. Leppin, *Wilhelm von Ockham*, 156–172.
32. See Erich Kleineidam, *Universitas studii Erfordensis: Überblick über die Geschichte der Universität Erfurt im Mittelalter 1392–1521*. Teil 2: Spätscholastik, Humanismus und Reformation: 1461–1521, 2nd ed. (Leipzig: Verlag, 1992), 140
33. WA.TR 5, 653,1–2 (Nr. 6419); 2, 516,6 (Nr. 2544a).
34. Guillelmi de Ockham, "Quodlibet VI q. 1." In *Opera Theologica. Opera philosophica et theologica*, vol. 9, ed. Joseph C. Wey (St. Bonaventure, NY: Editiones Instituti Franciscani Universitatis St. Bonaventurae, 1980), 587, l.53–58
35. The pairing of certain positions to certain ordered traditions is one of the fruits of the order-specific research strategy employed by recent Scholastic studies.

Dei in the *Via moderna*. Ockham explains in the second *Quaestio* of the seventeenth distinction of the first book of his *Commentary on the Sentences* while engaging with Thomas Aquinas:

> I simply reject this as false, because God can accept a good motion of the will, elicited by pure nature, out of his grace, and consequently such an act from God's graciousness would be meritorious due to that acceptance.[36]

One could understand "*ex puris naturalibus*" ("by pure nature") here as an expression of a Pelagianism that places all of its hope in human powers. Many Ockham interpreters did just this, including his plaintiffs in Avignon.[37] But if we place the accent on the divine capacity to accept, then there is also a strong emphasis on the divine will in these sentences which gives God priority over all other mediating ways, even the sacraments instituted by God himself.

Even if Luther had a Pelagian feeling when engaging with the *Via moderna*, he had also discovered its strong God concept in his early studies which contradicted Pelagianism to a large extent. Thus, he had started swimming in the tow of immediacy. Both mysticism and the *Via moderna* provided a comfortable space for him to bridge the distance between God and the believer. When he encountered Augustine and his teachings on justification, he recast immediacy language into the language of justification, enabling the young professor to express Pauline theology true to both the Pauline writings and the spiritual atmosphere of his time.

Thus, one can scarcely describe the doctrine of justification as a direct transformation of mystical thought. That description fits far better for Law and Gospel. Mysticism *did*, however, prepare the way for Augustinian theology's popularity and was therefore at least a contributing factor in the transformational processes which were also connected to Luther's engagement with anti-Pelagian theology. Here, we also see that Luther found formulations for God's proximity which feel quite mystical. For example, the first *Lecture on the Psalms* reads:

> God's justice is called our justice (because his grace is given to us), the work of God is our work (which he performs in us), similarly the Word of God

36. Guillelmi de Ockham, *Opera Theologica. Opera philosophica et theologica*, vol. 3, ed. Gerard Etzkorn (St. Bonaventure, NY: Editiones Instituti Franciscani Universitatis St. Bonaventurae, 1977), 469, l.10–13: "Istud reputo simpliciter falsum, quia bonum motum voluntatis ex puris naturalibus elicitum potest Deus acceptare de gratia sua, et per consequens talis actus ex gratuita Dei acceptatione erit meritorious." My translation.
37. See Josef Koch, "Neue Aktenstücke zu dem gegen Wilhelm Ockham in Avignon geführten Prozeß," in *Recherches de théologie ancienne et médiévale*, vol. 8 (1936), 82,21–24

> (which he speaks in us), the virtues of God (which are made in us), and many other things . . . for through the same justice God and we are just, similarly through his same Word God acts and we are what he is, that we are in him and his being is our being.[38]

The literal textbook case of this proximity between mystical thought and the doctrine of justification is, of course, the *Freedom of a Christian*, which takes the same image of the bride and groom and recasts it into the form that Staupitz and—much earlier—Bernard had prepared:

> The third incomparable benefit of faith is that it unites the soul with Christ as a bride is united with her bridegroom.[39]

This can certainly be read as a mystical costume for the doctrine of justification. In any case, however, it is entirely alien to the neo-Protestant construal of incompatibility between the Reformation's doctrine of justification and mysticism. Nevertheless, neo-Protestantism does pick up on something present in this passage and elsewhere, namely, that faith has the central function of justification rather than affective love between, say, the mystical bride and groom.[40] Here as elsewhere, Luther is not merely repeating what he has heard, but the mystics did not do that either. Both Luther and the mystical tradition continued to think productively, breaking the old paradigms but also remaining within them.

THE PRIESTHOOD OF ALL BELIEVERS

These processes are homing in on our third facet of transformation: the priesthood of all believers. Within the established medieval sacramental system, the priest was *the* social instance by which grace was made real and present. The priest mediated everything. Based on our previous encounters with the mystics, it should not surprise us in the slightest that Tauler also employs language at home in this world. Tauler does not go as far

38. AWA 2,259,1–3. 12–14: "Vocatur autem iustitia dei et nostra, quod illius gratia nobis donata sit, sicut opus dei, quod in nobis operatur, sicut verbum dei, quod in nobis loquitur, sicut virtutes dei, quas in nobis operatur, et multa alia . . . ut eadem iustitia deus et nos iusti simus, sicut eodem verbo deus facit et nos sumus, quod ipse est, ut in ipso simus et suum esse nostrum esse sit." My translation.

39. WA 7, 25,26–28: "Nit allein gibt der glaub ßovil, das die seel dem gottlichen wort gleych wirt aller gnaden voll, frey und selig, sondernn voreynigt auch die seele mit Christo, als eyne brawt mit yhrem breudgam." Translation after LW 31:351.

40. For more on how the emphasis was transferred from love to faith, see Berndt Hamm, "Von der Gottesliebe des Mittelalters zum Glauben Luthers. Ein Beitrag zur Bußgeschichte," in *Luther-Jahrbuch*, vol. 65 (Göttingen: Vandenhoeck & Ruprecht, 1998), 19–52.

as Luther; he never elevates all baptized believers to the priesthood, but he does allow it to become a possibility for mystical believers: "The God thinking man it is that shall be a priest, and shall enter the holy of holies, whereas the rest of the people shall remain outside."[41] This is a statement which, incidentally, is applied explicitly to women.[42] In any case, the single restriction of the "inner person" has set the stage for Luther's own treatment of priesthood. It will synthesize all possible interpretations of the unconditional nature of God's grace into a holistic Christian life. Anyone who has crawled out of baptism has attained the same status of grace as a consecrated priest or bishop. Tauler principally wanted God's grace to reign alone in the life of the believers, but Luther set it into radical effect. Luther denied any preconditions on the part of the believers, which had an unfathomably large effect on the believers themselves. For Tauler, priesthood still requires a socially special existence in mystical spirituality. Here it must be said that we only have the sermons that Tauler held for former Beguines, who were usually consecrated women; his sermons directed at laypeople have been lost, and with them most of the information about what he thought of laypersons.[43] The special existence of Tauler's mystic falls away as soon as the mystical-hypothetical-imagined "priest" becomes in fact a truly general one. In Luther's terms, that means remapping the basis of priesthood to baptism. Any baptized person now lives in the paradigm of the sovereign, gracious God which cannot tolerate any sort of distinction or special effort on the part of the humans involved. In the Middle Ages, there was only one possible point of contention about how one was elevated from the community of Christians to the priesthood: either through consecration or through spiritual gifts. Mystical critique of the clerical system had always pointed to the missing worthiness of the priest (a latent but persistent tension within *character indelibilis*). Tauler advises his listeners to not simply attend every mass celebrated but preferred going "to those Holy priests . . . whose sacrifice is pleasing to God."[44] This was a criterion that went over and above that

41. Tauler, *Die Predigten*, 164,34–165,1: "Dieser gotdehtiger mensche das ist ein inwendiger mensche, der sol ein priester sin." Trans. after: Tauler, *The Sermons and Conferences of John Tauler*, 648.
42. Tauler, *Die Predigten*, 165,15–17; cf. Thomas Gandlau, "Trinität Und Kreuz: Die Nachfolge Christi in Der Mystagogie Johannes Taulers." *Freiburger Theologische Studien 155* (Freiburg im Breisgau: Verlag Herder, 1993), 146–147, with the distinction between a sacramental and spiritual priesthood.
43. See Volker Leppin, "Tauler, Johannes (ca. 1300–1361)," in *Theologische Realenzyklopädie Online* (Berlin: De Gruyter, 2010), 745–748
44. Tauler, *Die Predigten*, 319,5–7.

of the Sacrament of Consecration. The system of filtering out people, however, had not been removed, it had only been defined more tightly to the qualities of the person. Luther's Reformational theology *does* bring about a major disruption to this system. His disruption of the system had played very nicely with and had probably been augmented by the raging anticlericalism of the time. Luther cannot be considered the singular cause of the Reformation's criticism of the priesthood, but his contribution to the new constitution of spirituality meant overhauling the medieval system of estates. Additionally, there is a valid comparison to be drawn between Tauler's inner person and Luther's. Zur Mühlen has provided us with the study here which confirms:[45] Luther took this conceptual pair from late-medieval mysticism and also transformed it thoroughly.

The conclusion is: Luther is deeply rooted in his mystical tradition, but he made nonlinear transformations. The question cannot be "whether something was there or not." We must examine which heterogeneous currents of tradition were connected with each other and how this was the case. I think I can claim that mysticism played a significant role in Luther's development. However, this observation does not imply that Luther simply coughed up what he had been fed. Mysticism provided a framework for him to develop his own, original theological thought. At times, he broke out of that framework, but only at times. By the end of his life, his theology was no longer entirely discernable as mystical, and his mysticism would be vehemently contested. But joining the later Protestant chorus of verdict against mysticism drowns out the many mystical voices that Luther sings in his theological development. The core of his theology cannot be understood without this mystical background. He started with mysticism, thought like a mystic, and gave later generations of Lutherans a form of mysticism with its own, unique proximity to God.

45. Zur Mühlen, *Nos Extra Nos,* 155–161.

7.

Becoming One Bread ("Kuchen"): Mystical Tendencies in Luther's Teachings on the Lord's Supper*

About thirty years ago, Albrecht Beutel published a remarkable article in which he took a very critical stance toward Luther research being conducted in Finland at the time. That tradition had identified the concept of *deificatio* as the center of Luther's theology.[1] This idea arose from conversations held with the Orthodox Church in Finland and was supposed to demonstrate that Luther and Lutheran theology was not only a recipient of the Patristic theology of the West, but also of that of the East, specifically Athanasius. Beutel reminded his readers of some facts that were not very present at the time, namely that one finds in Luther the "thought of the unio developed in the mystical tradition." He meant to exclude Luther, however, from what he described as "mystical *unio*-speculation."[2] One

* Translator's note: This chapter focuses on the concept of "Kuchen" in Luther's works to illuminate an aspect of apotheosis-like mysticism in his theology. The word presents us with a unique difficulty because existing translations have not found agreement on how to translate it and many of the passages where it occurs have not yet been translated in the American Edition of Luther's works. "Kuchen" in its Middle-High German usage refers to a mass of dough which does not necessarily have to be baked. We have chosen the term "bread" because of its commonality with this image as well as the Pauline idea of many believers being gathered together like grain into one loaf of bread (1 Cor 10:7).

1. Albrecht Beutel, *Antwort und Wort*. For more on the question of the reality of God for Luther, cf. *Luther und Ontologie. Das Sein Christi im Glauben als strukturierendes Prinzip der Theologie Luthers, Veröffentlichungen der Luther-Akademie Ratzeburg 21*, ed. Anja Ghiselli, (Helsinki: Luther-Agricola-Gesellschaft, 1993) 70–93; it has been reprinted in: Albrecht Beutel, *Protestantische Konkretionen. Studien zur Kirchengeschichte*, (Tübingen: Mohr Siebeck, 1998), 28–44; the following cites from this reprinted copy.
2. Beutel, *Antwort und Wort*, 44.

example of where Beutel identifies the Lutheran form of the *unio*-idea was the concept of the believer becoming one bread ("*Kuchen*") with Christ.[3] The debates got rather heated, and we should not dwell on those aspects here.[4] We can, however, derive some important insights by examining the German Ebeling school in conversation with the Finns and other international Luther scholars.

TRANSFORMATION OF MYSTICISM

Luther's "relatively common"[5] phrase "to be/become one bread" first shows up as a description of Christian life in a sermon on Ascension Day of 1522, which was on 29 May of that year: "For a Christian has the same power as does Christ, they are one bread [with Him] and they sit with Him for their entire life."[6] Here a twofold background is very helpful for understanding this. Firstly, it is obvious that the idiomatic expression of "becoming one bread" ("*Kuchen*") was already in circulation during Luther's time to express close proximity or agreement.[7] Luther used the phrase in this sense in the Ascension Day sermon. In 1522, he spoke of the faithful as having a spirit that caused them to speak "until we include and incorporate everyone with us and make them one communion with us, wherever this is possible."[8] The parallel concepts illustrate that the

3. Beutel, *Antwort und Wort,* 33–36.
4. Things have cooled off between the German and Finnish Luther scholars: The newest edition of Albrecht Beutel's Luther Handbook even contains its own lemma on Scandinavian Luther research (Risto Saarinen, "Lutherforschung in Skandinavien," in *Luther Handbuch* [Tübingen: Mohr Siebeck, 2017], 42–47); Volker Leppin, "Transformationen spätmittelalterlicher Mystik bei Luther," in *Transformationen: Studien zu den Wandlungsprozessen in Theologie und Frömmigkeit zwischen Spätmittelalter und Reformation* (Tübingen: Mohr Siebeck, 2015), 78–84). Generally speaking, the newer reference works have stopped treating this facet, which one reviewer described as a specificum of the Beutel *Luther Handbuch* (Gerhard Müller, "Luther Handbuch," *Theologische Literaturzeitung*, 132, no. 10 (2007): 1085–1087; Ilmari Karimies, "Mystik," in *Das Luther-Lexikon*, ed. Gury Schneider-Ludorff, Ingo Klitzsch, and Volker Leppin (Regensburg: Bückle & Böhm, 2014), 502–506; Volker Leppin, "Luther's Roots in Monastic-Mystical Piety," in *The Oxford Handbook of Martin Luther's Theology*, ed. Robert Kolb, Irene Dingel, and L'ubomír Batka (Oxford: Oxford University Press, 2014), 49–61.
5. Beutel, *Antwort und Wort*, 33; In footnote 45, Beutel draws attention to the seventy entries in the Tübinger Luther-Register.
6. Luther, *Predigt am 29. Mai 1522* (WA 10/3,145,10–12): "Dann ain Christen mensch hat gleich gewalt mit Christo, ist ain kůch und sytzt mit jm in gesampten leben."
7. Jacob Grimm, and Wilhelm Grimm, *Deutsches Wörterbuch*, vol. 11 (Leipzig: S. Hirzel, 1873), Column 2499; cf. Albrecht Beutel, "Antwort und Wort: zur Frage nach der Wirklichkeit Gottes bei Luther." In *Luther und Ontologie* (Helsinki: Luther-Agricola-Gesellschaft, 1993), Note 1, 33.
8. Luther, *Missive an Hartmut von Coronberg* (WA 10/2, 54,19–20): "biß das wyr yderman ynn uns trucken und leyben unnd eynen kuchen mit uns machen, wo es muglich were." Trans.

bread formulation could be used without soteriological or Christological significance while nevertheless having significant power to describe Christian existence. Elsewhere, Luther did not always use the phrase to describe Christian life. He even used it for negative examples, such as when the Ebionites mixed the Old and New Testaments and other inappropriate combinations. He also used the phrase to describe his opponents in the fights concerning the Lord's Supper, whom he considered to be "them all part of the same bread."[9]

This idiomatic expression is therefore used by Luther to describe a wide range of situations and topics. Next to the ones mentioned here, however, Luther uses the phrase "to become one bread" very pointedly in his treatment of the Lord's Supper. In 1522, the same year as the above sermon was held, Luther translated Erasmus's *Novum Instrumentum* text[10] of 1 Corinthians 10:17 as: "*Denn wyr viele, sind eyn brot vnd eyn leyb, die weyl wyr alle eynes brods teylhafftig sind*" ("For we many are one bread and one body, because we are all participants in one bread").[11] When we consider that "*Kuchen*" could essentially mean "bread" in 1500,[12] then we see Luther working in a semantic-associative space with this vocabulary in which it is possible to transfer the meaning of "being one bread" to the context of the Lord's Supper and therefore to soteriology in general. Accordingly, Luther cites 1 Corinthians 10:17 in his Maundy Thursday sermon from April 2, 1523 in an abbreviated form: "*Wir sind alle eyn brot, die wir essen von eynem brot*" ("We, who eat from one bread, are all one bread"—note how "*Kuchen*" has been replaced by "*brot*") and concludes: "*das wir ein kuch werden mit yhm*" ("that we become one bread with him"—here with "*kuch*").[13] Apparently, this sermon demonstrates Luther's discovery of the connection between the common idiomatic expression and the theology of the Lord's Supper. However, as the sermon on Ascension Day demonstrates, he had already used the phrase in a soteriological context before.

after: Martin Luther, "A Letter of Consolation to All Who Suffer Persecution. 1522," in *Luther's Works*, vol. 43, *Devotional Writings II*, trans. Martin H. Bertram, ed. Helmut T. Lehmann and Gustav K. Wiencke, 57–70 (Philadelphia, PA: Fortress Press, 1968), 62.

9. Luther, *Kurzes Bekenntnis vom heiligen Sakrament* (WA 54, 155,29). Trans. after Martin Luther, "Brief Confession Concerning the Holy Sacrament, 1544." In *Luther's Works*, vol. 38, *Word and Sacrament IV*, trans. Martin E. Lehmann, ed. Helmut T. Lehmann and Martin E. Lehmann, 279–319 (Philadelphia, PA: Fortress Press, 1971), 304n37.
10. NOVVM IN-| strumentum omne, dilgienter ab ERASMO ROTERDAMO| recognitum et emendatum non solum ad græcam ueritatem, ue-| rumetiam ad multorum utriusque linguæ codicum, eorumque ue-| terum simul et emendatorum fidem (. . .); (Basel: Froben, 1516), 44.
11. WA.DB 7,112. 114; cf. the later translation on p. 113, in which the "ein Brot sein" / "being one bread" is omitted.
12. See Beutel, *Antwort und Wort*, 34.
13. Luther, *Predigt zum Gründonnerstag* (WA 12, 485,5–8).

There are no further sources that I can find that could help us determine if Luther was thinking from soteriology to the teachings on the Lord's Supper before Ascension Day of 1522.

The phrase can obviously take on a mystical significance depending on the context. It certainly did in Luther's first recorded usage of it. In a sermon on the twenty-fourth Sunday after Trinity, on November 15, 1523, Luther declared:

> This is how it works for a monk: even if they do many good works, pray and read the mass, they are still not a Christian, they must occupy themselves with even greater things. It is necessary that I have Christ and he has me, I should be able to say: "Christ is mine with his life and his works and conversely I am his." In sum, nobody can become a Christian or blessed through their good works, for it has been decided that nobody ascends to heaven except for a Christian "No one ascends to heaven [cf. John 3]" "I descended."" If you want to ascend to heaven, then it is necessary that Christ is in me and that I become one bread ['*kuchen*'] with him. Then I will be with him where he is.[14]

Expressions like "Christ is mine . . . and conversely I am his" or "Christ is in me" make the mystical tones very prominent. The same can be said of: "Therefore, we are now described as being planted in or unified with Christ, just as if we were baked into the same bread" in Cruciger's *Sommerpostille.*[15] Both illustrate the important context of a singular bread in the doctrine of justification. In the *Sommerpostille*, the sacramental mediation for becoming the bread is baptism. There is no getting around the Lord's Supper as the best fit for it, though, a point made by the Maundy Thursday sermon from 1523.[16]

In that particular sermon, Luther explains his two uses of the Sacrament: that the faithful "become one bread with Christ" and that they "become one bread with each other and with their neighbors."[17] This double-structure already hints at parallels between this text and the *Freedom of a Christian,* since the latter also poses a double-thesis whose application is

14. Luther, *Predigt am 24. Sonntag nach Trinitatis 1523* (WA 11,204,1–8): "*Ita cum monacho est, quanquam faciat bona multa, oret, legat missam, tamen nondum Christianus est, muß hoher khummen: oportet habeam Christum et ipse me habeat, dicere debeo 'Christus meus est cum vita sua et opibus et rursum ego sum suus'. Summa: nemo operibus bonis fit Christianus neque beatus, quia conclusum est: nemo ascendit in celum nisi Christianus. 'Nemo ascendit in celum' Ioh. 3. 'Ego descendi'. Si volueris ascendere celum, oportet Christus in me sit, ut unus kuchen cum eo sim, tum ego ero, ubi ipse est.*" My translation.
15. *Crucigers Sommerpostille* (WA 22,97,12–13): "*Also heissen wir nu in Christo gepflantzet oder vereinigt, und gleich wie in einen kuchen gebacken.*" My translation.
16. Luther, *Predigt zum Gründonnerstag* (WA 12, 483–491). The *Kuchen* usages are only found in the shorter version of the sermon, which is probably the authentic one.
17. Luther, *Predigt zum Gründonnerstag* (WA 12, 485,1–4).

expanded in the context of works for salvation and serving one's neighbor. The same structure can be found in the sermon on Maundy Thursday about two-and-a-half years later. The connections go even deeper, though: the image of the bread in the sermon functions in a very similar way as does the image of the bride in the *Freedom of a Christian*. The following synopsis should help to visualize this:

Freedom of a Christian (1520) (WA 7,25,26–26,12, trans. after LW 31:351–52)	*Maundy Thursday Sermon* (1523) (WA 12, my translations)
The third incomparable benefit of faith is that it unites the soul with Christ as a bride is united with her bridegroom. By this mystery, as the Apostle teaches, Christ and the soul become one flesh [Eph. 5:31–32]. And if they are one flesh and there is between them a true marriage—indeed the most perfect of all marriages, since human marriages are but poor examples of this one true marriage—it follows that everything they have they hold in common, the good as well as the evil. Accordingly the believing soul can boast of and glory in whatever Christ has as though it were its own, and whatever the soul has Christ claims as his own. Let us compare these and we shall see inestimable benefits. Christ is full of grace, life, and salvation. The soul is full of sins, death, and damnation. Now let faith become between them and sins, death, and damnation will be Christ's, while grace, life, and salvation will be the soul's; for if Christ is a bridegroom, he must take upon himself the things which are his bride's and bestow upon her the things that are his. If he gives her his body and very self, how shall he not give her all that is his? And if he takes the body of the bride, how shall he not take all that is hers?	[486,2–4] Through what? . . . through faith, if you believe that Christ has given his body and his life for you. [485,8–10] Therefore we make everything which is his into ours, that our conscience would no longer trust in itself but rather would consider and trust in the pure grace of Christ. [486,8–10] See, this is how you will become one bread [*kuchen*] with Christ: we join him in entering a communion of his goods with him and he enters into a communion of our goods [485,11–486,2] What does Christ have? He has the fact that he is the Lord over death, devil, hell, and all creatures, he is all mighty, potent, wise, just, pious, and full of all virtues. See, all of these goods become our own. [486,5–7] Then you will become a lord over death, devil, hell and all creatures, powerful, pious and blessed, not through the justice of your lies, but rather through [the justice] of Christ who stands for you.

Here we have a most pleasing vision not only of communion but also of a blessed struggle and victory and salvation and redemption. Christ is God and man in one person. He has neither sinned nor died, and is not condemned, and he cannot sin, die, or be condemned; his righteousness, life, and salvation are unconquerable, eternal, omnipotent. By the wedding ring of faith he shares in the sins, death, and pains of hell which are his bride's. As a matter of fact, he makes them his own and acts as if they were his own and as if he himself had sinned; He suffered, died, and descended into hell that he might overcome them all. Now since it was such a one who did all this, and death and hell could not swallow him up, these were necessarily swallowed up by him in a mighty duel; for his righteousness is greater than the sins of all men, his life stronger than death, his salvation more invincible than hell. Thus, the believing soul by means of the pledge of its faith is free in Christ, its bridegroom, free from all sins, secure against death and hell, and is endowed with the eternal righteousness, life, and salvation of Christ its bridegroom. So, he takes to himself a glorious bride, "without spot or wrinkle, cleansing her by the washing of water with the word" [Cf. Eph. 5:26–27] of life, that is, by faith in the Word of life, righteousness, and salvation. In this way he marries her in faith, steadfast love, and in mercies, righteousness, and justice, as Hos. 2 [: 19–21] says. Who then can fully appreciate what this royal marriage means? Who can understand the riches of the glory of this grace? Here this rich and divine	[487,2–3] See, when you reach this point, what more could you want? You are already in paradise and you are blessed. [486,5–7] Then you will become a lord over death, devil, hell and all creatures, powerful, pious and blessed, not through the justice of your lies, but rather through [the justice] of Christ who stands for you. [487,2–3] See, when you reach this point, what more could you want? You are already in paradise and you are blessed.

bridegroom Christ marries this poor, wicked harlot, redeems her from all her evil, and adorns her with all his goodness. Her sins cannot now destroy her, since they are laid upon Christ and swallowed up by him. And she has that righteousness in Christ, her husband, of which she may boast as of her own and which she can confidently display alongside her sins in the face of death and hell and say, "If I have sinned, yet my Christ, in whom I believe, has not sinned, and all his is mine and all mine is his," as the bride in the Song of Solomon [2:16] says, "My beloved is mine and I am his." This is what Paul means when he says in 1 Cor. 15 [:57], "Thanks be to God, who gives us the victory through our Lord Jesus Christ[.]"	

Albrecht Beutel has already observed how tightly these passages "match the motive of joyful exchange."[18] He did not, however, explore the very pressing implications for the development of Luther's theological development. They are enormous. The image of the bread makes clear how salvation occurs as a form of transfer between Christ and humans. In other contexts, there are additional points of contact, such as in the Ascension Day sermon from 1522 when Luther connected the idea of the bread with the transfer of the *gleich gewalt mit Christo* (the same power as Christ)[19] an apparent allusion to the spiritual kingdom which *The Freedom of a Christian* describes as originating from the spiritual marriage of Christ and the church or believing soul.[20]

Not only the application of the bread-image is of interest here. So is the connection running throughout the theological history which we see

18. Beutel, *Antwort und Wort,* 34; such parallels have been demonstrated for the Lord's Supper by Eberhard Winkler, ["Motive der Mystik in Luthers Verständnis des Abendmahls." In *Lutherjahrbuch vol.78.* 137–152 (Göttingen: Vabdenhoeck & Ruprecht, 2011), 143,] as early as the *Sermon von dem hochwürdigen Sakrament des heiligen wahren Leichnams Christi.*
19. Luther, *Sermon zum Auffahrttag* (WA 10/3,145,11).
20. Luther, *Freiheitsschrift* (WA 7,27,21–28,5).

when we use the *Freedom of a Christian* as a point of comparison. The bridal image in *The Freedom* is the best-known, uncontested evidence of how mystical theology continued to work in Luther's spirituality throughout his Reformational period. He had read about the image of the soul as the bride of Christ from Bernard[21] and heard about it directly from Staupitz.[22] In other passages of the *Freedom of a Christian*, such as when it speaks of the internal and external person concerning freedom, there are other, direct mystical ideas at work, especially those derived from the *Theologia deutsch*.[23] That means that the older, Lutheran opinion that the imagery of the bridal soul is just a form of mystical wrapping paper for the doctrine of justification loses all tenability. When we consider just how deeply and variously Luther was embedded in late-medieval mystical discourse,[24] then we must understand the *Freedom of a Christian* as a mystical tract that argues that *unio* takes place through faith.[25] That is already a big transformation![26] The idea of becoming one bread, however, goes much, much further. *Unio* and the joyous exchange remain the same, but they have now been disassociated from at least two elements that the Reformation-thinking Luther would have thought of as burdens. The first was that Bernard required a gigantic commitment to theological allegory when reading the Bible in order to make his theology work. By 1523, at the latest, such allegorical reading had become problematic for Luther.[27] With 1 Corinthians 10:17, however, Luther has found an anchor point for his bread-*Kuchen* image which could use a literal reading of a biblical text to support a mystical interpretation and thus resolved the issue

21. See the classic work: Ulrich Köpf and Bernard of Clairvaux, "Religiöse Erfahrung in Der Theologie Bernhards Von Clairvaux," in *Beiträge Zur Historischen Theologie* (Tubingen: Mohr, 1980).
22. Johann von Staupitz, *Sämtliche Schriften*, vol. 2, *Lateinische Schriften: Libellus de exsecutione aeternae praedestinationis*, ed. Lothar Graf zu Dohna and Richard Wetzel (Berlin: De Gruyter, 1979), 142–147.
23. *Eyn geystlich edles Buchleynn. | von rechter vnderscheyd | vnd vorstand. was der | alt vnnd new mensche sey. Was Adams | vnnd was gottis kind sey. vnnd wie ,Adam | ynn vns sterben vnnd Christus | ersteen sall,* (Wittenberg: Grunenberg, 1516), f. A 3v: "Auch stend dise menschen yn einer freyheyt." / "These individuals are also standing in freedom."
24. See the more comprehensive analysis in Volker Leppin, *Die fremde Reformation: Luthers mystische Wurzeln* (Munich: C. H. Beck, 2016).
25. For more on how the emphasis of Luther's thought shifted from faith to love, see Berndt Hamm, *Der frühe Luther: Etappen reformatorischer Neuorientierung* (Tübingen: Mohr Siebeck, 2010).
26. For more on this concept in the context of Reformation history, see Volker Leppin, *Transformationen: Studien zu den Wandlungsprozessen in Theologie und Frömmigkeit zwischen Spätmittelalter und Reformation* (Tübingen: Mohr Siebeck, 2015).
27. For more on the persistence of allegorical interpretation, cf. Kenneth Hagen, and Martin Luther, *Luther's Approach to Scripture as Seen in His "Commentaries" on Galatians: 1519–1538* (Tübingen: Mohr, 1993).

of allegory. The second disassociation is from the ecclesiological usage of the bridal image as he heard it from Staupitz. Luther *kept* that image as it pertained to the Christian congregation becoming one *Kuchen* with each other, but he *rejected* it for the office-oriented, institutionalized church. By the mid-1520s, Luther was well on his way to leaving the medieval-hierarchical institution of the church behind him. He started to rethink the image of bread to further convey the basic idea of the bridal image. Years later, Luther would continue to mention the tight connection between the bridal image and the *Kuchen* image. His Christmas sermon from 1527 illustrates this nicely:

> This is how we can tell how Christ is ours and how he became one bread with us through faith so that he can weave us men into each other as well. He desires that we all become one flesh and body just as he became one flesh and body with us, which bodily marriage demonstrates as God said: "the two will become one flesh." That is why Saint Paul speaks about spiritual marriage (among other things) to the Ephesians: "We are members of his body, from his flesh and from his bones, and for this reason a man leaves his father and mother and clings to his wife and the two of them become one and one flesh. The mystery is great, but I am speaking about Christ and the congregation." Therefore, if we all become one body and one flesh, then we will also be purified with Christ through a spiritual marriage, which means that we will all be his bride and he will place us next to him on the Last Day to judge the entire world.[28]

SACRAMENTALIZATION: A SHIFT IN LUTHER'S UNDERSTANDING OF MYSTICISM

The above passage from the 1527 sermon shows us that the transformation in the *Kuchen*-image never fully intended to replace the bridal image. We have seen how there *were* aspects that Luther did not find to be useful,

28. Luther, *Ein ander Sermon vom Christtag* (WA 17/2, 329,21–33): "Also erkennet man, wie Cristus unser sey, und wie er mit uns ain kueche sey worden durch den glawben, damit er uns menschen auch in einander flecht, Das wil, dz wir alle ein flaisch und ein leib werden, wie er ein fleisch und ein leib mit uns ist, welchs die leiblich ee anzeigt, davon got sprach, 'es werden zway sein ein flaisch'. Darumb sagt S. Paulus zue den Ephesern vonn diser gaistlichen Ehe undern andern also: 'Wir sind gelider seines leibes, von seinem flaisch und von seinem gepaine, Umb des willen wirt ein mensch verlassen vater und mûtter und seynem weibe anhangen, und werden zwey ein fleisch sein, Das geheymnis ist groß, Ich sag aber von Christo und der gemaine.' Darumb wenn wir ein leib alle werden unnd ein flaisch, so werden wir myt Christo auch gerainiget durch eine gaistliche ee, das ist, wir werden alle seine breutte, und er wirt uns an dem Jungsten tag setzen zû richten mit jm die gantze welt." My translation.

but he certainly found enough useful content that he could continue to leverage. Even after reading 1 Corinthians 10:17, a central connection between the mystical experience and a sacrament remained in his theology. Luther's later writings would bring a further point of connection to this: the Word. On Quasimodigeniti Sunday, April 20, 1544, Luther preached:

> Just as God and the human being are one person, so do the human being and the Word which they hear become bread. The heart desires what the Word desires and vice versa. Thus, the human being is transformed into the Word, but the Word is not transformed into the human but rather the heart says: "This is truth, I want to remain there."[29]

The Word has superseded all else, reminding us of a basic phenomenon in Luther's mystical thought, a persistent transformation occurring in the theology of the Word.[30] Contrary to popular understanding, that transformation did not entail Luther simply replacing his mystical roots with the Word, but it did mean reembedding those roots in another framework that placed a greater emphasis on grace from without.

At this point in Reformation history, the Wittenberg movement was starting to grow substantially more complex. At its beginning, Luther was one of many theological minds in Wittenberg who were wholeheartedly preoccupied with late-medieval mysticism, especially that of John Tauler's heritage. Henrik Otto has given us a very helpful study of the comments on Tauler editions demonstrating how several theologians in early-sixteenth-century Wittenberg were intensely reading Tauler. One of them was Andreas Karlstadt.[31] Hans Peter Hasse has demonstrated that Thomas Münzer was also shaped by Tauler.[32] It seems that all three of the great antagonists within the Wittenberg Reformation in the 1520s had been reading him! However, Luther's intense occupation (and conflict) with these two other scholars in 1522/23 demonstrates that they were all reading Tauler quite differently and drew alternative consequences from

29. Luther, *Predigt am Sonntag Quasimodogeniti* (WA 49,381,8–11): "Sicut Deus et homo una persona, sic homo et verbum, quod audit, wird ein kuchen, das das hertz wil, was das wort wil, econtra. Sic homo mutatur in verbum, verbum non in hominem, sed das hertz spricht: Das ist die warheit. Dabey wil ich bleiben." My translation.
30. Leppin, *Transformationen*, 412.
31. Henrik Otto, *Vor-und frühreformatorische Tauler-Rezeption: Annotationen in Drucken des späten 15. und frühen 16. Jahrhunderts. Quellen und Forshungen zur Reformationsgeschichte*, vol. 75 (Heidelberg: Gütersloher Verlagshaus, 2003).
32. Hans-Peter Hasse, *Karlstadt und Tauler: Untersuchungen zur Kreuzestheologie. Quellen und Forschungen zur Reformationsgeschichte*, vol. 58 (Gütersloh: Gütersloher Verlagshaus Gerd Mohn, 1993).

him. The conflict began while Luther was away from Wittenberg in Wartburg Castle throughout 1521/22 due to the Edict of Worms. While he was gone, Andreas Karlstadt used the opportunity to carry out significant changes in Wittenberg. He was firmly remonstrated in Luther's Invocavit sermon from 1522. One of the key words that Luther used here was the same one that he had used in the context of his own mystical development: freedom. Freedom, as Luther put it, should not be transformed into a new compulsion.[33] By this point, he may have been aware that he was fighting against another strain of mysticism than his own. It all boiled down to the question as to whether images should be removed from the churches or not. In January 1522, the city council of Wittenberg had in fact decided to do just that but had not implemented it quickly. Andreas Karlstadt protested against this delay with argumentation that conveyed his mystical formation.[34] Luther *also* used mystical vocabulary to argue for the preservation of the images: those images should be preserved that do not stand in the way of the message of Jesus Christ. The production of images is not forbidden, only praying to them.[35]

Luther realized that order in the congregation was necessary. Anything else he understood to be pursuant to one's own interests instead of those of God. In a sermon from March 1, 1523, he raged against the *schwermer* (spiritualists or enthusiasts) who caused turmoil.[36] This concept of the *schwermer* grew increasingly important for Luther until he could subsume both Karlstadt and Thomas Müntzer into it.[37] This was an important process in Luther's development of mysticism, for he made clear to himself and those around him that any action that invoked God for its legitimacy must be accountable to an external authority. *Purely* internal spirituality could not be allowed for this reason. Let us not forget: Luther was a man who had propagated internal spirituality over against the external(ized) forms of the late Middle Ages. He was now searching for an external buffer against an uncontrollable internalized spirituality. He would find it in the word of God and in the sacraments.

Research into Luther often concludes at this point that Luther rejected mysticism *per se*. However, the evidence does not support this claim.

33. Luther, *Invokavitpredigten* (WA 10/3,26,14–27,1).
34. Andreas Karlstadt, "Von Abtuung der Bilder." In *Flugschriften der frühen Reformationsbewegung (1518–1524)*, vol. 1, ed. Adolf Laube, Annerose Schneider, and Sigrid Looss (Vaduz, Liechtenstein: Topos, 1983), 105–127.
35. Luther, *Invokavitpredigten* (WA 10/3,28,3–5).
36. Luther, *Predigt am 1. März 1523* (WA 11,42,26).
37. See Volker Leppin, "Schwärmer." In *Theologische Realenzyklopädie*, vol. 30 (Berlin: De Gruyter, 1999), 628–629.

Luther transformed mysticism and bound it to the Sacrament, and he was not the first to do so. The Middle Ages had a famous connection between the Eucharist and the Sacrament as John Tauler's Corpus Christi sermons demonstrate.[38] The festival celebrates *looking at* the Sacrament, but on that day, Tauler preached about consuming it with the memorable phrase: "we feed upon our God"[39] (see p. 29). This communion garnered special significance, for according to Tauler, "no act in our material existence is so close to us, or enters so intimately into our bodily life, as eating and drinking."[40] Tauler used this very heavy-handed description and interpretation of the eucharistic event to give prominence to the spiritual dimension of the Eucharist. He meant a deeply internalized attitude of penance which should be cultivated in a person's life with Christ. The eucharistic event was broken: "When we eat this food, we ourselves are eaten."[41] Tauler embedded this thought into an explicitly eucharistic context which argued all the way until the Eucharist had become the deepest, most profound mystical unity in which the human becomes divine:

> Thou shalt find out if thou art absorbed into God as His food, if thou are so changed as to find nothing in thyself except Him, and findest thyself nowhere else but in Him. For does He not say: "He that eateth My flesh and drinketh My blood abideth in Me and I in him." Therefore must thou be stripped of thy old self, as it were, by the divine mastication of thy soul—just as thou dost change thy food by chewing it. If anything will be turned into fire it is perforce no longer wood. If thou shalt be changed, as it were, into God thou must cease to be thyself.[42]

Tauler brings about a high concentration of eucharistic consumption, the incarnation of God, and human apotheosis in the idea of mystical

38. This phenomenon has long been neglected by researchers, but cf. Herman W. J. Vekeman, "La Mystique Eucharistique Des Cisterciennes Au XIII Siècle." In *Collectanea Cisterciensia*, vol. 66, no. 2. (Abbaye de Scourmont, 2004), 120–139 has drawn attention to it.
39. Johannes Tauler, *Die Predigten Taulers aus der Engelberger und der Freiburger Handschrift sowie aus Schmidts Abschriften der ehemaligen Strassburger Handschriften*, ed. Ferdinand Vetter (Berlin: Weidmannsche Buchhandlung, 1910), 293, 27.
40. Tauler, *Die Predigten*, 293,31–33. Trans. after: John Tauler, *The Sermons and Conferences of John Tauler,* trans. and ed. Walter Elliott (Washington, DC: Apostolic Mission House, 1910), 369; Cf. Tauler, *Predigten* (Hofmann) 208.
41. Tauler, *Die Predigten*, 294,3–4.
42. Tauler, *Die Predigten*, 295,25–34: "Also, liebes kint, hie an solt du bekennen, ob dich Got gessen und verslunden habe, ob du dich vindest in im und in dir, und du dich niergent anders envindest und nút anders in dir. . . . Wan sol die spise in des menschen nature gewandelt werden, so mûs si von not in ir selber entwerden. Wan ein ueklich ding, sol es werden des es nút enist, so mûs es al zemole des entwerden das es ist; . . . Solt du in Got gewerden, so mûst du din selbes entwerden." Trans. after: Tauler, *The Sermons and Conferences of John Tauler*, 371.

unification. This complex of ideas is very central to understanding Luther's Maundy Thursday sermon from 1523:

> The other fruit is that we are one bread with each other. One might say: "we who eat from one bread are also one bread with each other." Or perhaps: "we who drink from one drink are one drink with each other." How does that work? If I eat the bread, then it eats me in a spiritual way. Externally, I consume the bread, internally I draw upon all of the power and potential of the Body of Christ which feeds me and strengthens me like a natural bread does for the body. But he also takes my sins upon himself, my death and my hell, and we are baked into each other, we become one bread and one kuchen with each other. And we, who are one bread with Christ, have basically become one thing. I will make an analogy so that you understand. Does it not work this way? The grains which are ground up jump into each other, none of them keep their flour to themselves but rather they all get mixed up until they all become one thing.[43]

Tauler's idea is very obvious here, and Luther sees it at work in the Eucharist. Consuming the Sacrament leads to being consumed by Christ and ultimately to unity with Christ and the congregation. The only thing missing here is the idea of the apotheosis which has a much greater significance for Tauler than it does for Luther. Common to both, however, is the idea of the joyous exchange/unification.[44] As concerns this point, Luther remains in conversation with those whom he has termed "*schwermer*," those who are also deeply committed to the basic ideas of mysticism.

43. Luther, *Predigt an Gründonnerstag* (WA 12,488,1–14): "Die ander frucht ist die, das wyr untter eynander auch eyn brot sind. Nu sagt er 'die wir essen von einem brot, sind auch unter einander eyn brot'. Item 'die wir trincken von eynem tranck, sind auch unter eynander eyn tranck'. Wie geht das zu? Alßo, wann ich das brot esse, so isset es mich widerumb auch geystlich: Außwendig nehme ichs brot zu mir, ynnwendig nehme ich zw mir alle krafft und macht des leybs Christi, das speyst mich und erquickt mich wye eyn naturlich brot den leyb. So fasset er widerumb mein sunde auff sich, meyn todt, meyn hell, und backen also ynn einander, und werden eyn brot und eyn kuchen mit einander. Und so wyr denn mit Christo eyn kuchen sind, so wirckt das selbige soviel, das wyr auch unter einander eyn ding werden. Und das yhr des eyn gleichnis seht und vorsthet, Seht, ist es nicht also? Die korner, wenn sie tzermalen werden, so sprengen sie sich ynn einander, keyns behelt seyn mel bey yhm, sondern mengens ynn eynander, biß es als eyn ding wirt." My translation.
44. Reinhart Staats, "Das Bild Christi Im Abendmahl: Patristische Tradition in Lutherischer Abendmahlslehre Und in Lutherischer Naturfrömmigkeit," in *Mystik, Metapher, Bild Beiträge des VII. Makarios-Symposiums*, ed. Martin Tamcke (Göttingen: Universitätsverlag, 2008), 74–75, has impressively demonstrated that Luther very probably believed in the idea of metamorphosis in the Lord's Supper in commonality with the Early Church; cf. Luther, *Daß diese Worte Christi* (WA 23,205,20–24): "Also wir, so wir Christus fleisch essen leiblich vnd geistlich ist die speise so starck, das sie vns ynn sich wandelt, vnd aus fleischlichen, sundlichen, sterblichen menschen, geistliche, heilige, lebendige menschen macht, wie wir denn auch bereit sind, aber doch verborgen ym glauben vnd hoffnung."

The Sacrament and the Word have not superseded mysticism. They have become the occasion for mysticism to develop in the souls of the believers. In 1522/23, Luther became a sacramental mystic à la Tauler. As is so often the case in Luther's development, this movement is best described as a *transformation* and not a rupture.

THE IMAGE OF BREAD (KUCHEN) AS THE CENTRAL METAPHOR IN LUTHER'S THEOLOGY

The bread metaphor is not an appendix in Luther's theology. He uses it in many different contexts, such as in his interpretation of mystical authors or when he uses the Adam-Christ typology. During his sermon series on Genesis, Luther explained on April 26, 1523: "'Adam' is the Hebrew word for what German knows as 'mensch' ['human being'], and all of us are known as Adam since we all come from him and we are one bread."[45] "Bread" is not applied to the mystical relation to Christ through salvation but rather to the context with Adam which Luther does not understand simply as genetic propagation but as an existential conflation of today's humanity with its original human father. He uses the very same image here as he was using at around the same time to describe the soteriological relation with Christ, the Adam-Christ typology, once again a complete unification of Christ and humanity as derived from Paul (Rom 6) and the *Theologia Deutsch*. As we saw above (see p. 71), he had given the latter work the subtitle "A spiritual, noble little book on the proper distinction and understanding of what the old and new person is, what is Adam's child and what is God's, and how Adam will die in us and Christ will arise in us" in his 1516 edition.[46] Luther's usage of the bread-image to convey inclusion in the state of Adam leads him to develop the central anthropological foundation of salvation through Christ—and it sets the stage for him to make his own interpretation of the relation between the human person and Adam.

There are two important things to note here: first, this is done mostly in the service of soteriology and, second, the connection to the incarnation,

45. Luther, *Predigten über das erste Buch Mose* (WA 14,125,2–3); cf. WA 24,75,25–26: "'Adam' hebraice, 'mensch' germanice, omnes Adam dicimur a primo illo et sumus ein kuchen." My translation.

46. Luther, *Vorrede zur unvollständigen Ausgabe der "deutschen Theologie"* (WA 1,153): "Eyn geystlich edles Buchleynn. | von rechter vnderscheyd | vnd vorstand. was der | alt vnnd new mensche sey. Was Adams | vnnd was gottis kind sey. vnnd wie ,Adam | ynn vns sterben vnnd Christus | ersteen sall." (Wittenberg: Grunenberg, 1516), f. A 3v: "Auch stend dise menschen yn einer freyheyt." My translation.

which we saw above, remains. At Christmas 1533, Luther preached about the birth of Christ: "What is an oven if not the thing which melts us and makes [out of us] one bread [with Christ]."[47] The context illustrates how the mystically shaped metaphor of Kuchen is related to another, preferred metaphor of Luther: On March 15, 1522, amidst his sermons on Invocavit, Luther sharply critiqued Karlstadt and the turbulence he had caused in the city of Wittenberg,[48] saying that God is a "glowing furnace of love, reaching even from the earth to the heavens."[49] Interestingly, Luther used this image to describe the "fruit of this sacrament," by which he meant the Lord's Supper.[50] He had it in mind when he wrote of the faithful becoming one Kuchen with Christ. If we are strict with chronology, the concept of the "glowing oven" precedes that of the "Kuchen" idea, but they are close enough to each other both in terms of their usage as well as their time of occurrence that we can speak of a phase in Luther's thought in which the incarnation and the sacrament were thought of together. Right around this time, Luther is also talking about the unity of God and man in Jesus Christ as "*eine kuchen.*"[51] Johann Anselm Steiger has used such expressions to describe the *communicatio idiomatum* as the "axis and motor of Martin Luther's theology."[52] It certainly shows up throughout Luther's theological works, such as when he describes the relation of Christ to the Father as "thus it is all blended into one."[53] Luther's specifically Christological and Trinitarian usage of the bread image diverges from Bernard's usage, blurring the distinction between the inner-divine and inner-Christological *unio* on the one hand and the union of Christ and the faithful on the other hand.

47. Luther, *Predigt am 25. Dezember 1533* (WA 37,236,2–3): "quod solt backoffen sein, quae nos zuschmeltzt et faceret ein kuchen." My translation.
48. For a sober account of these events, see Natalie Krentz, *Ritualwandel und Deutungshoheit: die frühe Reformation in der Residenzstadt Wittenberg (1500–1533).* Spätmittelalter, Humanismus, Reformation, vol. 74 (Germany: Mohr Siebeck, 2014).
49. Luther, *Predigt am 15. März 1522* (WA 10/3,56,2–3): "glüender backofen foller liebe, der da reichet von der erden biß an den hymmel." Trans. after LW 51:95.
50. Luther, *Predigt am 15. März 1522* (WA 10/3,55,10): "*frucht dieses sacraments.*" Trans. after LW 51:95.
51. Luther, *Wochenpredigten über Joh 6–8* (WA 33,232,21. 23).
52. Johann Anselm Steiger, "Die communicatio idiomatum als Achse und Motor der Theologie Luthers. Der 'fröhliche Wechsel' als hermeneutischer Schlüssel zu Abendmahlslehre, Anthropologie, Seelsorge, Naturtheologie, Rhetorik und Humor," *Neue Zeitschrift für Systematische Theologie und Religionsphilosophie* 38, no.1 (De Gruyter, 1996): 1–28; For more on the Lord's Supper: 16–19. My translation.
53. Luther, *Das XIV. und XV. Kapitel S. Johannis* (WA 45,521,21–23): "alles jnn einen kuchen geschlagen" Trans. after: Martin Luther, "Sermons in the Gospel of St. John Chapters 14–16" In *Luther's Works*, vol. 24, trans. Martin H. Bertram, ed. Jaroslav Pelikan and Daniel E. Poellot, 1–422 (Saint Louis, MO: Concordia Publishing House, 1961), 66.

What remains central to Luther's argumentation, however, is the soteriological dimension. He frequently uses it to jump into ecclesiological musing that is tightly related to the ecclesiological theory developed in the *Freedom of a Christian*. In that text, Luther does not only develop the idea of a kingdom of the believers but also that of their priesthood.[54] And he used the same image of *Kuchen* to illustrate it. On May 30, 1535, the First Sunday after Trinity, he preached against the idea that "the clerical estate is different from and higher than the other normal Christians in the eyes of God."[55] He then explained:

> For how should it come to be that the Holy Sacrament is used to differentiate between Christians? Our Lord Christ instituted it primarily to console the conscience and to strengthen faith. Additionally, it should be uniform within Christianity as a bond to bind together Christians, so that they are the same as bread or dough ("*kuchen*") and not merely that they have one God, one Word, one Baptism, one Sacrament, one hope and confidence, but also that they have one body, such that one member gives their hand to the next and serves, helps and advises them, suffers with them, etc.[56]

Put this way, the image of *Kuchen* serves to express the pneumatologically conveyed unity of the body of Christ. It supersedes the idea we saw earlier of addressing the needs of one's neighbors in love. Instead, we have the much grander idea of a continuum of the hidden church as a sticky cake dough that cannot be separated. The hiddenness shows that the *Kuchen* image is not intended to convey what we can perceive through our external senses. What starts in the visible bread of the Lord's Supper quickly ascends into the spiritually hidden dimension of the fully described True Church which vastly exceeds any earthly institution.

* * *

The ideas in this chapter have hopefully convinced the reader of some basic insights for understanding Martin Luther and his theology. The first

54. Luther, *Freiheitsschrift* (WA 7,28,6–25).
55. Luther, *Predigt am 1. Sonntag nach Trinitatis* (WA 41,280,33–34): "der pfaffen stand ein sonderer und hôher stand sey fůr Gott denn der andern gemeinen Christen." My translation.
56. Luther, *Predigt am 1. Sonntag nach Trinitatis* (WA 41,281,14–23): "Denn wie kompt das heilige Sacrament dazu, das es sol gebraucht werden zum unterschied unter den Christen zu machen, so es doch der Herr Christus furnemlich hat eingesetzet zum trost des gewissens und sterckung des glaubens, Darnach, das es sol sein jnn der Christenheit gleich als ein band, damit die Christen zusamen verbunden sind. Das sie gleich wie ein brod oder ein kuchen sind, nicht allein damit, das sie zu gleich einen Got, ein wort, eine Tauffe, ein Sacrament, eine hoffnung und zuversicht haben, sondern auch ein leib sind, da ein glied dem andern handreichung thun und dienen sol, helffen, raten, mitleiden tragen &c." My translation.

is rather simple: the metaphor of being or becoming one bread ("*Kuchen*") has a biblical reference backing it up (1 Cor 10:17) and a mystical significance. It is the culmination of various strains of thought with a great deal of anthropology and soteriology.

But beyond that, the bread image shows us how Luther's continued usage of late-medieval content could nevertheless direct the developments of the early 1520s which he regarded as dangerous. Confronted with the Peasants War and the theologies of Thomas Müntzer and Andreas Bodenstein Karlstadt, which he viewed as disastrous, particularly due to the violence they unleashed upon society, Luther took a clearly profiled stance within a range of given mystical options to ensure the accountability of his mystical spirituality without losing it altogether. Word and Sacrament became the point of contact between internalized and externalized spirituality, and he eagerly employed the biblical metaphor of bread to bring it to a point. He hoped that these external forms could put a stop to the subjectivism that he saw in Karlstadt and others whom he slandered as "*schwermer.*" As external forms, they could claim objectivity. And yet Luther's theology remained mystical—previous chapters have demonstrated that Luther transformed mystical theology into a new coordinate system, and we see something very similar taking place here. Word and Sacrament, it turns out, have much more to do with late-medieval mysticism than research has previously believed! This pairing of concepts conveys unity with Christ which transcends the boundaries of earthly existence for the faithful. The fact that Luther makes this mystical description of the faithful's relation to Christ into the foundation of his ecclesiology demonstrates that Luther remained a mystic after defeating Karlstadt. In fact, he remained an ecclesial-sacramental mystic.

8.

Philosophy of Language, Monastic Meditation, and Pneumatic Speech: A Study of Luther's Disputation on the Sentence "*Verbum caro factum est*"

Some Luther scholars, most prominently among them Eberhard Jüngel,[1] tend to see a major part of what makes Luther's theology so special in his understanding of language.[2] This is just one approach of many that seek to identify Luther's substantial innovation over against his medieval roots. The language analysis also provides the opportunity to show Luther's uniqueness in his later writings, especially his academic disputations. One of these has been provided by Stefan Streiff who interpreted Luther's disputation on *The Word became flesh* as giving an understanding of what philosophy or theology could be for Luther.[3]

Contrary to the prevailing scholarly opinion, the disputations do not clearly show a new Luther in contrast to the medieval world. Graham

1. See among others Eberhard Jüngel, "Metaphorische Wahrheit: Erwägungen zur theologischen Relevanz der Metapher als Beitrag zur Hermeneutik einer narrativen Theologie," in *Evangelische Theologie*, vol. 34, no. Supplement (München: 1974): 71–122.
2. Among the fathers of this view is also Gerhard Ebeling; for a detailed critique see Graham White, *Luther as Nominalist. A Study of the Logical Methods Used in Martin Luther's Disputations in the Light of Their Medieval Background* (Helsinki: Luther-Agricola-Society, 1994), 60–81. For a more recent approach see the impressive work by Joachim Ringleben, *Gott im Wort: Luthers Theologie von der Sprache her. Hermeneutische Untersuchungen zur Theologie* (Tübingen: Mohr Siebeck, 2010), 57–58.
3. Stefan Streiff, "*Novis linguis loqui*": *Martin Luthers Disputation über Joh 1,14 "verbum caro factum est" aus dem Jahr 1539* (Germany: Vandenhoeck & Ruprecht, 1993).

White's pioneering study on Luther as a nominalist,[4] has shown that even the later Martin Luther still made use of the logical training he had benefited from in Erfurt while studying under Bartholomaeus Arnoldi of Usingen and Jodocus Trutfetter, both representatives of the Ockham Renaissance in Erfurt[5] around 1500. The following study will go down the path paved by White with a closer look at *The Word became flesh* disputation contrasted against its medieval background.

THE DISPUTATION "VERBUM CARO FACTUM EST" IN WITTENBERG 1539

Disputations were among the most important media of the early Wittenberg movement. Even if the disputation about the indulgences never actually took place, the *95 Theses* were printed as an official invitation to a disputation. Later, the disputations in Heidelberg and Leipzig provided milestones for the development of new ideas and the formation of the Reformation movement.

Nevertheless, disputation ceased as a phenomenon in the time between 1522 and 1533.[6] A certain distance toward traditional academic manners had arisen, and the Wittenbergers preferred biblical lectures to the more theoretical, argumentative genre of disputation. The need for learned theologians led to the return of this custom in 1533 when Caspar Cruciger, Johannes Bugenhagen, and Johannes Aepinus were the first to pass their doctoral promotion with a disputation under the auspices of the Reformation.[7] From now on, a new series of disputations started in the context of doctoral exams as well as free-form circle disputations that presented the wisdom of the masters. A special role was reserved for Martin Luther within that academic culture. In 1538 he was freed from his duty to hold disputations but encouraged to give them.[8] The first of

4. White, *Luther as Nominalist*.
5. Erich Kleineidam, *Universitas studii Erfordensis: Überblick über die Geschichte der Universität Erfurt im Mittelalter 1392–1521. Teil 2: Spätscholastik, Humanismus und Reformation: 1461–1521*, 2nd ed. (Leipzig: Verlag, 1992), 139–146; cf. Wolfgang Urban, "Die 'Via Moderna' an der Universität Erfurt am Vorabend der Reformation," in *Gregor von Rimini: Werk und Wirkung bis zur Reformation. Spätmittelalter und Reformation*, ed. Heiko Augustinus Oberman (Berlin: De Gruyter, 1981), 316–330; Simo Knuuttila, "Trutfetter, Usingen and Erfurtian Ockhamism," in *Was ist Philosophie im Mittelalter? = What is philosophy in the Middle Ages?. Akten des X. Internationalen Kongresses für mittelalterliche Philosophie der Société Internationale pour l'Étude de la Philosophie Médiévale, 25. bis 30. August 1997 im Erfurt*, ed. Jan A. Aertsen and Andreas Speer, 818–823 (Berlin: De Gruyter, 1998).
6. WA 39/2, XIII.
7. WA 39/2, XIV.
8. WA 39/2,1.

his totally free disputations was held on January 11, 1539, on John 1:14: "*Verbum caro factum est*" ("The Word became flesh").

An early-modern disputation followed a strict form: One of the professors—in this case Martin Luther—presented theses, purportedly not as a firm opinion but as open for discussion. Other masters then provided arguments contrary to them (*opponentes*), and then one or more professors answered their arguments (*respondents*). In the case here, Luther was the only one to respond and he did this in a way that makes clear that the theses were more than openers for discussion.[9] They presented his convictions.

The surviving manuscripts and prints include not only the theses but also three reports of the actual disputation.[10] The most extensive one is preserved in a Munich codex, written by the Wittenberg student Johann Spon between 1553 and 1557 (Version A).[11] Even if it is the longest text, it is not the nearest to the reported events. Both other reports are included in the *Codex Helmstedt* 773 (Versions B and C) preserved in the Wolfenbüttel Library, which was collected between 1545 and 1550, with Johannes Aurifaber among the scribes.[12] It would take greater efforts to clear the authenticity of all reports—so for the time being, I follow the Weimar Ausgabe edition that presents all three reports, including Luther's preface or opening statement.

THE OPENING STATEMENT: CRITIQUE AGAINST THE SORBONNE

Luther began the disputation with a comprehensive *Praefatio*, or preface, which presented its aim. Versions B and C give just short summaries of it, but C delivers a *pointed* statement: Theologians, Luther claims, are to argue for their issues as if against the devil himself.[13] A statement like this is no stretch of the imagination coming from Luther: He was fully convinced that the devil was around him in his everyday life, especially in the papacy.[14] Nevertheless, it is not reported in the longer presentation of the preface given in the Munich Manuscript A.

9. WA 39/2,1.
10. See WA 39/2,3.
11. WA 39/2,XXI.
12. WA 39/2 XIXp.
13. Luther, *Disputation "Verbum caro factum est"* (WA 39/2,6,33p).
14. See Volker Leppin, "Luther on the Devil," in *Encounters with Luther: New Directions for Critical Studies,* ed. Kirsi Irmeli Stjerna and Brooks Schramm, 30–41 (Louisville, KY: Westminster John Knox Press, 2016).

However, both reports agree that there is another adversary in Luther's eyes: the Sorbonne, the University of Paris.[15] Research has shown that Luther's remarks on medieval scholasticism are usually general and undifferentiated, but Luther gives an exact name for his opponent here. Even if Luther was well trained in the Erfurt school of philosophy, his knowledge about medieval philosophy and theology seems to have quickly faded so that he saw Scholasticism in general as evil. Against this background, it is astonishing to see him singling out the University of Paris. It is even more so if we take into account that Luther was not thinking of the Sorbonne in general, but rather dwelt on a peculiar, famous sentence which he ascribed to it: the Parisians, he claimed, had taught that the same should be true in theology as well as in philosophy.[16] This was stated in the preface to Bishop Étienne Tempier's condemnation of 219 articles held by masters of the Faculty of Arts in Paris in 1277.[17] In any case, Luther must have had some knowledge of this condemnation. He certainly contradicted it with vigor: "Neither can all the same things be true in the various fields of learning."[18] While the Parisians had pleaded for a universal, uniform concept of truth, Luther seems to do the opposite. He did not see the concept of truth as one for all spheres of knowledge, but at least according to this preliminary statement, there is a special truth in theology and another truth in philosophy.

Even if Luther seems to demonstrate good knowledge of the Parisian document, he might not have grasped it fully. Moreover, it seems as if he knew only the quoted sentence and did not know anything about its context. This is clear by a sequence of theses in his disputation directed immediately against the Paris condemnation. Here, Luther attacks the Parisians with a reference to 2 Corinthians 10:5 where Paul admonishes "take every thought captive to obey Christ." The Vulgate Latin text here reads "*in captivitatem redigentes omnem intellectum in obsequium Christi.*" This is exactly the phrase that shows up in Luther's thesis 8 where he alleges that the Parisian idea of one consistent truth would mean to act against Paul's rule. The Parisians do not give their intellect, especially not philosophy, into captive obedience to Christ.[19] What Luther did not

15. Luther, *Disputation "Verbum caro factum est"* (WA 39/2,7,9–10. 29p).
16. Luther, *Disputation "Verbum caro factum est"* (WA 39/2,7,24p): "Itaque hic disputabimus contra Parrhisienses, quod etiam sint vera in theologia, quae in philosophia vera sunt et e contra."
17. White, *Luther as Nominalist*, 374–376, also considers an Oxford condemnation in the same year.
18. Luther, *Disputation "Verbum caro factum est"* (WA 39/2,7,25p): "Neque enim possunt eadem omnia vera esse in diversis professionibus." Trans. after LW 38:244.
19. Luther, *Disputation "Verbum caro factum est"* (WA 39/2,4,6p): "Cum contra Paulus doceat, captivandum esse omnem intellectum [2 Cor 10:5] (haud dubie et philosophiam) in obsequium Christi."

mention (and presumably did not know) was the fact that the Paris condemnation *had* quoted the same sentence of Paul. It did so with the same intention as Luther had: to bring philosophy into obedience to Christ. The list of condemned articles rarely gives a reason for the condemnation, but it does in article 18:

> [Condemned article:] A philosopher cannot admit future resurrection, because it is impossible to explore it by reason. [Reason for condemnation:] Error, because even a philosopher has to hold his mind captive to obey Christ.[20]

The Parisians said exactly what Luther said in thesis 8—but Luther thought his argument to be one against the "the Sorbonne, the mother of errors."[21] Luther accused the condemnation of exactly the opposite of what they themselves had thought. The reason was that Luther could not understand the concept of more than one truth in the sense that *philosophical* truth should be the only accepted one. So, in his view, the Paris condemnation "taught that articles of faith are subject to the judgment of human reason."[22] Without knowing it, Luther was fighting on the side of the Parisians when he attacked them!

As interesting as Luther's misperception is, it reveals what he intended with the disputation. In his mind, theology was threatened by a concept that submitted it to the authority of philosophy. He aimed to free theology from a philosophical approach. The main goal of the disputation was to show "that God is not subject to reason and syllogisms but to the word of God and faith."[23]

In the preface, Luther did not just reverse the relation between theology and philosophy as he imagined it but also spoke about different truths in different disciplines. At least in this disputation, he did not claim that truth in an overall view should be defined by theology alone, but he separated truth into different spheres with different truths. He understood faith and reason to be fundamentally different. According to Luther's preface, this does not only mean a different approach to the truth, but it means different objects of inquiry: Theology, he argues, deals with the invisible

20. Étienne Tempier and Kurt Flasch, *Aufklärung im Mittelalter? Die Verurteilung von 1277. Das Dokument von Paris übersetzt und erklärt von Kurt Flasch* (Mainz: Dieterich, 1989), 113: "Quod resurrectio futura non debet concedi a philosopho, quia impossibile es team investigari per rationem.—Error, quia etiam philosophus debet captivare intellectum in obsequium Christi."

21. Luther, *Disputation "Verbum caro factum est"* (WA 39/2,3,7): "Sorbona, mater errorum." Trans. after LW 38:239.

22. Luther, *Disputation "Verbum caro factum est"* (WA 39/2,4,2p): "docuit captivare articulos fidei sub iudicium rationis humanae." Trans. after LW 38:239.

23. Luther, *Disputation "Verbum caro factum est"* (WA 39/2,8,4p): "quod Deus non sit subiecuts rationi et syllogismis, sed verbo Dei et fidei." Trans. after LW 38:244.

while philosophy has to do with visible things.[24] Luther followed an old distinction here reflecting the old monastic idea, represented for example by Hugh of St. Victor who explained *theologia divina* as a way to go further than the sciences which deal with the merely visible things. By faith, *theologia divina* is able to understand the *sacramenta* of God.[25] Luther used this as a basis to dismantle the medieval hierarchy of disciplines, which shaped the usual course at universities with the *artes* at the beginning of intellectual formation. Where does formation start and end? For Luther, the answer to both was theology.

PHILOSOPHY AND THEOLOGY: LUTHER'S CLAIM FOR A DOUBLE TRUTH

What Luther discussed in the preface, comes up again in the theses which start with a double statement:

> 1. Although the saying, "Every truth is in agreement with every other truth," is to be upheld, nevertheless, what is true in one field of learning is not always true in other fields of learning. 2. In theology it is true that the Word was made flesh; in philosophy the statement is simply impossible and absurd.[26]

The reports about the disputations show that the scholars repeatedly referred to these basic arguments, sometimes mixed up with the arguments of Christology in a narrower sense. For the moment, we will focus on the epistemological arguments. Luther himself as the disputation's respondent lavished praise on an argument brought by Veit Oertel from Winsheim,

24. Luther, *Disputation "Verbum caro factum est"* (WA 39/2,7,26–8,1): "Scitis autem, longe [Röm. 8, 24–25.] aliud esse credere, aliud intelligere, ut Paulus ait: Video non, spero, aliud etiam invisibilis, aliud visibile. Hic theologia et philosophia differunt." / "For you know it is one thing to believe and something quite different to understand, as Paul says. 'I do not see, I hope' [cf. Rom 8:24 f.] the one is indeed invisible, the other is visible. Here theology and philosophy differ." Translation after LW 38:244.
25. Hugh of Saint-Victor and Rainer Berndt, *Hugonis de Sancto Victore De sacramentis Christiane fidei. Corpus Victorinum, Textus historici* (Munich: Aschendorff, 2008), 10, 225, 19–24: "Homo ergo quia oculum carnis habet mundum uidere potest. et ea que in mundo sunt. Item quia oculum rationis ex parte habet animum similiter ex parte uidet. et et que in mundo sunt. Quia uero oculum contemplationis non habet. deum et que in deo sunt uidere non ualet. Fides ergo necessaria est. quia creduntur. que non uidentur et subsitant in nobis per fidem."
26. Luther, *Disputation "Verbum caro factum est"* (WA 39/2,3,2–4): "1. Etsi tenendum est, quod dicitur: Omne verum vero consonat, tamen idem non est verum in diversis professionibus. 2. In theologia verum est, verbum esse carnem factum, in philosophia simpliciter impossibile et absurdum." Trans. after LW 38:239.

a contemporary professor of rhetoric in Wittenberg.[27] He considered it to be his core argument:[28]

> The wisdom of God does not contradict itself. Philosophy is the wisdom of God. Therefore, philosophy does not contradict itself.[29]

Luther's answer to this conclusion is once again a sharp answer to the Sorbonne as he perceived it. He denies that any philosopher would admit that Christ could become flesh,[30] nevertheless, the Sorbonne claimed that this issue could be found within philosophy.[31] Thus, a clear view of philosophy shows the Parisian theologians to be bad philosophers who did not understand the real limits of philosophy as well as Luther did. His argument against the unity of philosophy and theology was now clearly led by theological principles, namely his understanding of justification and of the word of God.

According to Luther, the word of God distinguished into Law and Gospel could not fully be grasped by philosophy.[32] Following Romans 1, a phrase obviously alluded to by Veit Oertel,[33] Luther admitted that the Law might be understood by philosophical means, especially the *Decalogue* (the second table more so than the first one).[34] However, philosophy would never be able to understand the forgiveness of sins, incarnation, and eternal life.[35] Luther believed that trust in philosophical knowledge had led the Parisians—and, one might add, the majority of Scholastics in Luther's eyes—to the distinction of *meritum de congruo* and *meritum de condigno* in the teaching on justification. That belief of Luther's gives us an important insight into how closely these reflections on incarnation are connected to Luther's

27. Karl Hartfelder, "Veit Winsheim," in *Allgemeine Deutsche Biographie*, vol. 43 (Leipzig: Verlag, 1898), 462–463.
28. Luther, *Disputation "Verbum caro factum est"* (WA 39/2,13,4): "argumentum . . . principale" / "chief argument" Trans. after LW 38:248.
29. Luther, *Disputation "Verbum caro factum est"* (WA 39/2,13,2p): "Sapientia Dei sibi ipsi non contradicit. Philosophia est sapientia Dei. Ergo philosophia sibi ipsi non contradicit." Transl. after LW 38:247.
30. Luther, *Disputation "Verbum caro factum est"* (WA 39/2,14,19–21).
31. Luther, *Disputation "Verbum caro factum est"* (WA 39/2,13,12p).
32. Cf. Thomas Wabel, *Sprache als Grenze in Luthers theologischer Hermeneutik und Wittgensteins Sprachphilosophie* (Berlin: De Gruyter, 1988), 307.
33. See Luther, *Disputation "Verbum caro factum est"* (WA 39/2,13,26): "Minor probatur ex Paulo: Veritas Dei."
34. Luther, *Disputation "Verbum caro factum est"* (WA 39/2,13,6–10); for the passages pertaining to Romans 1:21 see Luther, *Disputation "Verbum caro factum est"* 14,6–8.
35. Luther, *Disputation "Verbum caro factum est"* (WA 39/2,13,9–11).

understanding of justification.[36] When Luther speaks here about incarnation, his goal is a soteriological one: understanding incarnation means understanding that Jesus Christ came *to save the faithful*. The argument here provides us with a third aspect of the difference between philosophy and theology. The pairings faith-understanding and visibility-invisibility are joined by the pairing Law-Gospel. Philosophy might reach into the sphere of the Law, but we can only understand the Gospel by means of theology, which in turn means the way of superhuman revelation.

What makes things a bit more confusing is the fact that Luther not only states this difference between theology and philosophy—but he also tries to argue that philosophy contains different truths within itself. His examples mainly consist of cases of different metrics (geometry is incapable of measuring weights, etc.).[37] These theses seem not to have been discussed at the University of Wittenberg, which is a real pity because they reveal something of Luther's understanding of truth. Nowhere in the disputation does he make any effort to define what truth would be in his eyes. If one considers his examples, one might see that none of the classical definitions of truth—convergence, consensus, or coherence—would fit what truth is here. Taking Luther's example that it would be wrong to measure a pint (*sextarius*) with a cubit (*ulna*)[38] one sees immediately that the example is inadequate. In the most popular medieval understanding of truth, namely the "*adaequatio intellectus ad rem*" (the convergence definition) in every part of philosophy the statement, "The content of a pint is one cubit" would be wrong, because the content of a pint must be given in terms of a liquid measure. Thus, Luther is referring to the question of the right application of terms or measures,[39] not a question of truth in general. Therefore, these examples make clear that Luther's insistence on two distinct truths in philosophy and theology respectively uses the concept of truth in a sense distinct from how the Parisian condemnation and today's philosophers use it: truth here has more to do with correct adaption or correct methods than with the underlying idea of a convergence between mental and extramental reality. With this in mind, one might understand why Luther also treats the main question of theology and philosophy primarily along the lines of methodology.[40] The

36. Luther, *Disputation "Verbum caro factum est"* (WA 39/2,13,13–15).
37. Luther, *Disputation "Verbum caro factum est"* (WA 39/2,5,15–20).
38. Luther, *Disputation "Verbum caro factum est"* (WA 39/2,5,15p): "31. Falsum est et error in genere mensurarum, sextarium pedali vel ulnari mensura metiri." / "31. It is false and an error in the area of measurement to measure a pint with the measure of a foot or of an ell." Trans. after LW 38:241.
39. For this critique see White, *Luther as Nominalist*, 142.
40. As far as I see, this is different from the two positions summarized by Dennis Bielfeldt, "Luther on Language," *Lutheran Quarterly* 16, no. 2 (Sum 2002): 195–220, calling the one the "new

question pertains to logic and its right application. It was not by chance, that he summarized his aim with the sentence, "God is not subject to reason and syllogism"[41] (see p. 143)—he dealt with the question of syllogisms in theology. Here, we might see the impact of his Erfurt training in philosophy, as the main works of his teachers there, Bartholomaeus Arnoldi of Usingen (*Exercitium Novae logices*)[42] and Jodocus Trutfetter (*Summulae totius logicae* from 1501)[43] were devoted to logic. Indeed, both give the impression that philosophy mainly consists in logic, a sentiment also held by many authors of the *Via moderna*. Luther shared this conviction but in a less accurate way.

As revealing as the argument about different truths within philosophy is, it does not express Luther's main concern. In fact, it obfuscates what Luther really wanted with his disputation. That is seen not only in these side arguments but also in the very first theses speaking about different truths in different disciplines.[44] An optimistic (or careless) reading could see here a kind of postmodern approach, giving weight and respect to different approaches to reality. At first glance, it does indeed sound like a theory of multiple truths without hierarchies.[45] As demonstrated above, this was not Luther's intention, which is clearly derived from one discipline—theology—and aims to free it from a supposed philosophical determination. Actually, the asymmetric construction goes even further: Luther not only frees theology from philosophy, but also tries to subdue philosophy to theology. This one-sidedness is immediately evident in thesis 15 which draws a clear distinction:

> 15. To be sure, theology encroaches upon the rules of philosophy, but, contrariwise, philosophy itself encroaches more often upon the rules of theology.[46]

meaning view" and the other the "different inference position." Both do not really pertain to Luther's argument, which is a more methodological one. The "inference position" might have some methodological impact, but it argues within a logical framework. In any case, we have to consider Luther's preface to his German Works here (see p. 154).

41. Luther, *Disputation "Verbum caro factum est"* (WA 39/2,8,4p): "quod Deus non sit subiecuts rationi et syllogismis, sed verbo Dei et fidei."
42. Here I use: Exercitium Nove logi|ces in Studio Erffurdien colle /|ctum per Magistrum Barthol|omeum Arnoldi de Usin|gen instauratum atque| emendatum, (Erfurt 1516).
43. *Summule totius logice*: "quod opus | maius appellitare libuit: per Jodo|cum Trutuetter Jsennachensem Theologum . . . in Gymna|sio nuper Erphordiensi utpote succus e floribus labo|riosissime compilate." (Erfurt: Wolfgang Schenk, 1501).
44. Luther, *Disputation "Verbum caro factum est"* (WA 39/2,3,1p): "in diversis professionibus" / "in other fields of learning." Trans. after LW 38:239.
45. For an interpretation in this sense see White, *Luther as Nominalist*, 314–320.
46. Luther, *Disputation "Verbum caro factum est"* (WA 39/2,4,22p): "15. Impingit quidem theologia in philosophiae regulas, sed ipsa vicissim magis in theologiae regulas." Trans. after LW 38:240.

Here one might be tempted to see Luther's defensive interest in protecting theology from philosophical assaults. However, that would not be extreme enough for this is a universal statement blaming philosophy for its disproportionate encroachment on theology. Even more interesting is the universal thesis 14:

> 14. But wherever [*ubiubi*] either the syllogistic form or philosophical reason encroaches [upon theology], this saying of Paul, "Let the woman be silent in church" [1 Cor 14:34], and that other passage, "Listen to him" [Matt 17:5], must be applied to it.[47]

The context makes this thesis somewhat ambiguous: One could propose that Luther formulates it in a series of theses arguing about what boundaries philosophy has to respect concerning theology. Thus, one could see it as a sentence merely freeing theology from philosophy. But this would not explain why Luther uses the strong term "*ubiubi*," which excludes wrong syllogistic sentences of philosophical thoughts *wherever* they might come up. Indeed, he does not speak about academic theology here, but about *ecclesia*, as he does in thesis 11, where he refers to the Parisian convictions and says they must be avoided by all Christians (*christianis*).[48] This differs from a scholarly distinction of spheres—it defines a special kind of philosophy as residing outside Christian borders. When we think about sixteenth-century society, this cannot be seen as an inclusive theory of different but equally valid approaches to reality—the hierarchy is clear: theology is concordant with the Christian world by definition, but philosophy only to the extent that it aligns with theology. Seeing and accepting philosophy as another kind of truth, in fact, means excluding it from legitimate existence within the Christian world.

LOGICAL PROBLEMS IN THEOLOGY

As we have seen, Luther heavily attacked syllogisms in the field of theology, demonstrating this with his heritage from the late-medieval *Via moderna*. When this tradition spoke about the Trinity, it invariably reached logical problems. We can find an example of this in the long passages about the Trinity in Ockham's *Summulae logicae*, which shows that this

47. Luther, *Disputation "Verbum caro factum est"* (WA 39/2,4,19–21): "14. Sed ubiubi impingit vel forma syllogistica vel ratio philosophica, dicendum est ei illud Pauli: Mulier in Ecclesia taceat, et illud: Hunc audite." Trans. after LW 38:240.
48. Luther, *Disputation "Verbum caro factum est"* (WA 39/2,4,13).

was not only a problem of theology, but even more so one of logic. The question was why the syllogism as a form of thought was wrong in this case when it seemed to work well in other applications. The clearest problem is the problem of appropriations in the divine persons: a divine person is identical with the divine essence; yet one can still say something in particular about a person that cannot be said about the essence in general.

This may be the simplest form of Luther's problem, and he presents it nicely in theses 18 and 19:

> 18. This common syllogism is good: The Father is the entire divine essence; the Son is the divine essence, therefore, the Son is the Father. 19. But again the premises are true and the conclusion is false; and this is not a case of truth agreeing with truth.[49]

This conclusion can be seen as early as in Ockham's *Commentary to the Sentences*.[50] From here, the problem might have been derived from Trutfetter's *Summulae* who tried to avoid at least some of the problems by insisting that the sentence: "Every divine essence is the Father" would be wrong because the Son and the Spirit are divine essences as well.[51] Luther was well-trained to deal with such a problem, and so we find similar arguments in his own *Commentary to the Sentences*, when he argues that the sentence, "The Son is the God who is the Father" is right, while the sentence, "The Son is God the Father" would be wrong[52].

However, in Biel as well as in young Luther, we can see that the problem was primarily discussed regarding the question of generation, which means the eternal birth of the son, but is somehow connected with the question of incarnation. Luther picked this up in his disputation about the Word becoming flesh, when he stated:

> This expository syllogism is good: The Father generates in divine things; the Father is the divine essence; therefore, the divine essence generates.[53]

49. Luther, *Disputation "Verbum caro factum est"* (WA 39/2,4,28–31): "18. Iste syllogismus communis: Omnis essentia divina est pater. Filius est essentia divina. Ergo filius est pater, est bonus. 19. Sed praemissae sunt verae, et conclusio falsa, et verum vero hic prorsus non consonat." Trans. after LW 38:240.
50. Guillelmi de Ockham, "Commentary to the Sentences Prol. q. 7," in *Opera Theologica*, vol. 1, ed. Gedeon Gál (St. Bonaventure: Inst. Franciscanum 1967), 204,1–3.
51. Trutfetter, *Summulae* U 6[r].
52. Luther, *Commentary to the Sentences l. 1 d. 4* (AWA 9,283, 19p). My translation.
53. Luther, *Disputation "Verbum caro factum est"* (WA 39/2,4,24p): "Iste syllogismus expositorius: Pater in divinis generat. Pater est essentia divina. Ergo essentia divina generat, est bonus." Trans. after LW 38: 240.

Luther was referring to a long debate here. His teacher, Bartholomaeus Arnoldi of Usingen had presented exactly this syllogism in his *Exercitium* as an example for a false consequence, using Pierre d'Ailly as an example. According to Usingen, Cardinal d'Ailly demonstrated that a false consequence derived from correct presuppositions proved that the form of a *syllogismus expositorius* was not just a formal one, but a material one, meaning that its value depended on the material implications of the terms used.[54] This argument is preserved in Luther's overall critique of syllogisms:

> 26. In these and similar statements the syllogism is a most excellent form, but it is useless with regard to the matter itself.[55]

Luther's position is not different, just less differentiated compared to d'Ailly's statement. So, the problem was not new for Luther when he dealt with it in his disputation—he had used a similar argument when he commented on the *Sentences* of Peter Lombard as early as 1509/10.[56]

Luther knew of this long history of debate, and he referred to it in the course of the disputation, remembering Peter Lombard's discussion of the generation of the Son.[57] In his collection of *Sentences*, in Book 1, distinction 5, Peter Lombard had stated that the divine essence would not be generated nor generate in any way,[58] a position questioned by Joachim of Fiore, but later on (as Luther correctly reports) confirmed by the Fourth Lateran Synod.[59] Luther also mentioned a lot of scholars who had discussed this problem[60]—he might have been aware of this by the long treatise on the question in Gabriel Biel's *Collectorium*.[61] Among

54. Usingen, *Exercitium Novae logices,* d 2^{v}.
55. Luther, *Disputation "Verbum caro factum est"* (WA 39/2,5,7p): "26. In his et similibus syllogismus est forma optima, sed nihil ad materiam." Trans. after LW 38:241.
56. Luther, *Commentary on the Sentences* (AWA 9,286): "Et ista ratio contra magistrum sic fieret: si pater generaret essentiam, tunc generaret se ipsum: Igitur Si generat filium, generat essentiam, quia eque est eadem filio vt patri." / "And this argument has emerged against the master: if the Father generates the essence, then he must generate himself. Therefore, if he generates the Son, then he generates the essence, for it [the essence] is the same for both the Son and the Father." My translation.
57. Luther, *Disputation "Verbum caro factum est"* (WA 39/2,17,17–18,12).
58. Peter Lombard, *Magistri Petri Lombardi Parisiensis episcopi Sententiae in IV libris distinctae*, vol. 1 (Grottaferrata (Romae): Coll. S. Bonaventurae Ad Claras Aquas, 1971), 81, 1.5.1.1.
59. Luther, *Disputation "Verbum caro factum est"* (WA 39/2,17,17–20); cf DH 803.
60. Luther, *Disputation "Verbum caro factum est"* (WA 39/2,17,22).
61. Gabriel Biel, *Gabrielis Biel Collectorium circa quattuor libros Sententiarum. Prologus et Liber primus*, ed. Wilfrid Werbeck and Udo Hofmann (Tübingen: Mohr Siebeck, 1973), 269–278, *Collectorium l. 1 d. 5 q. 1*

others, here, he could find the argument of Nicholas of Oyta about the value of the *syllogismus expositorius* in divine matters.[62]

These reports are of great interest because they show that in the 1530s Luther started engaging with scholastic discourse to a limited extent again. While a closer look at his polemics against the Sorbonne had shown that he was not very well acquainted with this case in particular, one *can* see that he tried to set his disputation *Verbum caro factum est* into a broader horizon of scholastic debates. It would be worth giving more attention to what exactly he read at this time and what was just a recollection of his earlier days when he was writing his own commentary on the *Sentences*, a task undertaken with the help of Biel's *Collectorium*.

However, his conclusions are very different from those drawn by Biel. Biel had given a clear logical solution for the Trinity problem, explaining that the attribute "generating" could be predicated immediately for Father. But Father itself was rendered as an indirect predication for the essence. So "generating" could not be predicated for essence immediately.[63] This was a clever answer in the horizon of late-medieval theory of predication and supposition. Luther rejected it decisively. Although he did not name Biel, his argument is directed straight against him:

> 12. Neither are the subtle inventions of mediate and immediate suppositions to be used nor to be taken advantage of in matters of faith.[64]

The alternative chosen by Luther was a clear distinction and avoidance of misunderstandings: Because divine essence means the whole Trinity, he insisted on not saying that one essence could generate another one, as this sounded as if there were ultimately two Godheads. Instead, one should only speak of the Father generating.[65] This is not really a solution for the problems inherent to this discussion, but more a way of cleaning up the language and reducing complexity. Luther skipped the problem of identity between the persons and the essence, merely stating that the essence was

62. Biel, *Collectorium l. 1 d. 5 q. 1* (Biel, *Collectorium,* 271 D 1p).
63. Biel, *Colelctorium l. 1 d. 5 q. 1* (Biel, *Collectorium,* 272 D 26–32).
64. Luther, *Disputation "Verbum caro factum est"* (WA 39/2,4,15p): "12. Nec utendum nec fruendum est subtilibus istis inventis, de suppositione mediata et immediata, in rebus fidei." Transl. after: Martin Luther, "The Disputation Concerning The Passage: 'The Word Was Made Flesh' (John 1:14) 1539." In *Luther's Works*, vol. 38, *Word and Sacrament IV*, 2nd ed., trans. Martin E. Lehmann, ed. Helmut T. Lehmann and Martin E. Lehmann, 235–277 (Philadelphia: Fortress Press, 1980), 240n12.
65. Luther, *Disputation "Verbum caro factum est"* (WA 39/2,18,5–10).

common to all three persons.[66] Obviously, he referred to basic commitments of the Trinitarian doctrine, but in contrast to Scholastic theology, he did not face the intellectual consequences resulting from it. Instead, he praised the magnitude of the matter.[67] This majesty of the divine Trinity is the reason that all syllogisms in this matter fail[68] which leads Luther to reject all attempts at finding solutions within the system of logic.

This is also the case when he comes to the Christological problem. In thesis 22 he raises the problem of the natures of Christ:

> 22. This syllogism is good in philosophy: Whatever was made flesh became a creature; the Son of God was made flesh: therefore, the Son of God became a creature.[69]

Again, the problem is not new for medieval thinkers. Biel deals with it in lengthy passages of his third *Book on the Sentences*,[70] repeatedly referring to the problem of *communicatio idiomatum*.[71] Graham White has shown that this kind of argument can also be found in John Mair's (a Scottish teacher in Paris) commentary on the *Sentences*.[72]

Luther's critique seems not to be pertinent when he argues that the Scholastics used "*kenophonia*" or "empty talk" to solve the problem.[73] He saw them indeed as having come to the core of Christological dogma, but then having to explain what happened in consequences like this one with means of linguistic theory. The question of language becomes very

66. Luther, *Disputation "Verbum caro factum est"* (WA 39/2,18,8p).
67. Luther, *Disputation "Verbum caro factum est"* (WA 39/2,18,11p).
68. Luther, *Disputation "Verbum caro factum est"* (WA 39/2,4,32p).
69. Luther, *Disputation "Verbum caro factum est"* (WA 39/2,4,36–39): "22. Iste syllogismus: Quidquid factum est caro, factum est creatura. Filius Dei est factus caro. Ergo filius Dei est factus creatura, est bonus in philosophia." Trans. after LW 38:241.
70. Gabriel Biel, *Collectorium l. 3 d. 7 q. un.* (*Gabrielis Biel Collectorium circa quattuor libros Sententiarum. Liber tertius*, ed. Wilfried Werbeck and Udo Hofmann, [Tübingen: Mohr Siebeck, 1979], 152–177).
71. Cf. Streiff, *Novis linguis*, 56–78.
72. Editio Ioannis Majoirs | doctoris parisienso: super Tertium sen-| tentiarum: de novo edita, Paris: grsanion 1517, 24^{v}: "possunt fieri tales rationes: christus est homo: vel ergo homo creatus vel increatus. non secundum: nullus est homo increatus ergo est homo creatus creatura" / "There could be such arguments as: Christ is a human being, thus: either a created human being or a not created one. The second possibility does not hold up, though. There is no human being which is not created and therefore he is a created human being as a creature." My translation As White, *Luther as Nominalist*, 128, points out, this fits very well to the argument conveyed in WA 39/2,10,34–35; actually Gabriel Biel is mentioned in the same context (see WA 39/2,11,35). So, we might see both, Biel as well as Mair, in the background; for interferences with Schwenckfeld's Christology see Wabel, *Sprache als Grenze*, 288–289.
73. Luther, *Disputation "Verbum caro factum est"* (WA 39/2,5,1).

decisive: Christians should speak "soberly and (as Augustine teaches) according to the prescript."[74] If there is any innovation in this language, Luther claims, it is still very old, at least as old as Augustine. Speaking according to the prescript mainly means avoiding dogmatically wrong consequences which in the context of this claim means refraining from philosophical speculation.[75]

A NEW LANGUAGE IN THEOLOGY?

Up to this point, the course of Luther's argumentation suggests that theological language mainly consists of avoiding problematic (philosophical or heretical) terms. This must be kept in mind when Luther speaks about "new languages" (*novae linguae*) in thesis 40.[76] Stefan Streiff took this phrase as the key for understanding the disputation. Within the context of the Ebeling-Jüngel tradition of Luther interpretation, it seems to indicate a new approach to the phenomenon of language, especially if we examine it alongside thesis 27:

> 27. Therefore, in articles of faith, one must have recourse to another dialectic and philosophy, which is called the word of God and faith.[77]

Nowhere else in the theses themselves nor in the *Wittenberg disputation* do we find a clear description of what kind of dialectics or philosophy is meant here besides the short description: "word of God and faith." This is certainly not a complete theory of language!

We err if we understand Luther's claim to apply in a special scholarly domain. The new language or new dialectics is not something that can be defined by special methods of understanding language—as Graham White states, "the basic difference between the two languages was that the old language was rule-governed, whereas the new one was not."[78] If we want to speak about something methodological in it, we have to refer to another text from the same year when the disputation was held. In 1539,

74. Luther, *Disputation "Verbum caro factum est"* (WA 39/2,4,13p): "sobrie, et (ut Augustinus docet) secundum praescriptum."
75. Luther, *Disputation "Verbum caro factum est"* (WA 39/2,4,14).
76. Luther, *Disputation "Verbum caro factum est"* (WA 39/2,5,36).
77. Luther, *Disputation "Verbum caro factum est"* (WA 39/2,5,9p): "27. Eundum ergo est ad aliam dialecticam et philosophiam in articulis fidei, quae vocatur verbum Dei et fides." Trans. after LW 38:241.
78. White, *Luther as Nominalist*, 303.

the first volume of Luther's German scriptures was edited, and he wrote a preface to it explaining how a theologian was to deal with the Bible. Here, he developed his famous understanding of theology as *oratio*, *meditatio*, and *tentatio* (prayer, meditation, and temptation).[79] Here, we have more than chronology to suggest an answer to the question of how theology should proceed after leaving philosophy behind. In the same preface, we also find Martin Luther harshly critiquing all books of human wisdom which are nothing compared to the Bible, using exactly the same argumentation that he employed in his disputation against philosophy: they do not teach eternal life.[80]

If our investigations are correct, then the dialectic Luther speaks about in theology, led by the word of God and faith, is not a form of academic training but rather has a more existential dimension.[81] This also means that it is not about *actively* dealing with the text, but about passivity when confronted by the word of God. The prayer at the beginning makes clear that the one who seeks understanding of Scripture cannot do this by their own means, but only with God's help. Meditation and temptation are also not active forms of appropriation, but passive ones. Thus, we find an approach to Luther's understanding of theology here that is not primarily one of philosophy or theology of language, but more a kind of spiritual reading, or, as medieval monks used to say, of *lectio divina*.

Indeed, the model Luther uses is deeply rooted in a monastic tradition where the scheme was used in multiple varying forms.[82] We can find it, for example, in Hugh of St. Victor[83] and in its most comprehensive form in the *Scala claustralium* of Guigo the Carthusian, who discerns *lectio*, *meditatio*, *oratio*, and *contemplatio*.[84] Yes, Luther *does* transform the series, making *oratio* the starting point to stress the passivity. However, he remained in

79. Luther, *Preface to his German Works* (WA 50,659,5–660,4); cf. Oswald Bayer, "Oratio, Meditatio, Tentatio. Eine Besinnung auf Luthers Theologieverständnis," in *Luther Jahrbuch*, vol. 55 (Vandenhoeck & Ruprecht, 1988): 7–59.

80. Luther, *Preface to his German Works* (WA 50,659,5–7): "Erstlich soltu wissen, das die heilige Schrifft ein solch Buch ist, das aller ander Buecher weisheit zur narrheit macht, weil keins vom ewigen leben Leret on dis allein." / "Firstly, you should know that the Holy Scriptures constitute a book which turns the wisdom of all other books into foolishness, because not one teaches about eternal life except this one alone." Trans. after: LW 34:285.

81. The same direction can be seen in thesis 15 of the *Disputatio de divintiate et humanitate Christi* (WA 39/2,94,7p); cf. for this Risto Saarinen, "Metapher und biblische Redefiguren als Elemente der Sprachphilosophie Luthers," *Neue Zeitschrift für Systematik und Religonsphilosophie* 30 (1988): 18–39, 31.

82. For this, see Martin Nicol, *Meditation bei Luther* (Göttingen: Vandenhoeck & Ruprecht, 1984)

83. See Hugh of St. Victor, *Eruditionis didascalia l. 5* (PL 176,797B) with "quinque gradus": l 15 lectio—meditatio—oratio—operatio—contemplatio; cf. Nicol, *Meditation*, 162.

84. Guigo, *Scala claustralium* (PL 184,475–484); cf. Nicol, *Meditation*, 19.

the monastic tradition, adopting this scheme and making it *the* structure of theological education.

Not only the chronological proximity suggests that the *Preface* is helpful in filling the gap left by the disputation when it comes to positively defining theology, but also the disputation itself smacks of this new conception of theology, stating that the new languages of theology are not scholarly ones, but pneumatic ones. In thesis 40, Luther says:

> 40. We would act more correctly if we left dialectic and philosophy in their own area and learned to speak in a new language in the realm of faith apart from every sphere.[85]

Interpreters who want to find a philosophy of language here have to accept the biblical background of the phrase "*novae linguae*." We find this phrase explicitly in Mark 16:17 as a promise for believers of Jesus Christ ("*linguis loquentur novis*"). But for Luther himself, a clearer relation is given in Act 2:4, even if the phrase here is not "*novis linguis*", but "*aliis linguis*."[86] We see this in another context quite close to the text given here, namely in his 1535 disputation about Daniel 4:24:

> Well, we have to learn a new grammar, new languages (*novas linguas*), as the Apostles spoke in new languages (*novis linguis*). The sentence of the Parisians is wrong and against God, namely that a human being, doing what is in him or herself, infallibly pleases God and acquires grace.[87]

Obviously, the context is the same as it would be later in the *Disputation* on John 1:14: the Parisian teaching on justification pictures the adversary, an old *ars*—grammar or dialectics—must be replaced by a new kind of language, designated by the same phrase: "*novis linguis*." Now, Luther evidently refers to Pentecost, remembering the other languages of the apostles in Acts 2. This makes it all the more apparent that the new language is not to be understood in terms of philosophy or any scholarship, but rather that Luther thinks of pneumatic speech as experienced by the apostles at Pentecost. As Risto Saarinen has figured out, this means human language

85. Luther, *Disputation "Verbum caro factum est"* (WA 39/2,5,35p): "[40] 40. Rectius ergo fecerimus, si dialectica seu philosophia in sua sphaera relictis discamus loqui novis linguis in regno fidei extra omnem sphaeram." Trans. after LW 38:242.
86. See Streiff, *Novis linguis*, 150–155.
87. Luther, *Disputation on Dan 4:4* (WA 39/1,69,27–30): "Bene, oportet novam discere grammaticam, novas linguas, sicuti Apostoli loquebantur novis linguis. Parisiensium propositio falsa est et contra deum, quod homo, si facit, quod in se est, placeat Deo et acquirat gratiam infallibiliter." My translation.

reaches its boundaries and even transcends them. The new language is an ineffable language[88] that fits quite well to the monastic piety tradition of meditation. Even transforming these biblical insights into scholarly language, Luther makes clear the difference between new language and old, scholarly language. Luther is not seeking philosophical intellect but the affects of faith (*affectus fidei*).[89] This is the end of the *Disputation*—and somehow the end of Luther's argument.

CONCLUSION

The picture drawn here shows both Luther's difference with Scholasticism as well as a surprisingly strong degree of continuity with it—and it shows that the difference basically inherits an inner-medieval difference. Luther invented none of the problems he raises concerning a philosophical understanding of the Trinity and the incarnation. They derive from Scholastic discourse which had long been aware of the logical problems given by one God in three persons and an infinite God adopting finite human nature. Luther did not invent these tensions, but he did use them in the context of his general criticism of Aristotelianism which he developed in his early years.[90]

His aim was clearly a theological one. Philosophy should not get a place beside theology, but obviously under theology or, if it would not accept this position, a place outside of Christianity altogether. Luther saw no place for an autonomous philosophy within Christianity and at a Christian university. This would also make clear, that he never really argued for a theory of double truth. As shown in this chapter, what he calls truth is not truth in the full theoretical understanding of this term, but he is thinking about methods, especially dialectic methods. His conviction that philosophy could not really contradict theology can be seen in his great treatise on the Lord's Supper, written in 1528 against Zwingli. Here he states that no consequence could contradict Scripture and faith.[91] It is sometimes impossible to harmonize all of Luther's convictions. This fact, taken with the observations collected above, underlines that Luther is not a theorist of double truth, but rather uses concepts in a sometimes-disjointed manner.

88. Saarinen, *Metapher*, 28.
89. Luther, *Disputation "Verbum caro factum est"* (WA 39/2,5,39p).
90. See Theo Dieter, *Der junge Luther und Aristoteles. Eine historisch-systematische Untersuchung zum Verhältnis von Theologie und Philosophie* (Berlin: De Gruyter, 2001).
91. Luther, *Confession Concerning Christ's Supper* (WA 26,286,31p): "Was nicht widder schrifft und glauben ist, das ist auch widder keine folge" / "What is not contrary to Scripture and the Creed is not contrary to any subsequent instance either." Trans. after LW 37:186.

What he wanted to say seems to be that the theological method should be distinct from that of logic. Furthermore, it should not ultimately be a method but a spiritual exercise, led by the monastic tradition of reading the Bible. Thus, the new language within this disputation does not give space for a new theory of language, but for a rather traditional approach to faith and Scripture, thus resonating with his general mystical conviction.

Bibliography

SOURCES

Augustine of Hippo, Saint. *St. Augustine: On the Spirit and the Letter.* Translated by W. J. Sparrow-Simpson. London: Society for Promoting Christian Knowledge, 1925.

_______. *Expositions of the Psalms*, Volume III/19. In *The Works of Saint Augustine (4th Release).* Electronic *Edition*, edited by John E. Rotelle, vol. 34. Charlottesville, VI: InteLex Corp., 2014.

_______. *Letters 156–210*, Volume II/3. In *The Works of Saint Augustine (4th Release).* Electronic Edition, edited by Boniface Ramsey, vol. 17. Charlottesville, VI: InteLex Corp., 2014.

Augustini Sancti Aurelii. *Confessiones Liber Septimus.* CSEL: Corpus Scriptorum Ecclesiasticorum Latinorum, vol. 33, edited by F. Tempsky and G. Freytag, 140–168. Prague: Tempsky, 1896.

_______. "Enarratio In Psalmum CXIX." In *Hipponensis Episcopi, Opera Omnia.* PL: Patrologia Cursus Completus Series Latina, vo1. 37, edited by Jacques-Paul Migne, 1597–1605. Paris: Apud Garnier Fratres, 1865.

_______. "Enarratio In Psalmum XXX." In *Hipponensis Episcopi, Opera Omnia.* PL: Patrologia Cursus Completus Series Latina, vo1. 36, edited by Jacques-Paul Migne, 222–256. Paris: Apud Garnier Fratres, 1865.

_______. "In Ioannen tractatus XX." In *Hipponensis Episcopi, Opera Omnia.* PL: Patrologia Cursus Completus Series Latina, vo1. 35, edited by Jacques-Paul Migne, 1556–1564. Paris: Apud Garnier Fratres, 1864.

_______. *De Spiritu et Littera. Opera. Corpus Scriptorum Ecclesiasticorum Latinorum*, vol. 60, Sect. VIII, Part 1, edited by Carolus F. Urba and Josephus Zycha. Vienna: F. Tempsky, 1913.

_______. *Epistulae. Corpus Scriptorum Ecclesiasticorum Latinorum*, vol. 57, Part 4, Epistle 185–220, edited by Carolus F. Urba and Josephus Zycha. Vienna: F. Tempsky, 1911.

Biel, Gabriel. *Gabrielis Biel Collectorium circa quattuor libros Sententiarum. Liber secundus.* Edited by Wilfrid Werbeck and Udo Hofmann. Tubingen: Mohr Siebeck, 1984.

_______. *Gabrielis Biel Collectorium circa quattuor libros Sententiarum. Prologus et Liber primus.* Edited by Wilfrid Werbeck and Udo Hofmann. Tübingen: Mohr Siebeck, 1973.

Clairvaux, Bernhard von. *Sämtliche Werke. Lateinisch/deutsch*, vol. 6, edited by Gerhard B. Winkler. Innsbruck: Tyrolia, 1995.

Eckhart, Meister. *Die deutschen Werke. Die deutschen und lateinischen Werke / Meister Eckhart*, vol. 4, edited by Josef Quint. Stuttgart: Kohlhammer, 1963.

_______. *Meister Eckhart: Deutsche Werke, Predigten*, vol. 4.1, *Die deutschen und lateinischen Werke*, edited and translated by Georg Steer. Stuttgart: Kohlhammer, 2003.

_______. *The Complete Mystical Works of Meister Eckhart.* Edited by Maurice O'C. Walshe. Foreword by Bernard McGinn. New York: Crossroad Publishing, 2009.

Erasmus, Desiderus. *NOVVM IN-| strumentum omne, dilgienter ab ERASMO ROTERDAMO| recognitum et emendatum non solum ad graecam ueritatem, ue-| rumetiam ad multorum utriusque linguae codicum, eorumque ue-| terum simul et emendatorum fidem (. . .).* Basel: Johann Froben, 1516.

Geiler of Kaysersberg. *Das buch Granatapfel. im la-| tein genant Malogranatus (. . .) Merers teyls gepredigt durch den hoch-| gelerten doctor Johannem Geyler vonn Keysersberg etc.*, Straßburg: Johann Knobloch 1516.

Guigo, *Scala claustralium* (PL 184,475–484).

Hugh of Saint-Victor. *Hugonis de Sancto Victore De sacramentis Christiane fidei. Corpus Victorinum, Textus historici.* Edited by Rainer Berndt, Monasterii Westfalorum. Munich: Aschendorff, 2008.

_______. "Eruditionis Didascalia, Liber Quintus." In *PL* 36. 790–798. Paris: Garnier, 1834.

Karlstadt, Andreas. "Von Abtuung der Bilder." In *Flugschriften der frühen Reformationsbewegung (1518–1524)*, vol. 1, edited by Adolf Laube, Annerose Schneider, and Sigrid Looss, 105–127. Vaduz, Liechtenstein: Topos, 1983.

Lombard, Peter. *Magistri Petri Lombardi Parisiensis episcopi Sententiae in IV libris distinctae*, 2 vols. Grottaferrata (Romae): Coll. S. Bonaventurae Ad Claras Aquas, 1971.

Luther, Martin. Ein | Betbuchlin/| mit eim Calender vnd | Passional/ hůbsch | zu gericht.| D.Mart.Lut, Wittenberg: Hans Lufft, 1538 (VD 16 L 4104).

_______. Ein bet-|bůchlin/ mit | eym Calender vnd | Passional/ hůbsch | zugericht.| Marti.Luther., Wittenberg: Hans Lufft, 1529 (Cited as VD16 L 4100).

_______. SERMON | D: Martin Luthers /| von der | Betrachtung | des | Leidens Christi /| In der Kirchen-Postill /| und | Im ersten Jenischen Theile | befindlich, (Leipzig: Heinrich, 1693) (VD 17 14:670203B).

_______. *Eyn sermon von der | betrachtung des heyligen leydens christi.| Doctor Martini Luther Augustiner zu Wittenbergk.* Nürnberg: Jobst Gutknecht, 1519.

_______, *Erfurter Annotationen 1509–1510/11*, Archiv zur Weimarer Ausgabe (AWA), vol. 9. Edited by Jan Matsuura. Weimar: Böhlau, 2009.

_______. "Eyn Sermon am grunen donnerstag." In *D. Martin Luthers Werke: kritische Gesamtausgabe.* WA: Weimarer Ausgabe, vol. 12, 476–493. Weimar: H. Böhlaus Nachfolger, 1891.

_______. "26. Predigt in Jessen. XII. Iulij In Iessen. 12. Juli 1533." In *D. Martin Luthers Werke: kritische Gesamtausgabe.* WA: Weimarer Ausgabe, vol. 9, 103–108. Weimar: H. Böhlaus Nachfolger, 1893.

_______. "26. Sermon am Auffahrttage. Am Auffartag das Evamgelium Marci am letsten: 'Als die aylff junger zů tiscg sassen.' 29. Mai 1522." In *D. Martin Luthers Werke: kritische Gesamtausgabe.* WA: Weimarer Ausgabe, vol. 10.III, 133–147. Weimar: H. Böhlaus Nachfolger, 1905.

_______. "3. Abschnitt. Johannes Schlaginhausens Nachschriften." In *D. Martin Luthers Werke: kritische Gesamtausgabe.* WA.TR: Tischreden Weimarer Ausgabe, vol. 2, 1–672. Weimar: H. Böhlaus Nachfolger, 1913.

_______. "3. Ein ander Sermon D. M. Luthers Am dinstag nach Invocavit." In *D. Martin Luthers Werke: kritische Gesamtausgabe.*WA: Weimarer Ausgabe, vol. 10.III, 21–30. Weimar: H. Böhlaus Nachfolger, 1905.

_______. "9. Predigt am Karfreitag. In die parasceues. 30. März 1537." In *D. Martin Luther's Werke: kritische Gesamtausgabe.* WA: Weimarer Ausgabe, vol. 45, 60–68. Weimar: H. Böhlaus Nachfolger, 1911.

———. "Adnotationes Quincuplici Psalterio adscriptae." In *D. Martin Luthers Werke: kritische Gesamtausgabe.* WA: Weimarer Ausgabe, vol. 4, 466–526. Weimar: H. Böhlaus Nachfolger, 1886.

———. "An die Burgermenster und Radherrn allerlen stedte ynn Deutschen landen." In *D. Martin Luthers Werke: kritische Gesamtausgabe.* WA: Weimarer Ausgabe, vol. 15, 27–53. Weimar: H. Böhlaus Nachfolger, 1899.

———. "Annotationes Martini Lutheri In Epistolam Pauli ad Galatas. Anno 1531." In *D. Martin Luthers Werke: kritische Gesamtausgabe.* WA: Weimarer Ausgabe, vol. 40.I, 39–691. Weimar: H. Böhlaus Nachfolger, 1911.

———. "Auslegung des dritten und vierten Kapitels Johannis in Predigten 1538–40, herausgegeben von G. Buchwald." In *D. Martin Luthers Werke: kritische Gesamtausgabe.* WA: Weimarer Ausgabe, vol. 47, 1–231. Weimar: H. Böhlaus Nachfolger, 1912.

———. "Auslegung deutsch des Vater unnser fuer dye einfeltigen leyen. 1519." In *D. Martin Luthers Werke: kritische Gesamtausgabe.* WA: Weimarer Ausgabe, vol. 2, 80–130. Weimar: H. Böhlaus Nachfolger, 1884.

———. "Brief an die Galater." In *D. Martin Luthers Werke: kritische Gesamtausgabe.* WA: Weimarer Ausgabe, vol. 57.II. Weimar: H. Böhlaus Nachfolger, 1939.

———. "Capitell am newen Jar tag ab Galatas. 3. Gal. 3, 23–29." In *D. Martin Luthers Werke: kritische Gesamtausgabe.* WA: Weimarer Ausgabe, vol. 10.I.I, 449–503. Weimar: H. Böhlaus Nachfolger, 1910.

———. "Crucigers Sommerpostille. [CCLVIII] Am sechsten Sontag nach Trinitatis, Epistel Roma. VI." In *D. Martin Luthers Werke: kritische Gesamtausgabe.* WA: Weimarer Ausgabe, vol. 22, 92–104. Weimar: H. Böhlaus Nachfolger, 1929.

———. "Das diese wort Christi (Das ist mein leiv etce) noch fest wider die Schwermgeister. 1527." In *D. Martin Luthers Werke: kritische Gesamtausgabe.* WA: Weimarer Ausgabe, vol. 23, 64–283. Weimar: H. Böhlaus Nachfolger, 1901.

———. "Das XIV. und XV. Capitel S. Johannis." In *D. Martin Luthers Werke: kritische Gesamtausgabe.* WA: Weimarer Ausgabe, vol. 45, 465–733. Weimar: H. Böhlaus Nachfolger, 1911.

———. "Das Zehend Capitel. Das Neue Testament. 1522. 1. Kor. 9, 26. 27; 10, 1–17." In *D. Martin Luthers Werke: kritische Gesamtausgabe.* WA.DB: Die Deutche Bibel, vol. 7, 112–114. Weimar: H. Böhlaus Nachfolger, 1931.

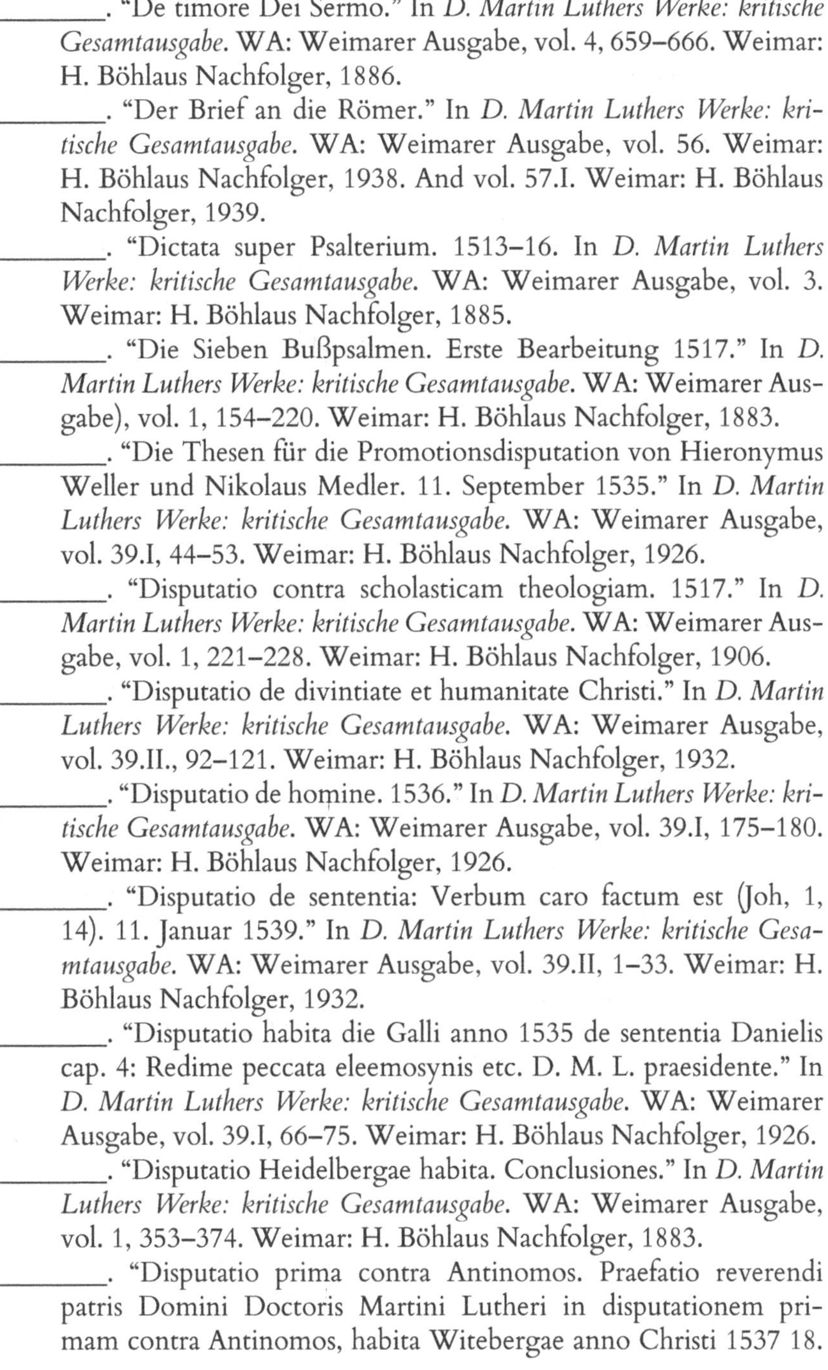

_______. "De timore Dei Sermo." In *D. Martin Luthers Werke: kritische Gesamtausgabe*. WA: Weimarer Ausgabe, vol. 4, 659–666. Weimar: H. Böhlaus Nachfolger, 1886.

_______. "Der Brief an die Römer." In *D. Martin Luthers Werke: kritische Gesamtausgabe*. WA: Weimarer Ausgabe, vol. 56. Weimar: H. Böhlaus Nachfolger, 1938. And vol. 57.I. Weimar: H. Böhlaus Nachfolger, 1939.

_______. "Dictata super Psalterium. 1513–16. In *D. Martin Luthers Werke: kritische Gesamtausgabe*. WA: Weimarer Ausgabe, vol. 3. Weimar: H. Böhlaus Nachfolger, 1885.

_______. "Die Sieben Bußpsalmen. Erste Bearbeitung 1517." In *D. Martin Luthers Werke: kritische Gesamtausgabe*. WA: Weimarer Ausgabe), vol. 1, 154–220. Weimar: H. Böhlaus Nachfolger, 1883.

_______. "Die Thesen für die Promotionsdisputation von Hieronymus Weller und Nikolaus Medler. 11. September 1535." In *D. Martin Luthers Werke: kritische Gesamtausgabe*. WA: Weimarer Ausgabe, vol. 39.I, 44–53. Weimar: H. Böhlaus Nachfolger, 1926.

_______. "Disputatio contra scholasticam theologiam. 1517." In *D. Martin Luthers Werke: kritische Gesamtausgabe*. WA: Weimarer Ausgabe, vol. 1, 221–228. Weimar: H. Böhlaus Nachfolger, 1906.

_______. "Disputatio de divintiate et humanitate Christi." In *D. Martin Luthers Werke: kritische Gesamtausgabe*. WA: Weimarer Ausgabe, vol. 39.II., 92–121. Weimar: H. Böhlaus Nachfolger, 1932.

_______. "Disputatio de homine. 1536." In *D. Martin Luthers Werke: kritische Gesamtausgabe*. WA: Weimarer Ausgabe, vol. 39.I, 175–180. Weimar: H. Böhlaus Nachfolger, 1926.

_______. "Disputatio de sententia: Verbum caro factum est (Joh, 1, 14). 11. Januar 1539." In *D. Martin Luthers Werke: kritische Gesamtausgabe*. WA: Weimarer Ausgabe, vol. 39.II, 1–33. Weimar: H. Böhlaus Nachfolger, 1932.

_______. "Disputatio habita die Galli anno 1535 de sententia Danielis cap. 4: Redime peccata eleemosynis etc. D. M. L. praesidente." In *D. Martin Luthers Werke: kritische Gesamtausgabe*. WA: Weimarer Ausgabe, vol. 39.I, 66–75. Weimar: H. Böhlaus Nachfolger, 1926.

_______. "Disputatio Heidelbergae habita. Conclusiones." In *D. Martin Luthers Werke: kritische Gesamtausgabe*. WA: Weimarer Ausgabe, vol. 1, 353–374. Weimar: H. Böhlaus Nachfolger, 1883.

_______. "Disputatio prima contra Antinomos. Praefatio reverendi patris Domini Doctoris Martini Lutheri in disputationem primam contra Antinomos, habita Witebergae anno Christi 1537 18.

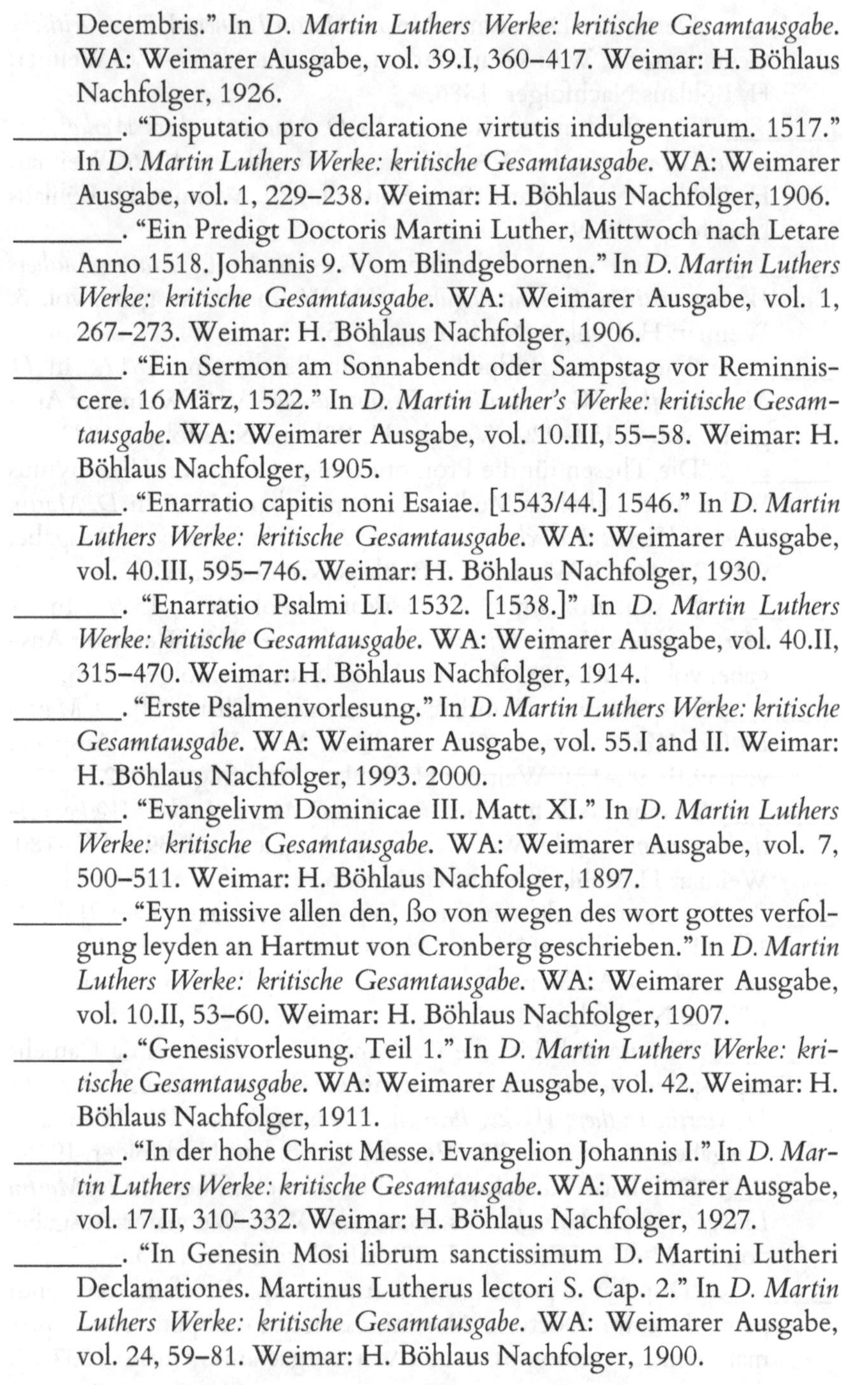

Decembris." In *D. Martin Luthers Werke: kritische Gesamtausgabe.* WA: Weimarer Ausgabe, vol. 39.I, 360–417. Weimar: H. Böhlaus Nachfolger, 1926.

_______. "Disputatio pro declaratione virtutis indulgentiarum. 1517." In *D. Martin Luthers Werke: kritische Gesamtausgabe.* WA: Weimarer Ausgabe, vol. 1, 229–238. Weimar: H. Böhlaus Nachfolger, 1906.

_______. "Ein Predigt Doctoris Martini Luther, Mittwoch nach Letare Anno 1518. Johannis 9. Vom Blindgebornen." In *D. Martin Luthers Werke: kritische Gesamtausgabe.* WA: Weimarer Ausgabe, vol. 1, 267–273. Weimar: H. Böhlaus Nachfolger, 1906.

_______. "Ein Sermon am Sonnabendt oder Sampstag vor Reminniscere. 16 März, 1522." In *D. Martin Luther's Werke: kritische Gesamtausgabe.* WA: Weimarer Ausgabe, vol. 10.III, 55–58. Weimar: H. Böhlaus Nachfolger, 1905.

_______. "Enarratio capitis noni Esaiae. [1543/44.] 1546." In *D. Martin Luthers Werke: kritische Gesamtausgabe.* WA: Weimarer Ausgabe, vol. 40.III, 595–746. Weimar: H. Böhlaus Nachfolger, 1930.

_______. "Enarratio Psalmi LI. 1532. [1538.]" In *D. Martin Luthers Werke: kritische Gesamtausgabe.* WA: Weimarer Ausgabe, vol. 40.II, 315–470. Weimar: H. Böhlaus Nachfolger, 1914.

_______. "Erste Psalmenvorlesung." In *D. Martin Luthers Werke: kritische Gesamtausgabe.* WA: Weimarer Ausgabe, vol. 55.I and II. Weimar: H. Böhlaus Nachfolger, 1993. 2000.

_______. "Evangelivm Dominicae III. Matt. XI." In *D. Martin Luthers Werke: kritische Gesamtausgabe.* WA: Weimarer Ausgabe, vol. 7, 500–511. Weimar: H. Böhlaus Nachfolger, 1897.

_______. "Eyn missive allen den, ßo von wegen des wort gottes verfolgung leyden an Hartmut von Cronberg geschrieben." In *D. Martin Luthers Werke: kritische Gesamtausgabe.* WA: Weimarer Ausgabe, vol. 10.II, 53–60. Weimar: H. Böhlaus Nachfolger, 1907.

_______. "Genesisvorlesung. Teil 1." In *D. Martin Luthers Werke: kritische Gesamtausgabe.* WA: Weimarer Ausgabe, vol. 42. Weimar: H. Böhlaus Nachfolger, 1911.

_______. "In der hohe Christ Messe. Evangelion Johannis I." In *D. Martin Luthers Werke: kritische Gesamtausgabe.* WA: Weimarer Ausgabe, vol. 17.II, 310–332. Weimar: H. Böhlaus Nachfolger, 1927.

_______. "In Genesin Mosi librum sanctissimum D. Martini Lutheri Declamationes. Martinus Lutherus lectori S. Cap. 2." In *D. Martin Luthers Werke: kritische Gesamtausgabe.* WA: Weimarer Ausgabe, vol. 24, 59–81. Weimar: H. Böhlaus Nachfolger, 1900.

_______. "Matthäus Kapitel 18–24 in Predigten ausgelegt 1537–1540, herausgegeben von G. Buchwald." In *D. Martin Luthers Werke: kritische Gesamtausgabe*. WA: Weimarer Ausgabe, vol. 47, 232–627. Weimar: H. Böhlaus Nachfolger, 1912.

_______. "Passional. Mart. Luther." In *D. Martin Luthers Werke: kritische Gesamtausgabe*. WA: Weimarer Ausgabe, vol. 10.II, 458–470. Weimar: H. Böhlaus Nachfolger, 1907.

_______. "Predigten der Jahre 1540 bis 4. August 1545." In *D. Martin Luthers Werke: kritische Gesamtausgabe*. WA: Weimarer Ausgabe, vol. 49, 1–805. Weimar: H. Böhlaus Nachfolger, 1913.

_______. "Predigten des Jahres 1523. Nachschriften Rörers." In *D. Martin Luthers Werke: kritische Gesamtausgabe*. WA: Weimarer Ausgabe, vol. 11, 9–228. Weimar: H. Böhlaus Nachfolger, 1900.

_______. "Predigten des Jahres 1528." In *D. Martin Luthers Werke: kritische Gesamtausgabe*. WA: Weimarer Ausgabe, vol. 27. Weimar: H. Böhlaus Nachfolger, 1903.

_______. "Predigten des Jahres 1531." In *D. Martin Luthers Werke: kritische Gesamtausgabe*. WA: Weimarer Ausgabe, vol. 34.I, 1–584. Weimar: H. Böhlaus Nachfolger, 1908.

_______. "Predigten des Jahres 1532." In *D. Martin Luthers Werke: kritische Gesamtausgabe*. WA: Weimarer Ausgabe, vol. 36. Weimar: H. Böhlaus Nachfolger, 1909.

_______. "Predigten des Jahres 1533." In *D. Martin Luther's Werke: kritische Gesamtausgabe*. WA: Weimarer Ausgabe, vol. 37, 1–248. Weimar: H. Böhlaus Nachfolger, 1910.

_______. "Predigten des Jahres 1534." In *D. Martin Luther' Werke: kritische Gesamtausgabe*. WA: Weimarer Ausgabe, vol. 37, 249–672. Weimar: H. Böhlaus Nachfolger, 1910.

_______. "Predigten des Jahres 1535." In *D. Martin Luthers Werke: kritische Gesamtausgabe*. WA: Weimarer Ausgabe, vol. 41, 1–492. Weimar: H. Böhlaus Nachfolger, 1910.

_______. "Predigten des Jahres 1536." In *D. Martin Luther's Werke: kritische Gesamtausgabe*. WA: Weimarer Ausgabe, vol. 41, 493–763. Weimar: H. Böhlaus Nachfolger, 1910.

_______. "Predigten des Jahres 1538." In *D. Martin Luthers Werke: kritische Gesamtausgabe*. WA: Weimarer Ausgabe, vol. 46, 113–537. Weimar: H. Böhlaus Nachfolger, 1912.

_______. "Predigten des Jahres 1539." In *D. Martin Luthers Werke: kritische Gesamtausgabe*. WA: Weimarer Ausgabe, vol. 47, 628–875. Weimar: H. Böhlaus Nachfolger, 1912.

_______. "Randbemerkungen Luthers." In *D. Martin Luthers Werke: kritische Gesamtausgabe*. WA: Weimarer Ausgabe, vol. 9, 1–115. Weimar: H. Böhlaus Nachfolger, 1893.

_______. "Resolutiones disputationum de indulgentiarum virtute. 1518." In *D. Martin Luthers Werke: kritische Gesamtausgabe*. WA: Weimarer Ausgabe, vol. 1, 522–628. Weimar: H. Böhlaus Nachfolger, 1883.

_______. "Secunda disputatio contra Antinomos cum praefatione secunda Martini Lutheri. 12. Januar 1538." In *D. Martin Luthers Werke: kritische Gesamtausgabe*. WA: Weimarer Ausgabe, vol. 39.I, 419–485. Weimar: H. Böhlaus Nachfolger, 1926.

_______. "Sermo de indulgentiis pridie Dedicationis." In *D. Martin Luthers Werke: kritische Gesamtausgabe*. WA: Weimarer Ausgabe, vol. 1, 94–99. Weimar: H. Böhlaus Nachfolger, 1883.

_______. "Sermo I. de passione Christi. 1518," and "Sermo II. de passione Christi. 1518." In *D. Martin Luthers Werke: kritische Gesamtausgabe*. WA: Weimarer Ausgabe, vol. 1, 335–345. Weimar: H. Böhlaus Nachfolger, 1906.

_______. "Sermo in Die S. Thomae. 1516." In *D. Martin Luthers Werke: kritische Gesamtausgabe*. WA: Weimarer Ausgabe, vol. 1, 111–115. Weimar: H. Böhlaus Nachfolger, 1883.

_______. "Sermo in Die sancti Matthaei. 21, September 1516." In *D. Martin Luthers Werke: kritische Gesamtausgabe*. WA: Weimarer Ausgabe), vol. 1, 81–85. Weimar: H. Böhlaus Nachfolger, 1883.

_______. "Sermo. Dominica Iubilate. 26. April 1523." In *D. Martin Luthers Werke: kritische Gesamtausgabe*. WA: Weimarer Ausgabe, vol. 14, 121–128. Weimar: H. Böhlaus Nachfolger, 1895.

_______. "Sermon vom Leiden und Kreuz. 16 April, 1530." In *D. Martin Luthers Werke: kritische Gesamtausgabe*. WA: Weimarer Ausgabe, vol. 32, 28–39. Weimar: H. Böhlaus Nachfolger, 1906.

_______. "Sermon von der Betrachtung des heiligen Leidens Christi. 1519." In *D. Martin Luthers Werke: kritische Gesamtausgabe*. WA: Weimarer Ausgabe, vol. 2, 136–142. Weimar: H. Böhlaus Nachfolger, 1884.

_______. "Sermon zu St. Michael zu Erfurt getan von Glauben und Werken. (Tag der elftausend Jungfrauen) 21. Oktober 1522." In *D. Martin Luthers Werke: kritische Gesamtausgabe*. WA: Weimarer Ausgabe, vol. 10.III, 352–361. Weimar: H. Böhlaus Nachfolger, 1905.

_______. "Vom abendmal Christi." In *D. Martin Luthers Werke: kritische Gesamtausgabe*. WA: Weimarer Ausgabe, vol. 26, 261–509. Weimar: H. Böhlaus Nachfolger, 1909.

_______. “Von der Freiheit eines Christenmenschen. 1520.” In *D. Martin Luthers Werke: kritische Gesamtausgabe.* WA: Weimarer Ausgabe, vol. 7, 20–38. Weimar: H. Böhlaus Nachfolger, 1897.

_______. “Von weltlicher Oberkeit, wie weit man ihr Gehorsam schuldig sei, 1523.” In *D. Martin Luthers Werke: kritische Gesamtausgabe.* WA: Weimarer Ausgabe, vol. 11, 245–280. Weimar: H. Böhlaus Nachfolger, 1900.

_______. “Vorrede zu Bugenhagens Ausgabe von Athanasii libri contra idolatriam. 1532.” In *D. Martin Luthers Werke: kritische Gesamtausgabe.* WA: Weimarer Ausgabe, vol. 30.III, 529–532. Weimar: H. Böhlaus Nachfolger, 1910.

_______. “Vorrede zu der unvollständigen Ausgabe der „deutschen Theologie”. December 1526.” In *D. Martin Luthers Werke: kritische Gesamtausgabe.* WA: Weimarer Ausgabe, vol. 1, 152–153. Weimar: H. Böhlaus Nachfolger, 1883.

_______. “Vorrede zu Justus Menius, Von dem Geist der Wiedertäufer. 1544.” In *D. Martin Luthers Werke: kritische Gesamtausgabe.* WA: Weimarer Ausgabe, vol. 54, 28–100. Weimar: H. Böhlaus Nachfolger, 1928.

_______. “Vorrede zum 1. Bande der Wittenberger Ausgabe der deutschen Schriften. 1539.” In *D. Martin Luthers Werke: kritische Gesamtausgabe.* WA: Weimarer Ausgabe, vol. 50, 657–661. Weimar: H. Böhlaus Nachfolger, 1914.

_______. “Vorrede zum ersten Bande der Gesamtausgaben seiner lateinischen Schriften. Wittenberg 1545.” In *D. Martin Luthers Werke: kritische Gesamtausgabe.* WA: Weimarer Ausgabe, vol. 54, 179–187. Weimar: H. Böhlaus Nachfolger, 1928.

_______. “Vorrede zur der vollständigen Ausgabe der “deutschen Theologie. 1518.” In *D. Martin Luthers Werke: kritische Gesamtausgabe.* WA: Weimarer Ausgabe, vol. 1, 375–379. Weimar: H. Böhlaus Nachfolger, 1906.

_______. “Wochenpredigten über Joh. 6–8.” In *D. Martin Luthers Werke: kritische Gesamtausgabe.* WA: Weimarer Ausgabe, vol. 33, 1–314. Weimar: H. Böhlaus Nachfolger, 1907.

_______. *Operationes in psalmos: 1519–1521.* AWA: Archiv zur Weimarar Ausgabe, vol. 2. Köln: Böhlau-Verlag KG, 1981.

_______. “Veit Dietrichs Nachschriften.” In *D. Martin Luthers Werke: kritisch Gesamtausgabe.* Tischreden. WA.TR: Weimar Ausgabe Tischreden, vol. 1, 1–308. Weimar: H. Böhlaus Nachfolger, 1912.

_______. “Tischreden aus Anton Lauterbachs Sammlung B.” In D. Martin Luthers Werke: kritisch Gesamtausgabe. Tischreden.

WA.TR: Weimar Ausgabe Tischreden, vol. 5, 425–701. Weimar: H. Böhlaus Nachfolger, 1919.

_______. "A Letter of Consolation to All Who Suffer Persecution. 1522." In *Luther's Works*, vol. 43, *Devotional Writings II*. Translated by Martin H. Bertram. Edited by Helmut T. Lehmann and Gustav K. Wiencke, 57–70. Philadelphia, PA: Fortress Press, 1968.

_______. "A Meditation on Christ's Passion 1519." In *Luther's Works*, vol. 42, *Devotional Writings I*. Translated by Martin H. Bertram. Edited by Helmut T. Lehmann and Martin. O. Dietrich, 3–14. Philadelphia, PA: Fortress Press, 1969.

_______. "Brief Confession Concerning the Holy Sacrament, 1544." In *Luther's Works*, vol. 38, *Word and Sacrament IV.* Translated by Martin E. Lehmann. Edited by Helmut T. Lehmann and Martin E. Lehmann, 279–319. Philadelphia, PA: Fortress Press, 1971.

_______. "Confession Concerning Christ's Supper. 1528." In *Luther's Works*, vol. 37, *Word and Sacrament III*. Translated by Robert H. Fischer. Edited by Helmut T. Lehmann and Robert H. Fischer, 151–372. Philadelphia, PA: Fortress Press, 1961.

_______. "Disputation against Scholastic Theology. 1517." In *Luther's Works*, vol. 31, *Career of the Reformer*. Translated by Harold J. Grimm. Edited by Helmut T. Lehmann and Harold J. Grimm, 3–16. Philadelphia, PA: Fortress Press, 1958.

_______. "Explanations of the Ninety-Five Theses or Explanations of the Disputation Concerning the Value of Indulgences. 1518." In *Luther's Works*, vol. 31, *Career of the Reformer*. Translated by Harold J. Grimm. Edited by Helmut T. Lehmann and Harold J. Grimm, 77–250. Philadelphia, PA: Fortress Press, 1958.

_______. "Heidelberg Disputation. 1518." In *Luther's Works*, vol. 31, *Career of the Reformer*. Translated by Harold J. Grimm. Edited by Helmut T. Lehmann and Harold J. Grimm, 35–70. Philadelphia, PA: Fortress Press, 1958.

_______. "Ninety-Five Theses or Disputation on The Power and Efficacy of Indulgences." In *Luther's Works*, vol. 31, *Career of the Reformer*. Translated by Harold J. Grimm. Edited by Helmut T. Lehmann and Harold J. Grimm, 17–33. Philadelphia, PA: Fortress Press, 1958.

_______. "Preface to the Wittenberg Edition of Luther's German Writings. 1539." In *Luther's Works*, vol. 34, *Career of the Reformer IV*. Translated by Robert R. Heitner. Edited by Helmut T. Lehmann and Lewis W. Spitz, 279–288. Philadelphia, PA: Muhlenberg Press, 1960.

_______. "Scholia. Chapter 5." In *Luther's Works*, vol. 25, *Glosses and Scholia.* Translated by Jacob A. O. Preus, ed. Hilton C. Oswald, 285–308. Philadelphia, PA: Fortress Press, 1972.

_______. "Scholia. Chapter 9." In *Luther's Works*, vol. 2, *Lectures on Genesis Chapters 6–14.* Translated by George V. Schick. Edited by Jaroslav Pelikan and Daniel E. Poellot, 264–549. Philadelphia, PA: Fortress Press, 1960.

_______. "Sermon at Coburg on Cross and Suffering. April 16, 1530." In *Luther's Works*, vol. 51, *Sermons I.* Translated by John W. Doberstein. Edited by Helmut T. Lehmann and John W. Doberstein, 197–208. Philadelphia, PA: Fortress Press, 1959.

_______. "Sermons in the Gospel of St. John Chapters 14–16." In *Luther's Works*, vol. 24. Translated by Martin H. Bertram. Edited by Jaroslav Pelikan, Daniel E. Poellot, 1–422. Saint Louis, MO: Concordia Publishing House, 1961.

_______. "Table Talk Recorded by Viet Dietrich, 1531–1533." In *Luther's Works*, vol. 54, *Table Talk.* Translated by Theodore G. Tappert. Edited by Helmut T. Lehmann and Theodore G. Tappert, 3–115. Philadelphia, PA: Fortress Press, 1967.

_______. "Temporal Authority: To What Extent it Should be Obeyed, 1523." In *Luther's Works*, vol. 45, *Christian in Society.* Translated by Albert T. W. Steinhaeuser. Edited by Helmut T. Lehmann and Walther I. Brandt, 75–130. Philadelphia, PA: Fortress Press, 1962.

_______. "The Disputation Concerning Man. 1536." In *Luther's Works*, vol. 34, *Career of the Reformer IV.* Translated by Lewis W. Spitz. Edited by Helmut T. Lehmann and Lewis W. Spitz, 133–144. Philadelphia, PA: Muhlenberg Press, 1960.

_______. "The Disputation Concerning the Passage: 'The Word Was Made Flesh' (John 1:14) 1539." In *Luther's Works*, vol. 38, *Word and Sacrament IV.* Translated by Martin E. Lehmann. Edited by Helmut T. Lehmann and Martin E. Lehmann, 235–277. Philadelphia, PA: Fortress Press, 1971.

_______. "The Freedom of a Christian. 1520." In *Luther's Works*, vol. 31, *Career of the Reformer I.* Translated by W. A. Lambert, Revised by Harold J. Grimm. Edited by Helmut T. Lehmann and Harold J. Grimm, 327–377. Philadelphia, PA: Fortress Press, 1957.

_______. "The Second Disputation against the Antinomians. January 12, 1538." In *Luther's Works*, vol. 73, *Disputations II.* Edited by Christopher Boyd Brown, 115–161. Saint Louis, MO: Concordia Publishing House, 2020.

_______. "To George Spalatin. Wittenberg, December 14, 1516." In *Luther's Works*, vol. 48, *Sermons I.* Translated by Gottfried G. Krodel. Edited by Helmut T. Lehmann and Gottfried G. Krodel, 32–36. Philadelphia, PA: Fortress Press, 1963.

_______. "To John von Staupitz. Wittenberg, May 30, 1518." In *Luther's Works*, vol. 48, Letters I. Translated by Gottfried G. Krodel. Edited by Helmut T. Lehmann and Gottfried G. Krodel, 64–70. Philadelphia, PA: Fortress Press, 1963.

_______. "To the Councilmen of All Cities in Germany That They Establish and Maintain Christian Schools. 1524." In *Luther's Works*, vol. 45, *Christian in Society*. Translated by Albert T. W. Steinhaeuser. Edited by Helmut T. Lehmann and Walther I. Brandt, 339–378. Philadelphia, PA: Fortress Press, 1962.

_______. "Sermon on St. Thomas' Day, Ps. 19.1, December 21, 1516." In *Luther's Works*, vol. 51, *Sermons I.* Translated by John W. Doberstein. Edited by Helmut T. Lehmann, 17–23. Philadelphia, PA: Muhlenberg Press, 1959.

_______. "Two Lenten Sermons, 1518." In *Luther's Works*, vol. 51, *Sermons I.* Translated by John W. Doberstein. Edited by Helmut T. Lehmann, 35–49. Philadelphia, PA: Muhlenberg Press, 1959.

_______. "Eight Sermons at Wittenberg, 1522." In *Luther's Works*, vol. 51, *Sermons I.* Translated by John W. Doberstein. Edited by Helmut T. Lehmann, 69–100. Philadelphia, PA: Muhlenberg Press, 1959.

_______. "Preface to the Complete Edition of a German Theology." In *Luther's Works*, vol. 31, *Career of the Reformer: I.* Translated by Harold J. Grimm. Edited by Helmut T. Lehmann, 75–76. Philadelphia, PA: Muhlenberg Press, 1957.

_______. "The Disputation Concerning the Passage: "The Word Was Made Flesh" (John 1:14) 1539." In *Luther's Works*, vol. 38, *Word and Sacrament: IV*. Translated and edited by Martin E. Lehmann. General editor: Helmut T. Lehmann, 237–277. Philadelphia, PA: Muhlenberg Press, 1971.

Mair, John. *Editio Ioannis Majoris | doctoris parisienso: super Tertium sen-| tentiarum: de novo edita*, Paris: Granjon, 1517.

Mauburnus, Johannes. *Rosetum exercitiorum spiritualium| et sacrarum meditationum: Jn quo etiam habant materia predi=| cabilis per totum anni circulum.* Basel: Wolff, 1504.

Ockham, Guillelmus de. *Opera philosophica et theologica. Opera Theologica*, vol. 1. Edited by Gedeon Gál. St. Bonaventure, NY: Editiones Instituti Franciscani Universitatis St. Bonaventurae, 1967.

_______. *Opera philosophica et theologica. Opera Theologica*, vol. 3. Edited by Gerard Etzkorn. St. Bonaventure, NY: Editiones Instituti Franciscani Universitatis St. Bonaventurae, 1977.

_______. *Opera philosophica et theologica. Opera Theologica*, vol. 9. Edited by Joseph C. Wey. St. Bonaventure, NY: Editiones Instituti Franciscani Universitatis St. Bonaventurae, 1980.

Porète, Marguerite. *Der Spiegel der einfachen Seelen*. Wege Der Frauenmystik. Edited by Louise Gnädinger. Munich: Artemis, 1987.

Roth, Friedrich Wilhelm Emil, "Aufzeichnungen über das mystische Leben der Nonnen von Kirchberg bei Sulz Predigerordens während des XIV. und XV. Jahrhunderts." *Alemannia*, 21 (1893): 103–148.

Scheel, Otto, ed. *Dokumente zu Luthers Entwicklung (bis 1519)*, 2nd ed. Tübingen: Mohr, 1929.

Schleiermacher, Friedrich Daniel Ernst. *Briefwechsel 1801–1802.* Edited by Andreas Arndt and Wolfgang Virmond. Berlin: De Gruyter, 1999.

Seuse, Heinrich. *Deutsche mystische Schriften*. Translated and edited by Georg Hofmann. Düsseldorf: Patmos-Verlag, 1966.

_______. *Deutsche Schriften.* Edited by Karl Bihlmeyer. Frankfurt: Minerva, 1961.

Spener, Philipp Jakob. *Pia desideria. Die Werke Philipp Jakob Speners. Studienausgabe*, vol 1.I. Edited by Kurt Aland. Gießen: Brunnen, 1996.

_______. *Pia desideria. Seminar editions*. Translated and edited by Theodore G. Tappert. Philadelphia: Fortress Press, 1964.

Staupitz, Johann. *Johann Von Staupitz, Salzburger Predigten 1512: Eine Textkritische Edition*. Edited by Wolfram Schneider-Lastin. PhD Dissertation. Tübingen, 1990.

_______. *Sämtliche Schriften, 2. Lateinische Schriften: Libellus de exsecutione aeternae praedestinationis*. Edited by Lothar Graf zu Dohna and Richard Wetzel. Berlin: De Gruyter, 1979.

Staupitz, Johann, and Rudolf K. Markwald. "A Mystic's Passion: The Spirituality of Johannes von Staupitz in His 1520 Lenten Sermons; Translation and Commentary." *Renaissance and Baroque*, vol. 3. New York: Lang, 1990.

Tauler, Johannes. *Sermones: des hoch| geleerten in gnaden erleüchten do|ctoris Johannis Thaulerii sannt | dominici ordens die da weißend | auff den nächesten waren weg im | gaist z wanderen durch überswe| bendenn syn. Von latein in teütsch | gewendt manchem menschenn z | sliger fruchtbarkaitt*. Augsburg: Hans Otmar, 1508.

———. *Die Predigten Taulers aus der Engelberger und der Freiburger Handschrift sowie aus Schmidts Abschriften der ehemaligen Strassburger Handschriften.* Edited by Ferdinand Vetter. Berlin: Weidmannsche Buchhandlung, 1910.

———. *Predigten: Vollständige Ausgabe.* Edited and translated by Georg Hofmann. Freiburg im Breisgau: Verlag Herder, 1961.

———. *Johannes Tauler: Sermons, trans. Maria Shrady, Classics of Western Spirituality.* Mahwah, NJ: Paulist Press, 1985.

———. *The Sermons and Conferences of John Tauler.* Edited and translated by Walter Elliott. Washington, DC: Apostolic Mission House, 1910.

Tempier, Étienne, and Kurt Flasch, "Aufklärung Im Mittelalter? Die Verurteilung Von 1277: Das Dokument des Bischofs von Paris." Excerpta Classica, vol. 6. Edited by Kurt Flasch. Mainz: Dieterich, 1989.

Theologia deutsch. de Francfordia, Johannes. *Eyn geystlich edles Buchleynn. von rechter vnderscheyd vnd vorstand. was der alt vn[d] new mensche sey. Was Adams vn[d] was gottis kind sey. vn[d] wie Ada[m] ynn vns sterben vnnd Christus ersteen sall.* Wittenberg: Rhau-Grunenberg, 1516.

Theologia deutsch. *'Der Franckforter', Theologia Deutsch.* Translated by Alois M. Haas. Einsiedeln: Johannes-Verlag, 1980.

Theologia deutsch. *"Der Franckforter": <"Theologia Deutsch">*, Kritische Textausgabe." Edited by Wolfgang von Hinten. Münchener Texte und Untersuchungen zur deutschen Literatur des Mittelalters. Munich: Artemis-Verlag, 1982.

Thomas à Kempis. *The Imitation of Christ: A Timeless Classic for Contemporary Readers.* Translated by William C. Creasy. Notre Dame, IN: Ave Maria Press, 2017.

———. *The Imitation of Christ.* Phoenix, AZ: Aquinas Press, 2017.

———. *Nachfolge Christi und vier andere Schriften.* Lateinisch und deutsch. Edited by Friedrich Eichler. Munich: Kösel-Verlag, 1966.

Trutfetter, Jodocus. *Summule totius logice: "quod opus | maius appellitare libuit : per Jodo|cum Trutuetter Jsennachensem Theologum (. . .) in Gymna|sio nuper Erphordiensi utpote succus e floribus labo|riosissime compilate.* Erfurt: Wolfgang Schenk, 1501.

Usingen, Bartholomaeus Arnoldi de. *Exercitium Nove logi|ces in Studio Erffurdien colle /|ctum per Magistrum Bartho|lomeum Arnoldi de Usin|gen instauratum atque| emendatum.* Erfurt: 1516.

von Paltz, Johannes. *Werke*, vol. 1, *Coelifodina*, and vol. 2, *Spätmittelalter und Reformation*. Edited by Christoph Burger and Friedhelm Stasch, Preface by Heiko A. Oberman. Berlin: De Gruyter, 1983.

_______. *Werke*, vol. 3: *Opuscula*. Edited by Christoph Burger. Spätmittelalter und Reformation: vol. 4. Berlin: De Gruyter, 1989.

Witte, Karl-Heinz, ed. *Der Meister des Lehrgesprächs, Der Audi-filia-Dialog: Des menschen val, adel vnd erlösunge. Nach der Handschrift CPC 1945 der Bibliothèque de Consistoire Colmar*, unpublished manuscript.

Zerbolt, Gerard. *La montée du cœur / De spiritualibus ascensionibus*. Introduction by Nikolaus Staubach. Edited and translated by Francis Joseph Legrand. Turnhout: Brepols, 2006.

_______. *The spiritual ascent: a devotional treatise*. Translated by J. P. Arthur. London: Burns & Oates, 1908.

LITERATURE

Aland, Kurt. *Der Weg zur Reformation: Zeitpunkt und Charakter des reformatorischen Erlebnisses Martin Luthers. Theologische Existenz heute*. Neue Folge, Nr. 123. Munich: C. Kaiser, 1965.

Aland, Kurt, and Barbara Aland. *Der Text des Neuen Testaments: Einführung in die Wissenschaftlichen Ausgaben sowie in Theorie und Praxis der modernen Textkritik*, 2nd ed. Stuttgart: Dt. Bibelgesellschaft, 1989.

Aland, Kurt, Ernst Otto Reichert, and Gerhard Jordan. *Hilfsbuch zum Lutherstudium*, vol. 4, durchgesehene und erw. Aufl. Bielefeld: Luther-Verlag, 1996.

Alimonti, Francesca Rita. *Maître Eckhart et la tradition spirituelle: les "Confessiones" de Saint Augustin dans les sermons latins. Analecta Augustiniana*, vol. 58. 265–286. Nerbini International, 1995.

Althaus, Paul. *Die Theologie Martin Luthers*. Gütersloh: Gütersloher Verlagshaus Mohn, 1962.

Auer, Albert. *Leidenstheologie im Spätmittelalter. Kirchengeschichtliche Quellen und Studien*, vol. 2. St. Ottilien: Eos Verlog der Erzabtei, 1952.

Barth, Hans-Martin. "Historie und Identifikation: Über Luthers Passions- und Osterpredigt." In *Pastoraltheologie*, 70–80. Göttingen: Vandenhoeck & Ruprecht, 1966.

Barth, Karl. *Kirchliche Dogmatik*, 8th ed. Bd. I/2. Zurich: Theologischer Verlag, 1990.

Bayer, Oswald. *Martin Luthers Theologie: eine Vergegenwärtigung*. Tübingen: Mohr Siebeck, 2003.

———. "Oratio, Meditatio, Tentatio. Eine Besinnung auf Luthers Theologieverständnis (Une réflexion sur la conception de la théologie chez Luther)." In *Luther Jahrbuch*, vol. 55. Göttingen: Vandenhoeck & Ruprecht, 1988.

———. *Promissio: Geschichte Der reformatorischen Wende in Luthers Theologie*. 2., durchgesehene, um ein Vorwort erweiterte Aufl.—reprograph. Nachdr. d. 1. Aufl., Göttingen, Vandenhoeck & Ruprecht, 1971. Darmstadt: Wissenschaftliche Buchgesellschaft, 1989.

———. "Vita Passiva: Luther und die Mystik." In *Die Kirchenkritik Der Mystiker*; vol. 2, *Frühe Neuzeit*. Edited by Mariano Delgado and Gotthard Fuchs. Fribourg: Academic Press, 2005.

Bell, Theo. "Divus Bernhardus: Bernhard von Clairvaux in Martin Luthers Schriften." *Veröffentlichungen des Instituts für Europäische Geschichte Mainz*, vol. 148. Mainz: Von Zabern, 1993.

Benzing, Josef. *Die Buchdrucker des 16. und 17. Jahrhunderts im deutschen Sprachgebiet*, 2nd ed. Wiesbaden: O. Harrassowitz, 1982.

Beutel, Albrecht. "Antwort und Wort: zur Frage nach der Wirklichkeit Gottes bei Luther." In *Luther und Ontologie*. Helsinki: Luther-Agricola-Gesellschaft, 1993.

———. *Protestantische Konkretionen: Studien zur Kirchengeschichte*. Tübingen: Mohr Siebeck, 1998.

———. "Theologie als Unterscheidungslehre." In *Luther Handbuch*. Edited by Albrecht Beutel, 450–454. Tübingen: Mohr Siebeck, 2005.

Beyer, Michael. "Martin Luthers Betbüchlein." In *Lutherjahrbuch*, vol. 74, 29–50. Göttingen: Vandenhoeck & Ruprecht, 2007.

Bielfeldt, Dennis. "Luther on Language." *Lutheran Quarterly* 16, no. 2 (Sum 2002): 195–220. https://search.ebscohost.com/login.aspx?direct=true&db=lsdar&AN=ATLA0001472763&site=ehost-live&scope=site.

Bizer, Ernst. *Fides ex auditu: Eine Untersuchung über die Entdeckung der Gerechtigkeit Gottes durch Martin Luther*, 3rd ed. Neukirchen: Verlag der Buchhandlung des Erziehungsvereins, 1966.

Blaumeiser, Hubertus. "Martin Luthers Kreuzestheologie: Schlüssel Zu Seiner Deutung Von Mensch Und Wirklichkeit; Eine Untersuchung Anhand Der Operationes in Psalmos (1519–1521)." *Konfessionskundliche Und Kontroverstheologische Studien 60*. Paderborn: Bonifatius, 1995.

Bornkamm, Heinrich. "Probleme der Lutherbiographie." In *Lutherforschung heute: Referate und Berichte Des 1. Internationalen Lutherforschungskongresses, Aarhus 18.-23. August 1956*, edited by Vilmos Vajta, 15–23. Berlin: Lutherisches Verlagshaus, 1958.

Brecht, Martin. *Martin Luther*, vol. 1, *Sein Weg zur Reformation 1483–1521*, 3rd ed. Stuttgart: Calwer Verlag, 1990.

Browe, Peter. *Die Verehrung der Eucharistie im Mittelalter*. Munich: M. Hueber, 1933.

Cognet, Louis. *Gottes Geburt in der Seele: Einführung in die deutsche Mystik*. Freiburg im Breisgau: Verlag Herder, 1980.

Courtenay, William J. *Capacity and Volition. A History of the Distinction of Absolute and Ordained Power.* Bergamo: P. Lubrina, 1990.

Degenhardt, Ingeborg. *Studien zum Wandel des Eckhartbildes*, Studien zur Problemgeschichte der antiken und mittelalterlichen Philosophie 3. Leiden: Brepols, 1967.

Dieter, Theo. *Der junge Luther und Aristoteles. Eine historisch-systematische Untersuchung zum Verhältnis von Theologie und Philosophie.* Berlin: De Gruyter, 2001.

Ebeling, Gerhard. "Luthers Psalterdruck vom Jahre 1513." In *Lutherstudien*, vol. 1. Tübingen: Mohr, 1971.

Elze, Martin. "Züge Spätmittelalterlicher Frömmigkeit in Luthers Theologie." *Zeitschrift für Theologie und Kirche* 62, no. 4 (1965): 381–402.

________. "Das Verständnis der Passion Jesu im ausgehenden Mittelalter und bei Luther." In *Geist und Geschichte der Reformation: Festgabe Hanns Rückert zum 65. Geburtstag*, edited by Heinz Liebing and Klaus Scholder, 127–151. Berlin: De Gruyter, 1966.

Enderlein, Wolfgang. "Rechtfertigungslehre und Mystik: Zum mystischen Kern der Rechtfertigungslehre bei Luther." *Theologische Zeitschrift* 70, no. 2. (2014): 118–141.

Evener, Vincent. *Enemies of the Cross: Suffering, Truth, and Mysticism in the Early Reformation.* Oxford: Oxford University Press, 2021.

Faupel-Drevs, Kirstin. "Vom rechten Gebrauch der Bilder im liturgischen Raum: mittelalterliche Funktionsbestimmungen bildender Kunst im Rationale divinorum officiorum des Durandus von Mende (1230/1–1296)." In *Studies in the History of Christian Thought*, vol. 89, 0081–8607. Leiden: Brill, 2000.

Forsberg, Juhani. "Die finnische Lutherforschung seit 1979." In *Lutherjahrbuch*, vol. 72, 147–182. Göttingen: Vandenhoeck & Ruprecht, 2005.

Gandlau, Thomas. "Trinität Und Kreuz: Die Nachfolge Christi in der Mystagogie Johannes Taulers." *Freiburger Theologische Studien 155*. Freiburg im Breisgau: Verlag Herder, 1993.

Gebrehiiwet, Mihreteab. "Christ-mysticism in the Theology and Spirituality of Martin Luther." PhD diss., Lutheran School of Theology at Chicago, 1976.

Ghiselli, Anja, Kari Kopperi, and Rainer Vinke, eds. *Luther und Ontologie: Das Sein Christi im Glauben als strukturierendes Prinzip der Theologie Luthers*: Referate der Factagung des Instituts für Systematische Theologie der Universität Helsinki in Zusammenarbeit mit der Luther-Akademie Ratzeburg in Helsinki, April 1–5, 1992. *Veröffentlichungen der Luther-Akademie Ratzeburg*. Helsinki: Luther-Agricola-Gesellschaft, 1993.

Gnädinger, Louise. *Johannes Tauler: Lebenswelt und mystische Lehre*. Munich: C. H. Beck, 1993.

Grane, Leif. *Modus loquendi theologicus: Luthers Kampf um die Erneuerung der Theologie (1515–1518)*. Leiden: Brill, 1975.

Grimm, Jacob, and Wilhelm Grimm. *Deutsches Wörterbuch*, vol. 11. Leipzig: S. Hirzel, 1873.

Grisar, Hartmann. *Luther*, vol. 1, *Luthers Werden. Grundlegung der Spaltung bis 1530*, 3rd ed. Freiburg im Breisgau: Verlag Herder, 1924.

Haas, Alois M. *Gottleiden—Gottlieben: Zur Volkssprachlichen Mystik Im Mittelalter*. Frankfurt am Main: Insel-Verlag, 1989.

________. *Kunst rechter Gelassenheit: Themen und Schwerpunkte von Heinrich Seuses Mystik*. Bern: P. Lang, 1995.

________. *Nim din selbes war: Studien zur Lehre von der Selbsterkenntnis bei Meister Eckhart, Johannes Tauler und Heinrich Seuse*. Freiburg, Schweiz: Universitätsverlag, 1971.

Hägele, Klaus. "Luther strikt mystisch verstehen! Ein Zwischenruf zum Reformationsjubiläum." *Deutsches Pfarrerblatt 113*, no. 10, 586–588. Verlagshaus Speyer, 2013.

Hagen, Kenneth, and Martin Luther. *Luther's Approach to Scripture as Seen in His "Commentaries" on Galatians: 1519–1538*. Tübingen: Mohr, 1993.

Hamel, Adolf. *Der junge Luther und Augustin: Ihre Beziehungen in der Rechtfertigungslehre nach Luthers ersten Vorlesungen 1509–1518 untersucht. 1.Teil: Der Sententiar von 1509/10 und Exeget der Psalmen von 1513–15 in seinem Verhältnis zu Augustin*. Gütersloh: Verlag C. Bertelsmann, 1934.

Hamm, Berndt. "Johann von Staupitz (ca. 1468–1524)—spätmittelalterlicher Reformer und 'Vater' der Reformation" *Archiv für*

Reformationsgeschichte—Archive for Reformation History 92, no. jg (2001): 6–42.

_______. "Was ist Frömmigkeitstheologie? Überlegungen zum 14. bis 16. Jahrhundert." In *Praxis Pietatis: Beiträge zu Theologie und Frömmigkeit in der frühen Neuzeit.* FS Wolfgang Sommer. Edited by Hans-Jörg Nieden, Marcel Nieden, and Elke Axmacher. Stuttgart: Kohlhammer, 1999.

_______. *Der frühe Luther: Etappen reformatorischer Neuorientierung.* Tübingen: Mohr Siebeck, 2010.

_______. *Frömmigkeitstheologie am Anfang des 16. Jahrhunderts. Studien zu Johannes von Paltz und seinem Umkreis. Beiträge zur historischen Theologie*, vol. 65. Tübingen: Mohr, 1982.

_______. "Die "Nahe Gnade"—innovative Züge der spätmittelalterlichen Theologie und Frömmigkeit." In *"Herbst des Mittelalters?" Fragen zur Bewertung des 14. und 15. Jahrhunderts*, edited by Jan A. Aertsen and Martin Pickavé. Berlin: De Gruyter, 2004.

_______. "Einheit und Vielheit der Reformation—oder: was die Reformation zur Reformation machte." In *Reformationstheorien. Ein kirchenhistorischer Disput über Einheit und Vielfalt der Reformation.* Edited by Bernd Moeller and Dorothea Wendebourg, 57–127. Göttingen: Vandenhoeck & Ruprecht, 1995.

_______. "Von der Gottesliebe des Mittelalters zum Glauben Luthers. Ein Beitrag zur Bußgeschichte." In *Luther-Jahrbuch*, vol. 65. Vandenhoeck & Ruprecht, 1998.

Häring, Herman. "Eschatologie." In *Augustin Handbuch*, edited by Volker H. Drecoll, 540–547. Tübingen: Mohr Siebeck, 2007.

Hartfelder, Karl. "Veit Winsheim." In *Allgemeine Deutsche Biographie*, vol. 43, 462–463. Leipzig: Verlag, 1898.

Hasse, Hans-Peter. *Karlstadt und Tauler: Untersuchungen zur Kreuzestheologie. Quellen und Forschungen zur Reformationsgeschichte*, vol. 58. First Print; Leipzig, Univ., Diss., 1991. Gütersloh: Gütersloher Verlagshaus Gerd Mohn, 1993.

Hendrikx, Ephraem. *Augustins Verhältnis zur Mystik: eine patristische Untersuchung*. Cassiciacum. Würzburg: Rita-Verlag, 1936.

Herrmann, Erik H. "Luther's Divine Aeneid: Continuity and Creativity in Reforming the Use of the Bible." *Lutherjahrbuch*, vol. 85. 85–109. Göttingen: Vandenhoeck & Ruprecht, 2018.

Hirsch, Emanuel. "Initium theologiae Lutheri." In *Der Durchbruch der reformatorischen Erkenntnis bei Luther.* Edited by Bernhard Lohse, 46–95. Darmstadt: Wissenschaftliche Buchgesellschaft, 1968.

Hoffmann, Adolf. "Sakramentale Heilswege bei Tauler." In *Johannes Tauler: ein deutscher Mystiker: Gedenkschrift zum 600. Todestag*. Edited by Ephrem Filthaut, 247–267. Essen: Driewer, 1961.

Joest, Wilfried. *Ontologie der Person bei Luther*. Göttingen: Vandenhoeck u. Ruprecht, 1967.

Jüngel, Eberhard. "Metaphorische Wahrheit: Erwägungen zur theologischen Relevanz der Metapher als Beitrag zur Hermeneutik einer narrativen Theologie" *Evangelische Theologie* 34, Supplement (1974): 71–122.

________. *Das Opfer Jesu Christi Als Sacramentum Et Exemplum*. Stuttgart: Diakonie-Verlag d. Gustav Werner Stiftung zum Bruderhaus, 1986/87.

Junk, Karsten. *Der menschliche Geist und sein Gottesverhältnis bei Augustinus und Meister Eckhart. Augustinus, Werk und Wirkung*, vol. 5. Paderborn: Ferdinand Schöningh, 2016.

Juntunen, Sammeli. *Der Begriff des Nichts bei Luther in den Jahren von 1510 bis 1523*. Helsinki: Luther-Agricola-Gesellschaft, 1996.

Karimies, Ilmari. "Mystik." In *Das Luther-Lexikon*, edited by Gury Schneider-Ludorff, Ingo Klitzsch, and Volker Leppin. Regensburg: Bückle & Böhm, 2014.

Kaufmann, Thomas. "Anpassung als historiographisches Konzept und als theologiepolitisches Programm. Der Kirchenhistoriker Erich Seeberg in der Zeit der Weimarer Republik und des 'Dritten Reiches'." In *Evangelische Kirchenhistoriker im "Dritten Reich"*, edited by Thomas Kaufmann and Harry Oelke. Gütersloh: Kaiser, Gütersloher Verlagshaus, 2002.

Kenney, John Peter. *The Mysticism of Saint Augustine: Rereading the Confessions*. New York: Routledge, 2005.

Khorkov, Mikhail. "Der Traktat 'Von dem ewigen Wort' und der augustinische Kontext in der Rezeption Der Lehre Von Der Gottesgeburt Am Oberrhein Im 15. Jahrhundert." *University, Council, City*. 203–218. Brepols, 2007.

________. Michail L'vovič Chor'kov. "Unbekannter Eckhart oder unbekannter Ruusbroec?: Zum Augustinistischen Kontext Der Meister-Eckhart-Rezeption Im 15. Jahrhundert." In *Meister Eckhart in Erfurt*. Edited by Andreas Speer and Lydia Wegener. Berlin: De Gruyter, 2005.

Kleineidam, Erich. *Universitas studii Erfordensis: Überblick über die Geschichte der Universität Erfurt im Mittelalter 1392–1521. Teil 2: Spätscholastik, Humanismus und Reformation: 1461–1521*, 2nd ed. Leipzig: Verlag, 1992.

Knuuttila, Simo. “Trutfetter, Usingen and Erfurtian Ockhamism.” In *Was ist Philosophie im Mittelalter? = What is philosophy in the Middle Ages? Akten des X. Internationalen Kongresses für mittelalterliche Philosophie der Société Internationale pour l'Étude de la Philosophie Médiévale, 25. bis 30. August 1997 im Erfurt*, edited by Jan A. Aertsen and Andreas Speer, 818–823. Berlin: De Gruyter, 1998.

Koch, Josef. “Neue Aktenstücke zu dem gegen Wilhelm Ockham in Avignon geführten Prozeß.” *Recherches de théologie ancienne et médiévale*, vol. 7 (1935): 353–380, vol. 8 (1936): 79–93, 168–197. Louvain: Peeters Publishers, 1935.

Köpf, Ulrich. “Martin Luthers theologischer Lehrstuhl.” In *Frömmigkeitsgeschichte und Theologiegeschichte: Gesammelte Aufsätze*. Tübingen: Mohr Siebeck, 2022.

_______. “Religiöse Erfahrung in der Theologie Bernhards von Clairvaux.” *Beiträge zur Historischen Theologie*. Tübingen: Mohr, 1980.

_______. “Martin Luther Als Mönch.” In *Luther* 55, no. 2, 66–84. Göttingen: Vandenhoeck & Ruprecht, 1984.

_______. “Martin Luther und Tauler.” In *Frömmigkeitsgeschichte und Theologiegeschichte: Gesammelte Aufsätze*, 515–539. Tübingen: Mohr Siebeck, 2022.

_______. “Monastische Traditionen bei Martin Luther.” In *Luther, zwischen den Zeiten: eine Jenaer Ringvorlesung*, edited by Christoph Markschies and Michael Trowitzsch, 17–35. Tübingen: Mohr Siebeck, 1999.

Krentz, Natalie. *Ritualwandel und Deutungshoheit: die frühe Reformation in der Residenzstadt Wittenberg (1500–1533). Spätmittelalter, Humanismus, Reformation* vol. 74. Tübingen: Mohr Siebeck, 2014.

Kunzelmann, Adalbero. *Geschichte der deutschen Augustiner-Eremiten. Cassiciacum,* vol. 5, *Die sachsisch-thüringische Provinz und die sächsische Reformkongreation bis zum Untergang der beiden*. Würzburg: Augustinus-Verl., 1974.

Langer, Otto. *Mystische Erfahrung und spirituelle Theologie: zu Meister Eckharts Auseinandersetzung mit der Frauenfrömmigkeit seiner Zeit*. Munich: Artemis, 1987.

Leppin, Volker. “‘Als wir diese spise essent, so werden wir gessen’: Reale und metaphorische Nähe Christi bei Johannes Tauler.” In *Metaphorik und Christologie*, edited by Jörg Frey, Jan Rohls, and Ruben Zimmermannm, 167–177. Berlin: De Gruyter, 2003.

_______. “Aristotelisierung, Immediatisierung Und Radikalisierung: Transformationen Der Sündenlehre Von Thomas Von Aquin Bis Martin Luther.” In *Transformationen*, 303–332. Mohr Siebeck, 2018.

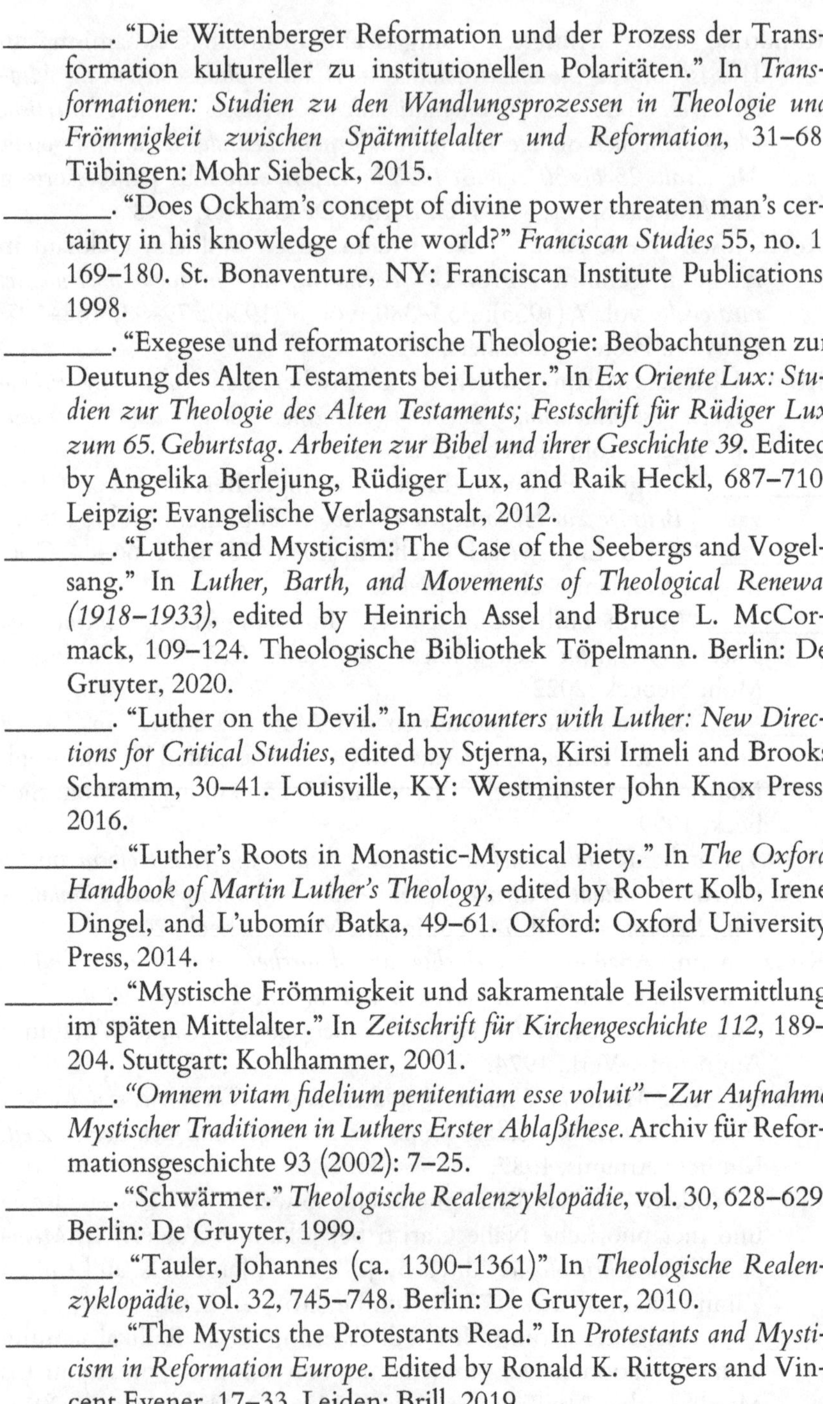

________. "Die Wittenberger Reformation und der Prozess der Transformation kultureller zu institutionellen Polaritäten." In *Transformationen: Studien zu den Wandlungsprozessen in Theologie und Frömmigkeit zwischen Spätmittelalter und Reformation*, 31–68. Tübingen: Mohr Siebeck, 2015.

________. "Does Ockham's concept of divine power threaten man's certainty in his knowledge of the world?" *Franciscan Studies* 55, no. 1, 169–180. St. Bonaventure, NY: Franciscan Institute Publications, 1998.

________. "Exegese und reformatorische Theologie: Beobachtungen zur Deutung des Alten Testaments bei Luther." In *Ex Oriente Lux: Studien zur Theologie des Alten Testaments; Festschrift für Rüdiger Lux zum 65. Geburtstag. Arbeiten zur Bibel und ihrer Geschichte 39*. Edited by Angelika Berlejung, Rüdiger Lux, and Raik Heckl, 687–710. Leipzig: Evangelische Verlagsanstalt, 2012.

________. "Luther and Mysticism: The Case of the Seebergs and Vogelsang." In *Luther, Barth, and Movements of Theological Renewal (1918–1933)*, edited by Heinrich Assel and Bruce L. McCormack, 109–124. Theologische Bibliothek Töpelmann. Berlin: De Gruyter, 2020.

________. "Luther on the Devil." In *Encounters with Luther: New Directions for Critical Studies*, edited by Stjerna, Kirsi Irmeli and Brooks Schramm, 30–41. Louisville, KY: Westminster John Knox Press, 2016.

________. "Luther's Roots in Monastic-Mystical Piety." In *The Oxford Handbook of Martin Luther's Theology*, edited by Robert Kolb, Irene Dingel, and L'ubomír Batka, 49–61. Oxford: Oxford University Press, 2014.

________. "Mystische Frömmigkeit und sakramentale Heilsvermittlung im späten Mittelalter." In *Zeitschrift für Kirchengeschichte 112*, 189–204. Stuttgart: Kohlhammer, 2001.

________. *"Omnem vitam fidelium penitentiam esse voluit"—Zur Aufnahme Mystischer Traditionen in Luthers Erster Ablaßthese.* Archiv für Reformationsgeschichte 93 (2002): 7–25.

________. "Schwärmer." *Theologische Realenzyklopädie*, vol. 30, 628–629. Berlin: De Gruyter, 1999.

________. "Tauler, Johannes (ca. 1300–1361)" In *Theologische Realenzyklopädie*, vol. 32, 745–748. Berlin: De Gruyter, 2010.

________. "The Mystics the Protestants Read." In *Protestants and Mysticism in Reformation Europe*. Edited by Ronald K. Rittgers and Vincent Evener, 17–33. Leiden: Brill, 2019.

_______. "Transformationen spätmittelalterlicher Mystik bei Luther." In *Transformationen: Studien zu den Wandlungsprozessen in Theologie und Frömmigkeit zwischen Spätmittelalter und Reformation*, 399–417. Tübingen: Mohr Siebeck, 2015.

_______. *Die fremde Reformation: Luthers mystische Wurzeln*, 2nd ed. Munich: C. H. Beck, 2017.

_______. *Geglaubte Wahrheit: das Theologieverständnis Wilhelms von Ockham*. Göttingen: Vandenhoeck & Ruprecht, 1995.

_______. *Sola: Christ, Grace, Faith, and Scripture Alone in Martin Luther's Theology*. Minneapolis: Fortress Press, 2024.

_______. *Wilhelm von Ockham: Gelehrter, Streiter, Bettelmönch*. Darmstadt: Primus, 2003.

Löhrer, Magnus. "Das augustinische Binom 'Sacramentum et exemplum'" und "die Unterscheidung des Christlichen" bei Gerhard Ebeling und Eberhard Jüngel" In *Mysterium Christi: Symbolgegenwart und theologische Bedeutung: Festschrift für Basil Studer*. Edited by Magnus Löhrer and Elmar Salmann, 377–403. Rome: Pontificio Ateneo S. Anselmo, 1995.

Lohse, Bernhard. *Luthers Theologie in ihrer historischen Entwicklung und in ihrem systematischen Zusammenhang*. Göttingen: Vandenhoeck & Ruprecht, 1995.

Mager, Inge. "Weshalb hat Martin Luther kein Passionslied geschrieben?" In *Passion, Affekt und Leidenschaft in der Frühen Neuzeit*, edited by Johann Anselm Steiger, 405–422. Wiesbaden: Harrassowitz in Kommission, 2005.

Manselli, Raoul. "Brüder Des Freien Geistes." In *Theologische Realenzyklopädie*, vol. 7, 218–220. Berlin: De Gruyter, 2010.

Manstetten, Reiner. *Esse est Deus: Meister Eckharts christologische Versöhnung von Philosophie und Religion und ihre Ursprünge in der Tradition des Abendlandes*. Freiberg im Breisgau: K. Alber, 1993.

Maurer, Wilhelm. *Von der Freiheit eines Christenmenschen: zwei Untersuchungen zu Luthers Reformationsschriften 1520/21*. Göttingen: Vandenhoeck & Ruprecht, 1949.

McGinn, Bernard. *The Presence of God*, vol. 1, *The Foundations of Mysticism*. New York: Crossroad, 1991.

_______. "How Augustine Shaped Medieval Mysticism." *Augustinian Studies*, 31, no. 1 (2006): 1–26.

Mieth, Dietmar. *Die Einheit von vita activa und vita contemplativa in den deutschen Predigten und Traktaten Meister Eckharts und bei Johannes Tauler: Untersuchungen zur Struktur des christlichen Lebens. Studien zur Geschichte der katholischen Moraltheologie.* Regensburg: F. Pustet, 1969.

Moeller, Bernd. "Thesenanschläge." In *Luthers Thesenanschlag—Faktum oder Fiktion, Schriften Der Luthergedenkstätten In Sachsen-anhalt,* edited by Joachim Ott and Martin Treu, 9–31. Leipzig: Evangelische Verlagsanstalt, 2008.

_______. "Das Berühmtwerden Luthers." In, *Luther-Rezeption. Kirchenhistorische Aufsätze zur Reformationsgeschichte.* Edited by Johannes Schilling, 15–41. Göttingen: Vandenhoeck & Ruprecht, 2001.

Moeller, Bernd, and Karl Stackman. *Luder, Luther, Eleutherius, Erwägungen zu Luthers Namen/ Bernd Moeller; Karl Stackmann. Nachrichten der Akademie der Wissenschaften zu Göttingen 1981,* vol. 7. Göttingen: Vandenhoeck & Ruprecht, 1981.

Molendijk, Arie L. *Zwischen Theologie und Soziologie: Ernst Troeltschs Typen der christliche Gemeinschaftsbildung: Kirche, Sekte, Mystik. Troeltsch-Studien,* vol. 9. Gütersloh: Gütersloher Verlagshaus, 1996.

Mother, Rudolf. "Leiden und Weisheit in der protestantischen Mystik." In *Leiden und Weisheit in der Mystik.* Edited by Bernd Jaspert, 243–270. Paderborn: Bonifatius, 1992.

Müller, Alphons Victor. *Luther und Tauler auf ihren theologischen Zusammenhang.* Bern: Ferd. Wyss, 1918.

Müller, Gerhard. Review "Luther Handbuch." *Theologische Literaturzeitung* 132, no. 10 (2007): 1085–1087.

_______. "In memoriam Wilhelm Maurer." In *LutherJahrbuch,* vol. 50, 16–19. Göttingen: Vandenhoeck & Ruprecht, 1983.

Ngien, Dennis. *The Suffering of God According to Martin Luther's Theologia Crucis.* American University Studies. Series VII, Theology and Religion, vol. 181, 0740–0462. New York: P. Lang, 1995.

Nicol, Martin. *Meditation bei Luther.* Göttingen: Vandenhoeck & Ruprecht, 1984.

Oberman, Heiko Augustinus. "'Iustitia Christi' und 'Iustitia Dei'. Luther und die scholastischen Lehren von der Rechtfertigung." In *Der Durchbruch der reformatorischen Erkenntnis bei Luther,* edited by Bernhard Lohse, 413–444. Darmstadt: Wissenschaftliche Buchgesellschaft, 1968.

_______. *Spätscholastik und Reformation,* vol. 1, *Der Herbst der mittelalterlichen Theologie.* Zürich: EVZ-Verlag, 1965.

_______. *The Harvest of Medieval Theology: Gabriel Biel and Late Medieval Nominalism.* Grand Rapids, MI: Eerdmans, 1967.

Ohly, Friedrich. "Geistige Süße bei Otfried." In *Schriften zur mittelalterlichen Bedeutungsfroschung*. Darmstadt: Wissenschaftliche Buchgesellschaft, 1977.

_______. "Süsse Nägel Der Passion: Ein Beitrag zur theologischen Semantik." *Saecula Spiritalia*, vol. 21. Baden-Baden: Koerner, 1989.

Ohst, Martin. *Pflichtbeichte: Untersuchungen zum Busswesen im Hohen und Späten Mittelalter*. Beiträge zur historischen Theologie, vol. 89. Tübingen: J.C.B. Mohr (P. Siebeck), 1995.

Otto, Henrik. *Vor-und frühreformatorische Tauler-Rezeption: Annotationen in Drucken des späten 15. und frühen 16. Jahrhunderts. Quellen und Forschungen zur Reformationsgeschichte*, vol. 75. Gütersloh: Gütersloher Verlagshaus, 2003.

Ozment, Steven E. *Homo spiritualis: A comparative study of the anthropology of Johannes Tauler, Jean Gerson and Martin Luther (1509–16) in the context of their theological thought*. Leiden: Brill, 1969.

Pesch, Otto Hermann. "Neuere Beiträge zur Frage nach Luthers 'Reformatorischer Wende'," *Catholica Münster* 37, no. 5 (1983): 259–287; 38 (1984): 66–133. Münster: Aschendorff, 2000.

_______. "Zur Frage nach Luthers reformatorischer Wende. Ergebnisse und Probleme der Diskussion um Ernst Bizer." In *Der Durchbruch der reformatorischen Erkenntnis bei Luther*. Edited by Bernhard Lohse, 445–505. Darmstadt: Wissenschaftliche Buchgesellschaft, 1968.

Peura, Simo. *Mehr als ein Mensch?: die Vergöttlichung als Thema der Theologie Martin Luthers von 1513 bis 1519*. Mainz: P. von Zabern, 1994.

Peura, Simo, and Antti Raunio, eds. *Luther und Theosis: Vergöttlichung als Thema der abendländischen Theologie. Schriften der Luther-Agricola-Gesellschaft, Helsinki*. Helsinki: Luther-Agicola-Gesellschaft, 1990.

Posset, Franz. "Goldene Worte: Augustinus und Bernhard in der Sicht des alten Luther (1531–1546)." *Catholica Münster* 54, no. 3 (2000): 220–239. Münster: Aschendorff, 2000.

_______. "Preaching the Passion of Christ on the Eve of the Reformation." *Concorida Theological Quarterly*, 59 (1995): 279–300.

_______. *The Front-Runner of the Catholic Reformation: The Life and Works of Johann von Staupitz*. Aldershot, UK: Ashgate, 2003.

Ringleben, Joachim. *Gott im Wort: Luthers Theologie von der Sprache her. Hermeneutische Untersuchungen zur Theologie*. Tübingen: Mohr Siebeck, 2010.

Ritschl, Albrecht. *Geschichte des Pietismus*, vol. 1, *Der Pietismus in der reformierten Kirche*. Berlin: De Gruyter, 1966.

Rittgers, Ronald. *The Reformation of Suffering: Pastoral Theology and Lay Piety in Late Medieval and Early Modern Germany*. New York: Oxford University Press, 2012.

Rittgers, Ronald K., and Vincent Evener. "Introduction." In *Protestants and Mysticism in Reformation Europe*. St Andrews Studies in Reformation History. Edited by Ronald K. Rittgers and Vincent Evener, 1–16. Leiden: Brill, 2019.

Rosenberg, Alfred. *Der Mythus des 20. Jahrhunderts: Eine Wertung der seelisch-geistigen Gestaltenkämpfe unserer Zeit*, 91st–94th ed. Munich: Hoheneichen-Verlag, 1936.

Ruh, Kurt. "Meister Eckhart und die Spiritualität der Beginen." In *Perspektiven der Philosophie*. Leiden: Brill, 1982.

Saak, Eric. *High Way to Heaven: The Augustinian Platform Between Reform and Reformation, 1292–1524*. Leiden: Brill, 2002.

Saarinen, Risto. "Lutherforschung in Skandinavien." In *Luther Handbuch,* edited by Albrecht Beutel, 42–47. Tübingen: Mohr Siebeck, 2017.

________. "Metapher Und Biblische Redefiguren Als Elemente Der Sprachphilosophie Luthers." *Neue Zeitschrift Für Systematische Theologie Und Religionsphilosophie* 30, 18–39. Berlin: De Gruyter, 1988.

________. *Gottes wirken auf uns: die transzendentale Deutung des Gegenwart-Christi-Motivs in der Lutherforschung. Veröffentlichungen des Instituts für Europäische Geschichte Mainz. Abteilung Religionsgeschichte*, vol. 137. Stuttgart: Steiner Verlag Wiesbaden, 1989.

Schlie, Heike. "Exzentrische Kreuzigungen um 1500: Zur Erfindung eines bildlichen Affektraumes." In *Golgatha in den Konfessionen und Medien der Frühen Neuzeit. Arbeiten zur Kirchengeschichte,* vol. 113. Edited by Johann Anselm Steiger and Ulrich Heinen, 63–91. Berlin: De Gruyter, 2010.

Schlüter, Dietrich M. "Philosophische Grundlagen der Lehren Johannes Taulers." In J*ohannes Tauler: ein deutscher Mystiker: Gedenkschrift zum 600. Todestag*, edited by Ephrem Filthaut, 122–161. Essen: Driewer, 1961.

Schneider, Hans "Staupitz' Ausschreiben zum Kapitel der deutschen Augustinerkongregation in Heidelberg 1518. Ein Quellenfund." *Blätter für pfälzische Kirchengeschichte und religiöse Volkskunde* 74, 361–372. Grünstadt: Verein für Pfälzische Kirschengeschichte, 2007.

Schröcker, Hubert. *Das Verhältnis der Allmacht Gottes zum Kontradiktionsprinzip nach Wilhelm von Ockham*. Berlin: Veröffentlichungen des Grabmann-Institutes 49, 2003.

Schwarz, Reinhard. "Vorgeschichte der reformatorischen Bußtheologie." *Arbeiten zur Kirchengeschichte* 41. Berlin: De Gruyter, 1968.

Seeberg, Reinhold. *Lehrbuch der Dogmengeschichte*, vol. 4. Basel: Benno Schwabe, 1953–1954.

Seegets, Petra. *Passionstheologie und Passionsfrömmigkeit im ausgehenden Mittelalter: der Nürnberger Franziskaner Stephan Fridolin (gest. 1498) zwischen Kloster und Stadt. (Spätmittelalter und Reformation.NR 10).* Tübingen: Mohr Siebeck, 1998.

Staats, Reinhart. "Das Bild Christi Im Abendmahl: Patristische Tradition in Lutherischer Abendmahlslehre Und in Lutherischer Naturfrömmigkeit." In *Mystik, Metapher, Bild Beiträge des VII. Makarios-Symposiums*, edited by Martin Tamcke, 67–82. Göttingen: Universitätsverlag, 2008.

Steer, Georg. *Scholastische Gnadenlehre in mittelhochdeutscher Sprache.* Munich: Beck, 1966.

Steiger, Johann Anselm. "Die communicatio idiomatum als Achse und Motor der Theologie Luthers. Der 'fröhliche Wechsel' als hermeneutischer Schlüssel zu Abendmahlslehre, Anthropologie, Seelsorge, Naturtheologie, Rhetorik und Humor." In *Neue Zeitschrift für Systematische Theologie und Religionsphilosophie* 38, no. 1. Berlin: De Greuyter, 1996.

_______. "Zorn Gottes, Leiden Christi und die Affekte der Passionsbetrachtung bei Luther und im Luthertum des 17. Jahrhunderts?" In *Passion, Affekt und Leidenschaft in der Frühen Neuzeit*, 179–201. Wiesbaden: Harrassowitz, 2005.

Stolle, Volker. "Wortglaube Und Passionsmystik: Zwei Seiten Des Lutherischen Verständnisses Der Realpräsenz Im Breslauer Vorbereitungsgebet." *Lutherische Theologie Und Kirche* 25, no. 3/4 (2001): 131–156.

Stracke, Ernst. *Luthers großes Selbstzeugnis 1545 über seine Entwicklung zum Reformator historisch-kritisch untersucht. Schriften des Vereins für reformationsgeschichte.* Leipzig: M. Heinsius nachfolger, Eger & Sievers, 1926.

Streiff, Stefan. *"Novis linguis loqui": Martin Luthers Disputation über Joh 1,14 "verbum caro factum est" aus dem Jahr 1539.* Göttingen: Vandenhoeck & Ruprecht, 1993.

Tomlin, Graham S. "The medieval origins of Luther's theology of the cross." *Archiv für Reformationsgeschichte* 89. Gütersloher Verlagshaus, 1998.

Troeltsch, Ernst. *The Social Teaching of the Christian Churches*. Translated by Olive Wyon. New York: Harper, 1960.

Ullmann, Carl. *Reformatoren vor der Reformation: vornehmlich in Deutschland und den Niederlanden*, vol. 1. FA Perthes, 1866.

Ulmer, Bernd. "Konversionserzählungen als rekonstruktive Gattung: Erzählerische Mittel und Strategien bei der Rekonstruktion eines Bekehrungserlebnisses," *Zeitschrift für Soziologie* 17, no. 1, 19–33. Stuttgart: De Gruyter, 1988.

Urban, Wolfgang. "Die 'Via Moderna' an der Universität Erfurt am Vorabend der Reformation." In *Gregor von Rimini: Werk und Wirkung bis zur Reformation. Spätmittelalter und Reformation.* Edited by Heiko Augustinus Oberman, 311–330. Berlin: De Gruyter, 1981.

van Aelst, José. "Vruchten van de passie: De Laatmiddeleeuwse Passieliteratuur verkend aan de hand van Suso's 'Honderd Artikelen'." *Middeleeuwse Studies En Bronnen 129.* Hilversum: Verloren, 2011.

van Dijk, Rudolf. "Spiritualität der 'inicheit'. Mystik und Kirchenkritik in der Devotio Moderna." In *Die Kirchenkritik der Mystiker. Prophetie aus Gotteserfahrung*, vol. 2. Edited by Mariano Delgado, 9–38. Stuttgart: Kohlhammer, 2005.

Vekeman, Herman W. J. "La Mystique Eucharistique Des Cisterciennes au XIII siècle." *Collectanea Cisterciensia*, 66, no. 2. 120–139 Abbaye de Scourmont, 2004.

Vogelsang, Erich. "Luther und Die Mystik." Lutherjahrbuch 19. 32–54. Göttingen: Vandenhoeck & Ruprecht, 1937.

von Harnack, Adolf. *Lehrbuch der Dogmengeschichte*, vol. 3, *Die Entwicklung des kirchlichen Dogmas*, 4th ed. Tübingen: Mohr, 1909.

von Hinten, Wolfgang. "Der Franckforter" ("*Theologia deutsch*"). In VerfLex 2 (1979): 802–808.

Wabel, Thomas. *Sprache als Grenze in Luthers theologischer Hermeneutik und Wittgensteins Sprachphilosophie*, vol. 92. Berlin: De Gruyter, 1998.

Wegener, Lydia. *Der 'Frankfurter' / 'theologia deutsch': Spielräume und grenzen des sagbaren.* Frühe Neuzeit, vol. 201. Berlin: De Gruyter, 2016.

Weilner, Ignaz. *Johannes Taulers Bekehrungsweg: die Erfahrungsgrundlagen seiner Mystik. Studien zur Geschichte der katholischen Moraltheologie*, vol. 10. Regensburg: Pustet, 1961.

Wetzel, Richard. "Staupitz und Luther." In *Martin Luther: Probleme seiner Zeit*, edited by Volker Press and Dieter Stievermann, 775–787. Stuttgart: Klett-Cotta, 1986.

White, Graham. *Luther as Nominalist: A Study of the Logical Methods Used in Martin Luther's Disputations in the Light of Their Medieval Background*. Helsinki: Luther-Agricola-Society, 1994.

Wieneke, Josef. *Luther und Petrus Lombardus: Martin Luthers Notizen Anläßlich Seiner Vorlesung über Die Sentenzen Des Petrus Lombardus Erfurt 1509/11*. Dissertationen / Theologische Reihe. St. Ottilien: EOS-Verlag, 1995.

Wiesenhütter, Alfred. *Die Passion Christi in der Predigt des deutschen Protestantismus von Luther bis Zinzendorf*. Berlin: Furche-Verlag, 1930.

Winkler, Eberhard. *Motive der Mystik in Luthers Verständnis des Abendmahls. Lutherjahrbuch*, vol. 78, 137–152. Göttingen: Vandenhoeck & Ruprecht, 2011.

Winterhager, Wilhelm Ernst. "Martin Luther und das Amt des Provinzialvikars in der Reformkongregation der deutschen Augustiner-Eremiten." In *Vita Religiosa Im Mittelalter*, edited by Franz J. Felten and Nikolas Jaspert, 707–738. Berlin: Duncker u. Humblot, 1999.

Witte, Karl-Heinz. *Der Meister des Lehrgesprächs und sein "In-principio-Dialog": ein deutschsprachiger Theologe der Augustinerschule des 14. Jahrhunderts aus dem Kreise deutscher Mystik und Scholastik: Untersuchung und Edition*. Munich: Artemis, 1989.

_______. "Der 'Traktat von Der Minne', Der Meister des Lehrgesprächs und Johannes Hiltalingen von Basel. Ein Beitrag Zur Geschichte der Meister-Eckhart-Rezeption in der Augustinerschule Des 14. Jahrhunderts," *Zeitschrift Für Deutsches Altertum Und Deutsche Literatur* 131, no. 4 (2002): 454–487.

Wriedt, Markus. *Gnade und Erwählung: eine Untersuchung zu Johann von Staupitz und Martin Luther*. Veröffentlichungen des Instituts für Europäische Geschichte Mainz, vol. 141. Mainz: von Zabern, 1991.

Zecherle, Andreas. Review. "Lydia Wegener: Der› Frankfurter‹/› Theologia Deutsch‹. Spielräume und Grenzen des Sagbaren." *Beiträge zur Geschichte der deutschen Sprache und Literatur* 139, no. 4. Edited by Svetlana Petrova, et al. 633–637. Berlin: De Gruyter, 2017.

_______. "Die 'Theologia Deutsch.' Ein spätmittelalterlicher mystischer Traktat." In *Gottes Nähe unmittelbar erfahren: Mystik im Mittelalter und bei Martin Luther*, edited by Berndt Hamm and Volker Leppin, in collaboration with Heidrun Munzert. Spätmittelalter und Reformation neue Reihe, vol. 36, 1–95. Tübingen: Mohr Siebeck, 2007.

Zekorn, Stefan. *Gelassenheit und Einkehr: zu Grundlage und Gestalt geistlichen Lebens bei Johannes Tauler. Studien zur systematischen und spirituellen Theologie*, vol. 10. Würzburg: Echter, 1993.

Zumkeller, Adolar. "Das Ungenügen der menschlichen Werke bei den deutschen Predigern des Spätmittelalters." *Zeitschrift Für Katholische Theologie* 81, no. 3 (1959): 265–305.

_______. "Erbsünde, Gnade, Rechtfertigung und Verdienst nach der Lehre der Erfurter Augustinertheologen des Spätmittelalters." *Cassiciacum*, vol. 35. Würzburg: Augustinus-Verlag, 1984.

Zur Mühlen, Karl-Heinz. "Zur Rezeption der Augustinischen Sakramentsformel 'Accedit verbum ad elementum, et fit sacramentum' in der Theologie Luthers." In *Zeitschrift für Theologie und Kirche (ZThK)* 70 (1973): 50–76. Tübingen: Mohr Siebeck.

_______. "Die Erforschung des 'jungen Luther' seit 1876." In *Luther-Jahrbuch*, vol. 50, 48–125. Göttingen: Vandenhoeck & Ruprecht, 1983.

_______. *Nos Extra Nos: Luthers Theologie Zwischen Mystik Und Scholastik.* Beiträge Zur Historischen Theologie, vol. 46. Tübingen: Mohr Siebeck, 1972.

_______. *Reformatorisches Profil. Studien zum Weg Martin Luthers und der Reformation.* Göttingen: Vandenhoeck & Ruprecht, 1995.

Scripture Index

People Index

Subject Index

Living by Faith: Justification and Sanctification, by Oswald Bayer (2003).

Harvesting Martin Luther's Reflections on Theology, Ethics and the Church, essays from *Lutheran Quarterly*, edited by Timothy J. Wengert, with foreword by David C. Steinmetz (2004).

A More Radical Gospel: Essays on Eschatology, Authority, Atonement, and Ecumenism, by Gerhard O. Forde, edited by Mark Mattes and Steven Paulson (2004).

The Role of Justification in Contemporary Theology, by Mark C. Mattes (2004).

The Captivation of the Will: Luther vs. Erasmus on Freedom and Bondage, by Gerhard O. Forde (2005).

Bound Choice, Election, and Wittenberg Theological Method: From Martin Luther to the Formula of Concord, by Roberg Kolb (2005).

A Formula for Parish Practice: Using the Formula of Concord in Congregations, by Timothy J. Wengert (2006).

Luther's Theological Music: Principles and Implications, by Robin A Leaver (2006).

The Preached God: Proclamation in Word and Sacrament, by Gerhard O. Forde, edited by Mark C. Mattes and Steven D. Paulson (2007).

Theology the Lutheran Way, by Oswald Bayer (2007).

A Time for Confessing, by Robert W. Bertram (2008).

The Pastoral Luther: Essays on Martin Luther's Pastoral Theology, edited by Timothy J. Wengert (2009).

Preaching from Home: The Stories of Seven Lutheran Women Hymn Writers, by Gracia Grindal (2011).

The Early Luther: Stages in a Reformation Reorientation, by Berndt Hamm (2013).

The Life, Works, and Witness of Tsehay Tolessa and Gudina Tumsa, the Ethiopian Bonhoeffer, edited by Samuel Yonas Deressa and Sarah Hinlicky (2017).

The Wittenberg Concord: Creating Space for Dialogue, by Gordon A. Jensen (2018).

Lutheran Quarterly Books

Luther's Outlaw God: Volume 1: Hiddenness, Evil, and Predestination, by Steven D. Paulson (2018).

The Essential Forde: Distinguishing Law and Gospel, by Gerhard O. Forde, edited by Nickolas Hopman, Mark C. Mattes, and Steven D. Paulson (2019).

Luther's Outlaw God: Volume 2: Hidden in the Cross, by Steven D. Paulson (2019).

Minister's Prayer Book: An Order of Prayers and Readings, Revised Edition, edited by Timothy J. Wengert, Mary Jane Haemig, Chris Halverson, and Robert Harrell (2020)

The Augsburg Confession: Renewing Lutheran Faith and Practice, by Timothy J. Wengert (2020).

Luther's Outlaw God: Volume 3: Sacraments and God's Attack on the Promise, by Steven D. Paulson (2020).

Stories from Global Lutheranism: A Historical Timeline, by Martin J. Lohrmann (2021).

Teaching Reformation: Essays in Honor of Timothy J. Wengert, edited by Luka Ilić and Martin J. Lohrmann (2021).

Experiencing Gospel: The History and Creativity of Martin Luther's 1534 Bible Project, by Gordon A. Jensen (2023).

Face to Face: Martin Luther's View of Reality, by Robert Kolb (2024).

A New Song We Now Begin: Celebrating the Half Millennium of Lutheran Hymnals 1524–2024, edited by Robin A. Leaver (2024).

Sola: Christ, Grace, Faith, and Scripture Alone in Martin Luther's Theology, by Volker Leppin (2024).

United with Christ: Martin Luther and Christian Mysticism, by Volker Leppin (2025).